JOURNAL OF AN EMBASSY

FROM THE

GOVERNOR-GENERAL OF INDIA

TO THE COURTS OF

SIAM AND COCHIN CHINA

JOURNAL OF AN EMBASSY

FROM THE

GOVERNOR-GENERAL OF INDIA

TO THE COURTS OF

SIAM AND COCHIN CHINA;

EXHIBITING A VIEW OF THE ACTUAL STATE OF THOSE KINGDOMS.

BY

JOHN CRAWFURD, ESQ., FRS., FLS., FGS., &c.

LATE ENVOY

SECOND EDITION

IN TWO VOLUMES

VOL. I

GYAN

Published by

GYAN

Gyan Publishing House
5, Ansari Road
Daryaganj, New Delhi-110002
Phone: 011-47034999, 9811692060
E-mail: books@gyanbooks.com

Distribution Network
gyanbooks.com
India, USA, Canada, UK, Australia, France

ISBN : 978-81-212-3644-7 (Set)
ISBN : 978-81-212-2075-0 (HB)
First Published, 1830

2nd Impression 2020

Printed at: Gyan Press, Delhi.

The book at your disposal is the edition of an old book originally published long back. The Text quality of this book may not be at par as compared to our other books but many readers approached us to reprint this important book so that it could satiate their hunger. We request all the readers of this book to help us to improve its quality by providing the necessary text of those pages which are not properly visible. Your valuable support in this case will be highly appreciated and acknowledged and our future readers will be benefitted immensely.

JOURNAL OF AN EMBASSY

FROM THE

GOVERNOR-GENERAL OF INDIA

TO THE COURTS OF

SIAM AND COCHIN CHINA;

EXHIBITING A VIEW OF THE

ACTUAL STATE OF THOSE KINGDOMS.

BY

JOHN CRAWFURD, ESQ., FRS., FLS., FGS., &c.

LATE ENVOY.

SECOND EDITION.

IN TWO VOLUMES.

VOL. I.

LONDON:
HENRY COLBURN AND RICHARD BENTLEY,
NEW BURLINGTON STREET.
1830.

VIEW OF THE TOWN AND ROADS OF SINGAPORE FROM THE GOVERNMENT HILL.

CONTENTS

OF THE FIRST VOLUME.

CHAPTER I.

CHAPTER II.

CHAPTER III.

CHAPTER IV.

CHAPTER V.

CHAPTER VI.

CHAPTER VII.

CHAPTER VIII.

CHAPTER IX.

CHAPTER X.

ILLUSTRATIONS.

VOL. I.

VOL. II.

WOOD CUTS.

VOL. I.

VOL. II.

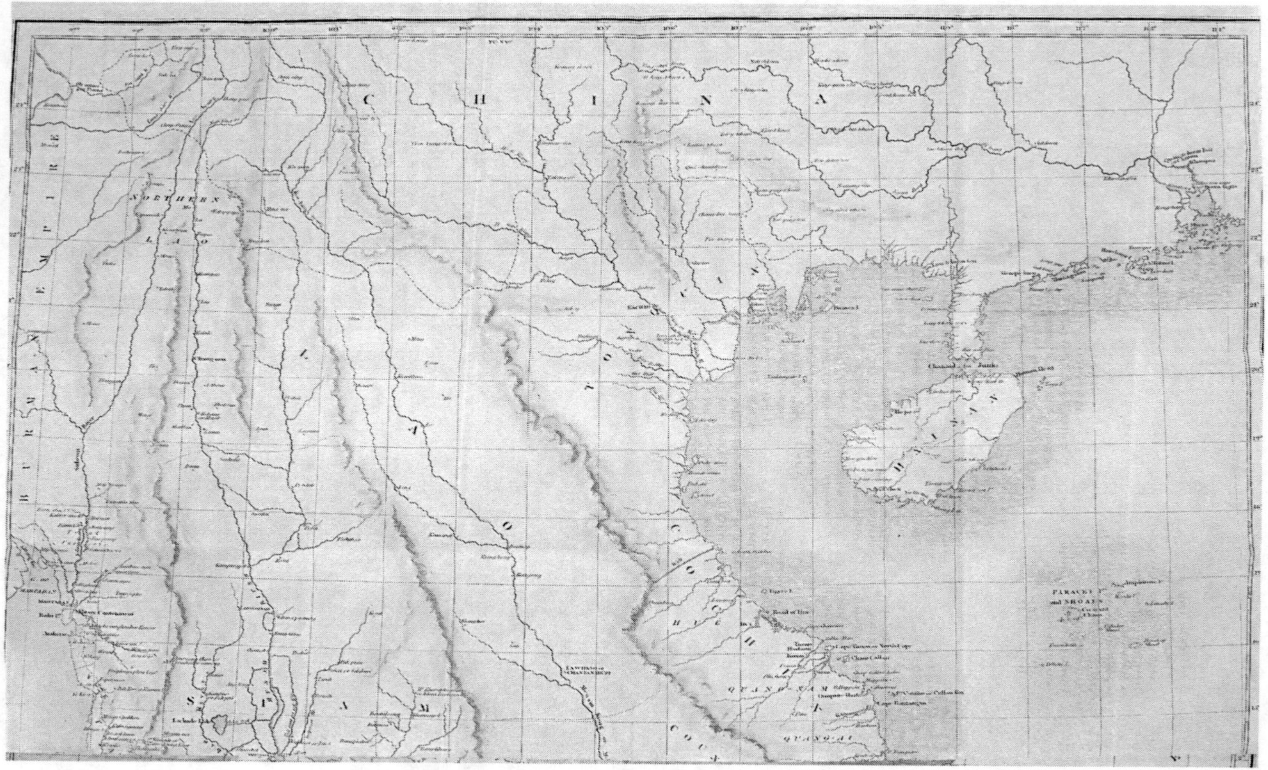
C H I N A
NORTHERN
L A O
B U R M A N E M P I R E
H A I N A N
Q U A N G N A M
Q U A N G - A I
S I A M

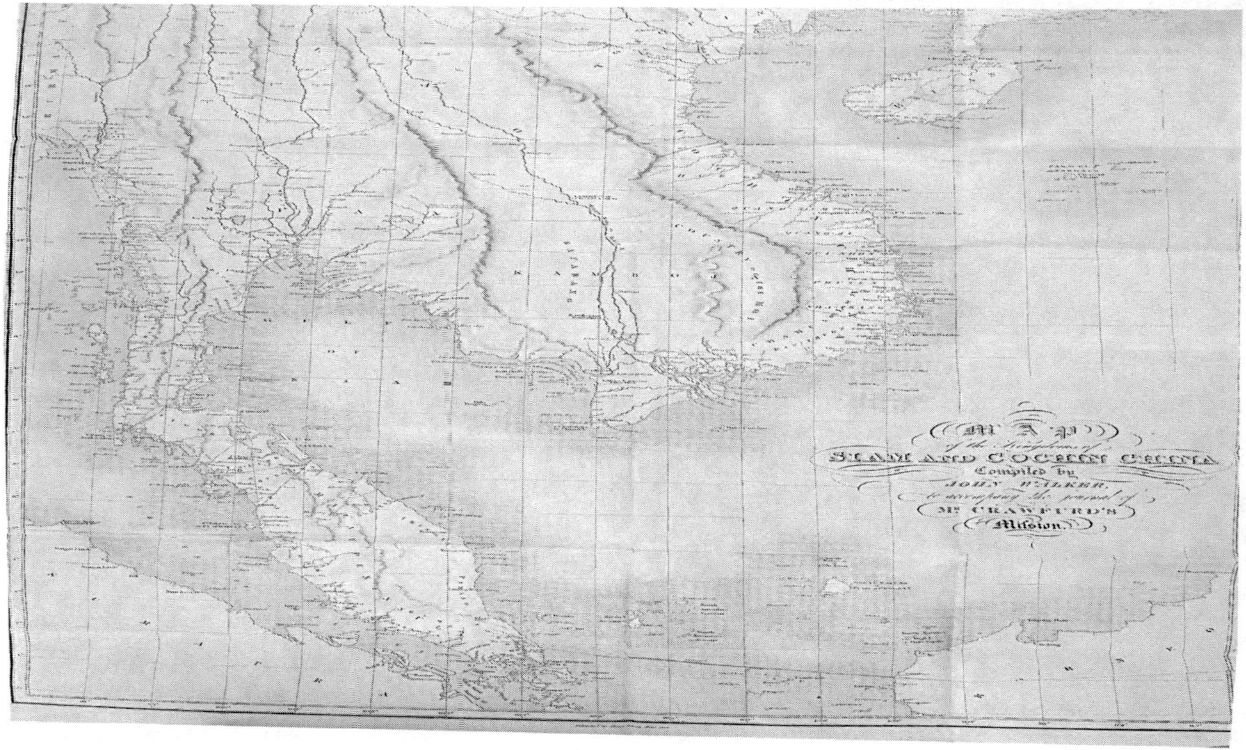
MAP
of the Kingdoms of
SIAM AND COCHIN CHINA
Compiled by
JOHN WALKER,
to accompany the Journal of
Mr. CRAWFURD'S
Mission.

JOURNAL OF AN EMBASSY

TO

THE COURTS OF SIAM

AND

COCHIN CHINA.

CHAPTER I.

Nature of the Mission.—Departure from Calcutta.—Islands Preparis and Narcondam.—Sayer Islands.—Coast of Siam.—Arrival at Penang.—Invasion of the neighbouring Malayan principality by the Siamese.—Incidents at Penang.—Description of the Settlement.

I RETURNED to India in the month of May, 1821, and in September was nominated by the late Marquis of Hastings, then Governor-general of India, to proceed on a mission to the Courts of Siam and Cochin China. The circumstances which led to this appointment are sufficiently detailed in my instructions, which will be found in the Appendix to the present work. My companions were Captain Dangerfield and Lieutenant Rutherford, of the Indian army, and Mr. Finlayson, of His Majesty's Medical Service. Captain

Dangerfield was appointed my assistant, and to succeed in case of accident; Mr. Rutherford commanded our small escort of thirty Sepoys; and Mr. Finlayson was attached to the mission in quality of medical officer and naturalist. I had the good fortune to find in Captain Dangerfield a skilful astronomer, surveyor, and geologist; and Mr. Finlayson with zeal and talents had made highly respectable acquirements in botany and zoology. The John Adam, an Indian-built ship of about 380 tons burthen, was appointed for the accommodation of the mission.

Having received my instructions, and being charged with letters addressed from the Governor-general to the Kings of Siam and Cochin China, accompanied by such presents as are required by the usages of the East, we embarked, on the 21st of November, 1821, and dropped down the river with the ebb-tide, which took us as far as the Government manufactory of gunpowder, about eight miles below Calcutta, carrying us within a stone's throw of the left bank of the river, and along the most picturesque part of it; that bend of the Hoogly which Europeans call Garden Reach, a series of beautiful and magnificent country-houses belonging to some of the principal merchants of Calcutta.

Nov. 23.—There being no wind yesterday to enable us to stem the flood-tide, we could only make progress during the ebbs, and from the intricacy of the navigation, this only during daylight. This morning a favourable breeze sprung up from the north-east, which enabled us to stem the flood-tide, and we successively passed Fultah and the James and Mary Sand, and anchored at Culpee for the night. The passage of the James and Mary Sand, formed by the junction of the Rupnarain with the Hoogly, is the most dangerous part of the navigation of the river. The bank is a hard sand, and the channel constantly changing. In running down we had met the Forbes, a ship of 600 tons, which had struck upon it, and was consequently obliged to return to Calcutta for repair. No ship which draws above fifteen feet when loaded can navigate the Ganges with safety and economy. The ships of the East India Company, usually of the burthen of 1000 and 1200 tons, and drawing above twenty-two feet water, are totally unfit for this purpose; they take in their cargo 100 miles from Calcutta, and, besides this inconvenience, commonly lose many of their crew from the great insalubrity of the stations where they usually lie.

Nov. 24.—Calms with light winds not enabling us to stem the flood-tides, we reached today no farther than the land which, with the north end of Saugor Island, forms Channel-creek, or Lackams Channel. In the evening, being close to the shore, a small party of us landed. The country farther than the eye can see is here covered with an almost impenetrable forest of low wood, the trees of which do not exceed eight or ten feet high. The timber which they afford is fit only for firewood. The soil is entirely alluvial, and the successive depositions of strata are distinctly preceptible on the shore. The land could not be less than twelve feet above the level of the sea or river at high-water, and might therefore be cultivated with advantage. The crew of the pilot-boat which accompanied us, assured us that the place abounds with deer and tigers, and that it was dangerous, on account of the latter, even to attempt to cut a little firewood within a few yards of the shore. We had not, indeed, penetrated above a few yards into the wood, when we discovered in the soft soil many traces of deer, and those of one tiger.

Nov 25.—We sailed from Culpee in the morning, and in the evening anchored below Kadegree, and opposite the Island of Saugor. Three years ago, a plan was set on foot to clear this island; and the Government of Bengal, knowing that its culture, on the part of the natives, was hopeless, departed from its usual policy, and made extensive grants to a society of English gentlemen and others at Calcutta, who subscribed a large sum towards the purpose of clearing and bringing it into culture. The project has been attended with but very partial success, chiefly owing to natural obstacles. The island is low, being little better than a sand bank, a few feet above high-water mark. The soil is scanty and sterile, and there is no command of water for artificial irrigation. In the first attempts at clearing it, the nearest lands to the shore were chosen; but so little coherence was there in the soil, when the roots of the trees were removed, that on more than one occasion the high tides, which took place during gales of wind in the S. W. monsoon, swept away the whole cleared land. When it is considered that abundance of unreclaimed land of the finest description exists in almost every part of India, the capital laid out on this unprofitable project may be considered as little better than a sacrifice to the unwise and narrow-minded, anti-colonial policy of the East India Company.

Nov. 28.—During the two last days we moved by slow degrees, under the pilot's charge, over the reefs and sands which obstruct the entrance into the Hoogly. The pilot left us last night in nine and a half fathoms water, and we now proceeded under the auspices of the north-east monsoon, having a six-knot breeze, serene weather, and a cloudless sky. In the complicated and difficult navigation of the Hoogly, it has taken us seven days to sail one hundred and forty miles; which is the distance between the town of Calcutta, and what is called the Reef Buoy, the extreme limit of the dangers of the river. With the assistance of a steam-boat, ships might be towed down in two days without difficulty. The freshes in the river, which continue two months, and during which the ebb-tide is sometimes found to run at the rate of eight miles an hour, might prove an obstacle to their employment at that season; but, at all other periods of the year, they might surely be used to advantage, whether for towing vessels or conveying passengers. Under such favourable circumstances, and in a country where either wood or coals may be had for fuel, it is some reflection upon our want of enterprise in India, that steam-vessels have not yet been established.* In quitting or approaching the Hoogly, it is impossible not to be struck with the extraordinary difficulties which the early European navigators had to contend against, in navigating it, before the establishment, as at present, of an intelligent and experienced, although most costly class of pilots. Some share of their success is to be ascribed to the convenient size of the very small vessels which they employed,

* The first steam-vessel used in India, was built about three years after this passage was written. There are at present about ten, of all descriptions, in the Hoogly—some belonging to the Government, and others used for conveving passengers, or towing ships up and down.

and a large one to their courage and enterprise. The reputation of the country to which it opened a road, no doubt powerfully prompted them to the undertaking. With all the difficulties and dangers of the Ganges, the English, if their Indian conquests be any advantage to them, owe almost as much gratitude to it as the Hindoos themselves, for unquestionably to it they are indebted for their Indian empire. It is the great military road which enabled us to conquer the richest provinces of Hindustan, the acquisition of which enabled us eventually to conquer and maintain the rest of our possessions.

Dec. 3.—During the last four days we proceeded on our voyage without any occurrence worth mentioning. This morning at daybreak the Island of Preparis appeared in sight, and being considerably to windward, we bore down upon it with the intention of landing, and availing ourselves of the opportunity that offered of gaining some knowledge of the natural history of a place so near to the Indian capital, but of which, notwithstanding, little or nothing is known. We were, however, disappointed; for the north-east wind blew so strongly upon the eastern shore, the only safe one to approach, that we could not venture to land. We came within a short mile, however, of two small islands lying to the northern extremity of the principal one, called by navigators the "Cow and Calf." At the depth of ten or twelve fathoms, the lead brought up fragments of coral rock, which we plainly saw under the ship's bottom, with some sharks swimming over them. We skirted the eastern shore of the large island itself, the highest part of which may be about two hundred feet above the level of the sea. It is entirely covered with a forest of considerable height, leaving only a narrow beach of white sand, having a few ledges of rocks here and there scattered through it. The Island of Preparis is seven miles in length from north to south, and uninhabited except by monkeys and squirrels.

The western side and southern end are surrounded by a coral reef, which in several parts appears above water, and upon which three small islands have been formed. The approaches to the Preparis are imperfectly known and very dangerous, and have occasioned many shipwrecks. In the year 1817, the Francis and Charlotte, a transport, bringing part of his Majesty's 78th Regiment from Java, after the restoration of the Dutch colonies, struck, at night, on the reefs to the southern end of the Preparis, and was lost. The troops were conveyed to the main island, where the greater part of them had to remain feeding on a little biscuit saved from the wreck, with some shell-fish picked up on the shore, and devoured at night by mosquitoes, until relief was brought to them from Calcutta.

Dec. 4.—Last night we passed the Island of Narcondam, visible by moonlight, and this morning had a fine view of it from the deck. The island rises in the form of a cone abruptly from the sea, and is of small extent: it bears all the exterior forms of a basaltic formation, and its summit even exhibits the appearance of the exhausted crater of a volcano. Barren Island, of similar size and appearance, lying within seventy miles of it, has a volcano, which has been in a state of activity since the year 1791. In ordinary weather Narcondam is visible, as we now experienced, at fifty miles distance, and in clear weather at seventy. By an observation, not taken, however, under very favourable circumstances, we made its height 2589 feet above the level of the sea.

Dec. 7.—We sailed during the last two days with delightful weather and favourable winds; and early this morning found ourselves (the coast of Siam, visible for the first time in the distance, on our left) near the Sayer Islands, the most northerly of which is in latitude 8° 43′ north, and in longitude 97° 48′ east: they are six in number. At noon one party landed on the largest island, usually called the Great Sayer, and another on that lying immediately west of it. The coasts of the whole group are bold, and the navigation easy. A ship of large size might come within fifty yards of the Great Sayer, without danger. We found the two islands which we visited, to consist entirely of granite,—presenting an appearance of irregular stratification,—of a very large grain, with narrow veins of quartz running here and there through it. Immediately over the rocks, which are washed by the sea, vegetation commences; and the islands are covered with a forest of trees, rather undersized if compared with the magnificent woods of the great Indian Archipelago. The sea which surrounds them abounds in fish, and on the rocks are found a rich supply of shells, and some corals, of which considerable collections were made. A few storks, of a lead-blue colour, were the only birds we saw; and the only inhabitant of the forest appeared to be the large bat *(Vespertilio)*, of which great numbers were seen; which proves that wild fruits abound, as these constitute their principal food. The Sayer Islands are uninhabited, and deserve to be so, for the granite of which they consist is covered with a mould so thin, that it would not suffice for raising a sufficient supply of the plants necessary to the subsistence of man. These islands are the last of the chain which extends along the coast of Siam for eight degrees, and which navigators have called the Mergui or Tennasserim Archipelago. They are also the last of the long chain which, with but a partial interruption, the delta of the Irrawadi, covers the eastern coast of the Gulf of Bengal. It deserves to be remarked, that a similar chain of islands extends along the eastern coast of the Gulf of Siam; while the western coasts of both, but especially of the former, have comparatively few such islands along their shores. A similar observation may be made in regard to harbours. The eastern coast of the Bay of Bengal abounds with them, but there is not one on the western. There are several fine harbours on the eastern coast of the Siamese Gulf, but scarcely one which deserves the name on the western.

Dec. 8.—During the night we steered a course to bring us close to the shore of the mainland of Siam; and in the morning found ourselves within a mile and a half of it, in the latitude of 8° 14′ N., and within five miles of the narrow straits which divide Junk-Ceylon from the continent. The coast is here bold, and safe to approach. The country inland, as far as we could see, was mountainous, leaving along the coast a narrow belt of two or three miles of lower land; still elevated, however, perhaps eighteen or twenty feet above the sea. Nothing was to be seen, at first, but one universal forest of stately trees. We afterwards, however, saw one neat village within a mile of the Papra Strait. On the shore we observed a few fishermen drying their nets, while their canoes lay on the beach. One canoe pushed off, as we believed with the intention of coming on board; but in this we were disappointed, although we did not fail to endeavour to make our wish for an intercourse intelligible by signals. At length we sent a boat to the shore; and after considerable hesitation, two individuals consented to come on board, but not until one of our men was left behind as a hostage for their safety. This extraordinary timidity arises from the situation in which these poor people are placed. They live on the territory disputed between the hostile Burmans and Siamese, and consequently are in a state of perpetual distrust and insecurity; while they are rarely visited by European shipping. Our visitors proved to be a Siamese and a creole Chinese of Siam, who had so much of the native blood of the country in him, that in complexion and features he was no longer distinguishable as a Chinese, and could only be recognized as claiming the name by the fashion in which he wore his hair. We addressed them in Malay, but they understood but a few words, and we could carry on no conversation with them. The coast abounds in fish, and for the value of two rupees we obtained a very large supply of an excellent description. As it fell calm, a party landed at ten o'clock, to examine more nearly the appearance of the country. The beach is a beautiful white sand, with a few ledges of rocks interspersed at considerable distances. We landed on one of the latter, which appeared to proceed from a point of land elevated above the surrounding country, and which promised a favourable opportunity for geological examination. We found both this point, and every other part of the coast which we examined, to consist of the same large-grained granite which composes the Sayer Islands, perhaps a little more diversified by the occasional appearance of gneiss, and of a darker and smaller-grained granite.

On coming on board in the afternoon, we made sail, still keeping close to the shore, and soon passed the western opening of the narrow strait which divides Junk-Ceylon from the continent. Sandy points form the mouth of the strait on each side, which is not more than half a mile broad. It was low water, and so shallow is it, that the sea was breaking over a reef which crosses it, and which, at all times, renders it unnavigable for large vessels: even boats, indeed, can pass only at high-water. A severe squall forced us to keep at a respectable distance from the coast of Junk-Ceylon, but still we had a distinct view of the shore, and even of much of the interior. The shore is bold and precipitate, and the coast frequently so deeply indented, as to give to many of the headlands at a distance, the appearance of islands. The aspect of the country presents a perpetual succession of hills or mountains, apparently so close upon each other, that there can be little room for extensive valleys capable of affording room for profitable cultivation. The whole appeared covered with an immense forest, and not a single habitation or a single patch of culture was discernible. A view of the eastern or sheltered side of the island would, no doubt, have presented a somewhat more favourable aspect, but it is sufficiently known that the island is but thinly inhabited and poorly cultivated.

Dec. 9.—During all night and to-day, we have had a great deal of rain and blowing weather. This prevented us from landing, as we intended, on Junk-Ceylon, and other islands which we passed. We were now within the Straits of Malacca, and the limits of the Malay name and navigation. This is discovered by the sudden alteration of names of places, always significant in the Malay language; and especially by the constant occurrence of the word Pulao, or Pulo, meaning an island, in the vernacular language of that people. In the course of the day we passed Pulo Raja, the Brothers, and Pulo Butung.

Dec. 11.—In the morning we had a near view of Trutao, Langkawi, and Lada, large islands which are inhabited. Langkawi in particular, not less than twenty-five miles long, contains a considerable portion of the population of the Malay state of Queda. Penang was visible in the course of the forenoon, and at ten o'clock at night we got into the harbour. This morning we landed, and our whole party was received into the hospitable and elegant mansion of my friend Mr. Phillips, the Governor of the island. Mr. Phillips's residence is called Suffolk, after the native county of the first owner, Mr. Francis Light, the founder of the settlement. In the time of this gentleman, the ground was little more than an ordinary pepper garden, but the taste of Mr. Phillips has rendered it the most beautiful spot of the kind in India, after Barrackpoore, the country residence of the Governor-general: it is, in short, an English gentleman's mansion and park, where clove and nutmeg trees (in full bearing during our visit) are substituted for oaks, elms, and ashes. The grounds contain from two to three hundred spotted deer.

We found the settlement in a state of alarm, consequent upon an invasion of the territory of the King of Queda by the Raja of Ligor, a dependent prince or chief of Siam, of which Queda is a vassal. This chieftain, a few days before, had suddenly made his appearance at Queda in the night-time with an overwhelming force. A trifling scuffle ensued between his people and the Malays, in which some of the principal chiefs of the latter were killed, but the greater number of the people took to flight without offering the least resistance. The King, after leaving his treasure and property, of which he had more than usually fall to the lot of Malay princes, and having several of his family made prisoners, took refuge at Penang, to which the Siamese chief sent an insolent and threatening message and letter, to demand him. In this letter he hinted pretty directly at the punishment of any one who should screen the fugitive prince. The terror of this threat alarmed the timidity of the native inhabitants, and the usual supply of grain and other necessaries, for which Penang almost entirely depends upon Queda, being interrupted, the settlement was subjected to considerable temporary inconvenience.

We had scarcely landed, when we were met by the commander and the pilot of a Siamese ship, thus far on her voyage from Calcutta to Bungkok. I had frequently seen these two men at Calcutta, and availed myself of my acquaintance with them, to add to our information. They were both, especially the pilot, shrewd and well-informed men, and the details they communicated respecting their country, supplied more useful and practical knowledge than all we had before obtained from printed sources. They were descendants of Mohammedan settlers from Arcot on the Coromandel coast, and inherited the religion and language of their country. They told us that they had quitted Calcutta with a very favourable opinion of our nation; and they stated, that they had already communicated accounts of our mission to the Raja of Ligor, with the view of being transmitted to Siam.

Penang, *Dec.* 12.—I had resided three years at Prince of Wales's Island, and then knew the place well, but I had not seen it for ten; and when I went over George Town and the cultivated part of the island this morning, I found the whole so much changed, that I could hardly recognize it. The town, which had been once almost entirely burnt down, was now constructed of more solid materials, and many new roads had been formed through the country; which, however, presented a less busy and active scene than in former times, and even exhibited some marks of decay, which I am told are since more evident.

Dec. 13.—Accompanied by Captain Dangerfield and Mr. Finlayson, I made, this morning, an excursion to the falls of water at the foot of the hills which supply the flour-mills of Lowe Ami, an old and enterprising Chinese inhabitant of the town. The bed of the rivulet which supplies the mills, afforded us an opportunity of examining the rock, which was throughout granite. The huge blocks of stone which were on the surface, were of red granite a good deal decomposed. The more deep-seated rock was a hard grey granite, exhibiting many distinct crystals of quartz and mica.

Dec. 17.—We paid this morning a visit to Mr. Brown, at Glugar, about five miles from George Town. Mr. Brown is the greatest proprietor in the island, and a person distinguished for his enterprise and intelligence. He raises on his own estates, yearly, about eight thousand piculs of pepper, or more than a million of pounds; worth, at the present time, not less than twenty thousand pounds sterling. The estate of Glugar is of a poor soil, and unfit for the growth of pepper. Mr. Brown has planted it with nutmeg and clove-trees, which are in full bearing, and have a very thriving appearance, the effect of skilful culture and of great care, despite of the sterility of the soil. Although it was not the usual season of the mangostin, Mr. Brown produced a few very delicious ones, highly acceptable to such of our party as had never tasted this fine fruit, the most acceptable to the European palate of all tropical ones.

Dec. 22.—This morning we ascended the Flagstaff Hill, the height of which is 2223 feet above the level of the Government House at Suffolk, and about 2300 feet above the level of the sea. The ascent is steep, yet not abrupt or difficult. A stranger to the vegetation of warm climates is here presented with a very favourable view of the luxuriant and magnificent spectacle of a tropical forest. The greater part of Prince of Wales's Island consists of a rapid succession of hills and narrow valleys, clothed with a forest of the tallest trees, in a livery of perpetual green. These trees, rising often to the height of a hundred and thirty feet, from the close pressure of the forest, are as straight as an arrow, and throw out no branches until within fifteen or twenty feet of their tops. Where the soil is dry, the exclusion of the sun's rays prevents the growth of grass or underwood, with the exception of rattans and the gigantic parasites, which, extending fantastically from tree to tree, give a tropical forest so singular and unexpected a character. This scene, however, is more splendid than useful. The timber of the forest trees is generally of inferior quality, and very little of it is applicable to useful purposes. In passing through these woods, the paucity of animal life is peculiarly striking:—it is seldom that those of Penang are disturbed, except by the loud shrill noise of the grasshopper, or the occasional chattering of a herd of monkeys.

On the top of the hill, water boils at 207½ of Fahrenheit. At 1800 feet above the level of the sea, the character of the vegetation begins to change. The operation of forming the road exposes the external part of the structure of the mountain, which is a yellow-coloured clay, intermixed with gravel, resulting from the disintegrated granite, of which the island seems entirely composed. The granite itself is here and there exposed on the highest parts of the hill, and appears in abundance in the valleys.

Dec. 24.—Last night two messengers arrived from the Raja of Ligor, bearing a letter to my address. They waited upon us this morning, feigning the great joy of their master, the Governor of Ligor, at hearing that the Governor-general of India was sending an envoy to Siam, They disclaimed, on his behalf, all hostile or unfriendly intentions towards us in the invasion of Queda. As an earnest of the Ligor chief's sincerity, the messengers informed us that he had not failed to punish certain of his followers, who had presumed to enter the British territories on the opposite coast in a hostile manner; the officer who commanded having received thirty strokes of a rattan, and each of the private soldiers five a-piece. In respect to the offenders in question, the fact was this:—A Siamese detachment, of an officer and thirty men, had crossed the river which forms the boundary between the Queda and British territory, and, with or without authority, commenced plundering our frontier villages. A native sergeant, with twelve sepoys, was sent in pursuit, and took prisoner and disarmed the whole Siamese party without resistance. They were sent back to the chief of Ligor, and their conduct disavowed. The appearance of the messengers was sufficiently uncivilized:—their dresses were scanty in amount, and not of the best description in point of quality. Above all, their bare and shaggy heads gave them a wild and unpromising aspect. Notwithstanding this, Mong Narrain, the principal, was a man of intelligence, and spoke with an air of much confidence and apparent frankness.

Dec. 28.—Juragan Soliman, an old Malay trader, came to call upon me. He had travelled into several parts of the interior of the Malayan peninsula, and often gone across it to the opposite coast. According to him, from Trang, on the western coast, to Ligor on the eastern, the distance, by elephants, is but three days' journey; and a man on foot can travel despatch in two. From Queda to Sungora, the nearest Siamese province to the Malays, on the side of the Gulf of Siam, he says that merchandize is carried on elephants in five days. This last route is so safe and expeditious, that a great deal of merchandize is sent by it; and it is not uncommon for native vessels from Siam, to send back half their returns in this direction, as well for expedition as to divide the risk. The state of Queda is divided from Patani, the bordering Malayan principality to the north-east, by a chain of mountains, one of the peaks of which, called *Titih Bangsa*, is very lofty; I should suppose, from the comparison made by my informer with other mountains, not less than 6000 feet high. From the mouth of the river Muda, in the territory of Queda, in lat. 5°. 40′. N., to nearly the foot of the Patani hills, is a voyage of ninety-six hours in boats, by a very winding course. From thence four hours' journey on elephants carries the traveller across the mountains to Kroh, in the Patani territories, where there are tin mines. These mines are said to be rich, but unskilfully worked. The Juragan, that is to say, the trading commander, computes that they yield at present 1500 bahars, of three Chinese piculs each, annually, which I suspect is considerably exaggerated. When asked what manner of people the Patanis were, he replied in a style very characteristic of the language and manner of the Malays: "They are simple and uncultivated men, and you may hold them by a hair, if you have only the discretion not to pull it too hard."

Dec. 29.—We paid a second visit to Mr. Brown at Glugar. He brought to meet us an old Chinese inhabitant of Penang, named Che-wan, one of the few survivors of the original settlers of the island. Che-wan left his native country, the province of Fo-kien, at three-and-twenty, and has never since returned to it. He is now at the age of sixty, preparing for himself a splendid tomb, after the Chinese fashion, cut from hewn granite, in a very beautiful and romantic spot. There is an inscription on it in Chinese and English; and this simple monument will last for ages, and after many a revolution of those ephemeral structures which Europeans raise in this country, for mere comfort or utility. Che-wan in conversation is lively, communicative, and sensible. His details are characterized by a degree of European precision and good sense, which one rarely meets with in the East, except among his countrymen. He has visited many parts of the interior of the Malayan peninsula, and several provinces of Siam, as well as the capital of that country. He has a bad opinion of the court of Siam, and thinks the government inferior even to that of Cochin China, which he has also visited; or as he expresses it in the Malay language, "There is less compassion for the people."

Jan. 4, 1822.—We took leave of our kind friends at Suffolk this morning, and re-embarked to pursue our voyage; our party being increased by the addition of three interpreters. Two of these spoke and wrote the Siamese and Malay languages, through the last of which they interpreted to us. The third was a Chinese, who spoke both English and Malay fluently: he was to be our only medium of communication with the Cochin Chinese, for it was in vain to look for an interpreter in the Anam language who spoke any dialect understood by us. The government of Penang, conformably to the instructions received from Bengal, committed to us the conduct of a negociation for the settlement of their claim of sovereignty to the island, and for the adjustment of the disputes between Queda and Siam.

I shall take this opportunity of giving my reader a short account of the Island of Penang, or Prince of Wales's Island, a place of some importance in the commerce of the East, and of which there are no recent or authentic details before the public.

Penang is about sixteen miles in length from north to south, and from seven to eight in breadth, lying between the latitudes of 5°. 16′.

and 5°. 30′. North. By far the greater part of the island is mountainous, rocky, sterile, and covered with a forest of tall trees. A portion of the south and of the eastern parts is level, and these alone constitute the cultivated and inhabited quarter of the island. The highest hills are above 2000 feet in height, and on these the thermometer is about ten degrees lower than on the plain. The harbour, which was the principal inducement to its occupation, is formed by the island, with the mainland two miles distant. The whole island, like the countries in its neighbourhood, is one mass of granite, exhibiting very little variety. In the valleys, traces of alluvial deposits of tin are found. The soil is every where thin and scanty, seldom exceeding a few feet in depth, and often not many inches: it consists, in the plains, of disintegrated granite washed down from the mountains, which, in a few favoured spots, where the best husbandry is conducted, is mixed with a little vegetable mould. The mountains, from the thin soil with which they are covered, and the impracticability of carrying on the labours of agriculture on their steep and precipitate sides and ridges, may be looked upon as condemned to perpetual sterility. The seasons are irregular: rain is frequent throughout the year; but the regular wet season is of short continuance, beginning with September and ending with

November. The coldest months are December and January; and the hottest, June and July. In rural economy, the rainy season is the spring of the year; and January, February, and March, constitute autumn. In the former the rice crop is sown, and in the latter it is reaped. But the great irregularity of the seasons is exhibited in the progress of the pepper plant towards fructification; for the same individual plant blossoms twice a-year, namely, in April and in October, and affords two crops, one of which is reaped in January, and the other in June.

The husbandry of Penang is favourably distinguished from that of any of the rest of our Eastern possessions, and, when we consider the barren and limited nature of the spot, may be quoted as a remarkable proof of the efficacy, as well as safety, of European colonization. This colonization has sprung out of necessity or accident. The land could not be cultivated without the aid of European enterprise and capital, and therefore Europeans were allowed, as a matter of mere exigency, to become proprietors of the soil. The landed proprietors of Penang consist, however, of persons of all the races which inhabit it; but the chief proprietors, and the *only* improvers, are the two most industrious classes—the Europeans and the Chinese. The terms of the grants of land are in perpetuity, on payment of a trifling yearly quit-rent to the state, of one-fifth of a Spanish dollar for an orlong, a measure of one and one-third English acres. Fifteen hundred and seventy of these grants have been given, and about 12,000 acres of the area of the island are in a state of culture.

Notwithstanding these favourable tenures, the natural barrenness of the island and the limited extent of its territory, necessarily exclude from its husbandry all such productions as demand either peculiar fertility of soil or an extensive range for their growth. In an agricultural point of view, it may be strictly said to be unfit for the growth of rice or any other grain,—of the sugar-cane, cotton, coffee, and indigo—the grand staples of tropical husbandry; but, in the culture of articles where skill can compensate for natural defects, the agriculture of Prince of Wales's Island is much superior to that of any other country of Asia. This is especially seen in the culture of pepper, and in the production of such fruits as find a ready market from the frequent resort of strangers. So neat and perfect a specimen of husbandry nowhere exists in the East as the pepper culture of Penang,—the joint effect of the superintending activity of Europeans, and the industrious labour of the Chinese. In Penang, the average of all pepper vines gives an annual product of two catties, or forty-two and two-thirds of an ounce avoirdupoise. In Malabar, the produce of a vine is no more than seven and one-fifth of an ounce, and according to the monopoly culture of Bencoolen, but six and a-half ounces. Agreeably to this estimate, an acre planted with pepper yields, at Penang, 2040 lbs., in Malabar, 344 lbs., and in Bencoolen, 310 lbs. In the expense of culture, there is, to be sure, a wide difference. To clear an acre of land at Penang, to supply the young plants, and to plant themselves, and their vegetating props, costs a hundred and twenty Spanish dollars. After incurring all this charge, with loss of interest of capital for four years, until the gardens begin to bear, they are let to Chinese cultivators on lease, the farmer paying one-third of the net produce as rent, and restoring the pepper gardens in good order. It is evident that very little of what is strictly rent enters into the elements of the proprietor's revenue, which is chiefly composed of the profits of stock.

The fruits cultivated at Penang, in the greatest perfection and quantity, are the orange, the plantain, and the pine-apple; all excellent, but the two last better than I have any where else found them. Both are in season throughout the year, and a hundred pines, of a middling size, are procurable in the market for a Spanish dollar. Those weighing six and seven pounds may be had at the rate of fifty for the same money.

The mangusteen and durian, the two most costly fruits, are imported from the neighbouring coasts of the peninsula, but are cheap and abundant in their season.

The fisheries at Penang constitute a valuable property among a population, the great bulk of which consumes no other animal food, and a large proportion of this. The Chinese are the fishmongers, and the Malays and other islanders are the fishermen. The modes of taking fish are innumerable. The smaller kinds are caught by hand-nets, a few with the line, but the greater quantity by the seine, and, above all, by stake-nets, with which a portion of the shallowest part of the harbour is covered. The most delicate, and one of the most abundant, of the fishes taken is the pomfret.

When the English took possession of Penang, in 1786, it was wholly uncultivated, and had no other inhabitants than a few occasional Malayan fishermen. It now contains* about 39,000, according to a regular yearly census, taken ever since 1815. This population consists of the following motley ingredients, viz. Indian islanders, Chinese, natives of the Coro-

* By the census taken in 1824, the population of the island, including the annexed territory on the opposite coast, was found to have increased to 55,000, chiefly in consequence of emigration from the Malay state of Queda, produced by the invasion of the Siamese.

mandel and Malabar coasts, usually called Chouliahs by Europeans, natives of Bengal, Burmans and Siamese, Europeans and their descendants, with a few Arabs, Armenians, Persees, and African negroes, to which is added a floating population of about 1500. The Indian islanders amount to 15,456, and have greatly increased within the last few years, in consequence of the anarchy and disorder prevalent in some of the neighbouring Malayan states. The tribes of which they chiefly consist are Malays, Achinese, Battaks, and Bugis. They find employment as fishermen, woodcutters, constructors of native houses, and field-labourers. We seldom find them employed as artisans, and not often as traders. The Chinese amount to 8595, and are landowners, field-labourers, mechanics of almost every description, shopkeepers, and general merchants. They are all from the two provinces of Canton and Fo-kien, and three-fourths of them from the latter. About five-sixths of the whole number are unmarried men, in the prime of life: so that, in fact, the Chinese population, in point of effective labour, may be estimated as equivalent to an ordinary population of above 37,000, and, as will afterwards be shown, to a numerical Malay population of more than 80,000! The Chouliahs amount to 6417; they are employed as porters, field-labourers, as clerks and police-officers, as shopkeepers and as merchants, and, occasionally, as mechanics. The natives of Bengal amount to 4624, and form a far less valuable part of the population than the two last classes. About 1700 consist of military and camp followers, about 1300 are convicts, and the remainder settlers, employed as labourers, domestic servants, and shopkeepers. The rate of wages paid to the different classes, when engaged in similar labour, affords a very striking picture of their relative skill, industry, and physical strength—in a word, perhaps of their relative state of civilization. A Malay field-labourer works only six and twenty days in the month, and receives but two dollars and a-half as wages; a Chouliah works twenty-eight days, and receives four dollars; and a Chinese works thirty days, and receives six dollars. The labour of a Chinese, therefore, to himself and the public is worth fifty per cent. more than that of a Chouliah; the Chouliah's, seventy-five per cent. more than that of a Malay; and the Chinese no less than one hundred and twenty per cent. beyond the latter. When skill is implied in the labour to be performed, the disparity is still more remarkable. A Chinese carpenter at Penang receives fifteen dollars a-month, a Persee also fifteen, a Chouliah eight, and a Malay six. I have little doubt but a scale might be constructed upon this principle, which would exhibit a very just estimate of the comparative state of civilization among nations, or, which is the same thing, of the respective merits of their different social institutions.

Notwithstanding the deaths by the cholera morbus, which carried off 1131 persons, or near one thirty-second part of the inhabitants, the population of Penang has increased since 1815, the first year in which an accurate census was made, by 5243. The cholera first made its appearance at Penang in October, 1819, in the midst of the rainy season, and disappeared in the end of February,—thus continuing for a period of four months. It chiefly raged during the first, second, third, and fourth weeks, and in the fifth began sensibly to diminish. It reappeared in the beginning of May, 1821, in a season perfectly the reverse, and continued for two months, with a character of far less virulence, however, than on the first occasion. The weak, the ill-fed, and the ill-lodged, were as usual the principal victims. The natives of the continent of India, evidently the weakest of the inhabitants in point of physical frame, lost in the first attack between a fourteenth and a fifteenth part of their whole numbers; the Malays and other islanders, certainly ill-fed and lodged, but with frames more vigorous and better suited to the climate, lost but one forty-second of their number; the Chinese, well-fed, well-lodged, with robust frames, lost but one one-hundred-and-thirteenth part of their numbers; and, lastly, the mortality among Europeans and their immediate descendants, amounted to no more than one in two hundred. The mortality was incomparably greatest in marshy and swampy situations; and the deaths most frequent after a rainy night. The mortality in the town was five and two-thirds in a hundred, and in the country but one and one-third.

Penang is supplied with rice from Bengal, from Achin; but, above all, from the territories of the King of Queda. The Achin rice is of very inferior quality; but the Bengal and Queda bring nearly the same price in the Penang market. It may be considered about twenty-five per cent. dearer than at Calcutta, and above thirty-five per cent. dearer than at Queda. The whole, under proper arrangements, ought to come from the latter country; but the Prince of Queda, in contravention of an existing treaty, and contrary to good policy, charges a duty of twenty per cent. on all the rice exported to Penang; and contrives, by arbitrary regulations, to restrict the production to certain districts in which the impost cannot be evaded, while the trade is in the hands of petty dealers, who are incapable of conducting it with skill and economy. The daily consumption of rice in Penang, excluding the military population, about one thousand seven hundred, is 32,000 pounds, which gives a consumption for each individual of seventeen-twentieths of a pound. There should be deducted from this calculation the small portion of wheat used by a few of the inhabitants, and the rice consumed in the distillery of arrack and by cattle, which is, however, inconsiderable. Perhaps three-quarters of a pound a-day will be very near the real consumption per head. I am thus particular in giving this statement, because nowhere else is there afforded an opportunity of ascertaining a fact of this nature, with so much precision.

The history of this little establishment is very shortly told. After the war which ended in the peace of 1783, and during which we had had to struggle for naval superiority with the French, the want of a good harbour in the Bay of Bengal, as a resort for our ships of war, became evident; and Penang, after other abortive and injudicious attempts had been made, was at length fixed upon, under the administration of Sir John Macpherson. The person who recommended it to the attention of the Government of India, was a Mr. Francis Light, who had traded and resided for a number of years at Siam and Queda, and who had a title of nobility from the former country. The settlement was formed in the year 1786, and this gentleman appointed to the charge of it, under the title of Superintendant. There is no foundation whatever for the idle story which has gained currency, of Mr. Light's having received Penang as a dowry with a daughter of the King of Queda. It was made over to the East India Company, in consideration of a yearly payment of 6000 Spanish dollars, to compensate for any loss of revenue which might arise to this petty prince from its occupation. It soon rose to considerable prosperity; and in the year 1791, five years after its occupation, we were already at war with the Prince of Queda on account of it. In the year 1800 we received an accession of territory by a cession of waste and uninhabited land on the opposite shore, three and twenty miles along the coast, and three miles inland, which now contains near 6000 inhabitants. The place still continued to prosper, to increase in wealth and population, and to prove of much utility to the general interests of Indian commerce. In the year 1805, however, this utility was strangely exaggerated, and an extensive plan formed for converting it into a grand naval depôt and dockyard, though neither the island nor its vicinity produced a stick of timber fit for shipbuilding. The authorities at home thought themselves warranted, on some vague conception of its merits, to create it into a separate Presidency, and to load it with a burthensome and expensive civil establishment. On a reduced scale, the civil establishment even now amounts to the enormous sum of *five and fifty thousand pounds sterling a-year!* and the military charge, which cannot be so correctly estimated, is certainly not under *thirty thousand,*—making an aggregate expenditure of *eighty-five thousand pounds sterling a-year!**

The real utility of Penang consists in its being a place of convenient resort for both our military and commercial navy, especially in time of war; but, above all, in its constituting a depôt, or emporium, at which is concentrated, for the convenience of the distant and general trader, the scattered traffic of numerous petty and barbarous tribes, separately trifling; but when thus united, of real importance. In none of these views, however, was it probably the most eligible situation which might have been selected. In passing through the Straits of Malacca from the west, it is a good deal out of the direct track, and the time wasted in visiting it is considerably increased by some difficulties in entering and quitting the harbour. The Island of Junk-Ceylon would, as a naval station, have been greatly preferable; and for commercial purposes, Singapore is incomparably superior. Junk-Cey-

* The settlements of Singapoor and Malacca have been recently annexed to Penang, and an enormous increase made to the civil and military establishments wholly uncalled for.

lon is, however, not likely to be a competitor; and Penang, although it will lose, by means of Singapore, the more valuable native commerce that comes from the East, will preserve, from its situation, the trade of its immediate neighbourhood, which will embrace the greater portion of the pepper trade, the trade in Areca nut, and a very considerable share of that in tin. A respectable opinion will be formed of the utility of Prince of Wales's Island as an emporium, when it is stated that the value of its exports and imports in 1820 amounted to 4,808,688 Spanish dollars.*

The whole revenue afforded by Prince of Wales's Island amounts to about two hundred thousand Spanish dollars, or very little more than one half the expenditure. Financial resources so respectable, however, ought to be adequate to the maintenance of an establishment on a plan still sufficiently liberal, and infinitely better suited to the purposes of good government than the present cumbrous and burthensome one.

The sources from which the Penang revenue is derived are—duties upon the trade; and excise duties, in the form of licences or monopolies, with a variety of minor items, such as quit-

* In 1824-25, the exports and imports had increased to 5,265,902 Spanish dollars.

rents, &c. The imposts upon trade amount to about 90,000 dollars, and the excise duties to about 96,000. In a port, the great utility of which consists in the facilities which it should afford to the common trade of the nation, and the commerce of which is but a mere transit trade, no duties whatever ought to be levied upon merchandize, because, however trifling their amount, the very act of subjecting the petty cargoes of the ignorant native traders to the examination and control of the officers of customs is, from the vexation necessarily attending it, a serious obstacle to their resort. A trifling duty upon tonnage, if any duty at all be worth levying, would be less easily evaded, more easily and cheaply levied, and in all probability equally productive.*

The excise duties are levied upon the consumption of opium, spirits, hemp used as an intoxicating drug, betel and pepper leaves, and pork. The monopoly of the vend of each of these is sold to a farmer by public sale from year to year. Some of these objects of taxation

* The Custom-House duties have recently been abolished at Penang, but the formalities somewhat unreasonably kept up. The abolition of this impost arose out of an attempt of the local Government to levy duties on the trade of Singapoor and Malacca. The subject was brought forward in Parliament—the Home Authorities interfered, and the imposition of duties at all the three settlements was judiciously prohibited.

are themselves very injudiciously selected. The tax on pork can be no better than a capitation tax on the Chinese, in a situation where the bulk of the rest of the population is Mohammedan. The tax on betel-leaf, which, besides being extremely unproductive, is one which falls peculiarly heavy upon the poorest class of the population, and exempts many of the rich. The most judicious and suitable subjects of taxation are opium, spirits, and hemp used as an intoxicating drug. The great consumers of opium are the Chinese and the Malays, and to a smaller extent the Siamese, Burmans, Chouliahs, and Bengallis. The regular and constant consumers of arrack, or native spirits, are the Chinese, but they seldom or never drink to the extent of inebriety. The native Christians, the Chouliahs, and the Bengallis, drink irregularly, but when they do, always to excess. The Burmans and Siamese are looked upon as hard drinkers. The Malays are extremely temperate.

In former times a tax was levied on gambling, more productive than all the rest put together; but on the institution of the Court of Justice, it was presented by the Grand Jury as a nuisance, and abolished. This was, perhaps, being too fastidious. The Chinese, the Malays, native Christians, Burmans, and Siamese, are violently, and without a revolution in their manners, not certainly to be brought about by mere municipal regulation, incurably addicted to gambling. The Chinese especially, habitually repair to the gaming-table after a day of severe toil. It would, perhaps, have been better to have regulated and controlled this propensity, than vainly to have attempted to eradicate it. The consequence of attempting the latter has been, that gaming still goes on clandestinely—heavy fines are levied by the police, and its officers are afforded a pretext for vexatious interference in the private concerns of the inhabitants.

The industry, activity, and energy of the population of Penang, in comparison to that of other Asiatic countries, is exemplified in its capacity to pay taxes. Excluding the military and convicts, amounting together to above 3000, and who scarcely in any respect contribute to the finances, the population of Penang pay, exclusive of custom-house duties, 112,759 dollars, which exhibits a rate of taxation of three dollars, thirteen cents, per head.*

* The inhabitants of our territorial dominions on the Continent, Custom-house duties included, pay only five shillings per head, or about a third part of the amount stated in the text, yet they are the most heavily taxed of the two. The annual revenue of our Continental dominions is about 22,000,000 sterling. Were our subjects there as well governed or as industrious as even the inhabitants of Penang, the revenue ought to be 66,000,000, and the people less oppressed!

CHAPTER II.

Departure from Penang.—Description of the Principality of Queda.—Description of the Dinding Islands.—Account of Perak.—Arrival at Malacca.—Incidents there.—Description of the Place.—Visit to the Carimon Islands.—Arrival at Singapore.—Incidents there.—Ancient settlement of the Malays.—Chinese Navigation.—Account of the race of Malays called Ourang-laut.

Jan. 5.—We went out of the harbour of Penang by the Southern channel, through which ships drawing no more than eighteen feet may always pass without risk, and thus save a day or two in their route to the Eastward. In passing out we landed upon the little island of Jărjak, about a mile and a half long, and separated from Penang by a deep and narrow channel. We found it to consist, like other places which we had visited in the neighbourhood, of the usual grey granite. It was at this place that the construction of naval docks was contemplated; but neither here, nor any where else in the vicinity of Penang, is there a sufficient rise and fall of the tide, or any other peculiar advantage for such a purpose.

Jan. 7.—During the three last days our progress had been impeded by calms, and light or unfair breezes, a very usual occurrence in these places. To-day we passed the southern limits of the Malay state of Queda. The principality of Queda, of which a rapid sketch will not here be out of place, is about one hundred and ten geographical miles in length, from north to south. Its breadth is unequal, and every where inconsiderable; for the utmost width of this portion of the peninsula itself is but one hundred and thirty miles; and this it shares every where with Patani, a chain of high mountains running north and south, dividing its breadth between them. The boundary to the north, between Queda and Siam, is Lănggu, in latitude 6° 50′, and that between it and Perak Kurao, about the latitude of 5°. Besides the territory on the main, several large islands belong to this state. The principal of these is Lăngkawi, which is twenty-five miles long, and which has a considerable share of culture and population. Trutao, the next in size, is fifteen miles in length, and has but few inhabitants. The character of this territory in general is, that of being extremely woody, marshy, and mountainous. From Lănggu to Kurao, inclusive—for both these give names to rivers—there are counted not less than six-and-thirty streams. Six of these are of very considerable size, and might be useful both to commerce and agriculture. In the range of hills in the interior, there are many mountains of a great height; and Jărai, a detached one near the western coast, is supposed to be six thousand feet high. Although the country is little cultivated, it does not seem to be destitute of fertility; and its capacity of production is satisfactorily shown in its power of supplying the principal consumption of Penang, now possessed of a population nearly equalling its own. The country is supposed to contain from 40 to 50,000 inhabitants, divided, according to ancient custom, into one hundred and five petty districts, each of forty-four families. By another old institution, the country was classified and sub-divided into petty divisions, each of twenty-four houses.* If we can rely upon the information of Commodore Beaulieu, who visited this country in 1620, it must have contained, seven years before his visit, a population of 60,000 souls; for he tells us that an epidemic which raged about that time, carried off 40,000, or two-thirds of the whole number.

The indigenous inhabitants of the territory of Queda, consist of four classes; namely, Malays,

* Called tăngga, or stairs; every dwelling-house having a stair to it.

Samsams, Siamese, and Sămangs; but chiefly of the two former, among whom the second are said to be the most numerous. By Samsams are meant people of the Siamese race, who have adopted the Mohammedan religion, and who speak a language which is a mixed jargon of the languages of the two people; a matter which, in the opinion of the latter, brings some reproach with it. The following is a specimen. "Saya na pai naik keh bun gunung." "I want to ascend the mountain;" in which the first word is Malay, the two next Siamese, the fourth Malay, the fifth and sixth Siamese, and the seventh or last Malay again.

The Sămang are the same Negro race found from the Andamans to New Guinea. They are here distinguished into two races, the Sămang and Bila; the latter holding no intercourse whatever with the inhabitants of the plains, but the former frequenting the villages, and carrying on some traffic with the more civilized inhabitants. Neither have any fixed habitation, and roaming through the woods, exist chiefly on the produce of their hunting, feeding indiscriminately upon every description of animal, whether quadruped or reptile. They appear to be a timid and harmless race.

The revenue of the petty chief of Queda amounted to about 42,000 Spanish dollars a-year. The country, from the earliest knowledge of Europeans, has been a tributary or vassal state of Siam; and, besides contributing in war to the assistance of the paramount state, in men, arms, and provisions, by immemorial usage, the King of Queda sends to Siam, in common with other Malayan princes, a triennial token of submission, in the form of a little tree of gold, which hence comes to be applied by the Malays of these parts to any tribute whatever. About the beginning of the seventeenth century, Queda was conquered by Achin, which held it for some years in a state of vassalage.

Jan. 9.—Yesterday morning we were in sight of the islands usually called in the maritime charts the Dindings, (correctly Pangkur, for Dinding is the name of a place on the opposite main,) and the group of islets farther south, called by the Malays, Pulo Sambilan, or the Nine Isles. We gratified our curiosity by landing on the largest Dinding. The sea-breeze carried us in between this island and the mainland of Perak, with which it forms a beautiful and safe harbour, running north and south, and seemingly sheltered from every wind. After rounding the south point of the island, of which we sailed within one hundred yards, we came upon a little cove, with a sandy beach, and here landed. The island consists of abrupt hills of a few hundred feet high, clothed with tall wood almost to the water's edge. Except in one or two spots, such as that on which we landed, there was no beach, the coast being formed of great blocks of granite, the only rock which we any where perceived. Tin ore is asserted to be found on the island. It is utterly uncultivated and uninhabited; but near the landing-place we observed two or three temporary and unoccupied huts thrown up, consisting of a few boughs of trees and some long grass. This is a famous haunt of pirates, and our Malay interpreters informed us that these huts were of their construction. In the seventeenth century, the Dutch occupied the island as a post to control the trade of the country, and chiefly to secure a monopoly of the tin of the Malay principality of Perak. Dampier, who visited this place in the year 1689, gives an accurate description of it. Relying upon his known fidelity, we sought for the remains of the Dutch fort, and found it exactly as he described it. The brick walls are still standing after a lapse of one hundred and thirty-two years; concealed, however, from the first view, by the forest which has grown round them. The fort was merely a square building of masonry of about thirty feet to a side. A platform, about sixteen feet high, contained the guns and troops, and in the walls were eight round embrasures for cannon, and sixteen loop-holes for fire-arms. The governor and officers' apartments were in the upper-story. There was but one entrance to the fort, and this by a flight of steps towards the sea-side. Dampier tells us that the governor had a detached house near the sea, where he passed the day, but which, for security, he always abandoned for the fort at night; and accordingly we found, in the situation he mentions, the terrace on which the house in question stood, with fragments of broken bottles and coarse china-ware scattered here and there in its neighbourhood. The whole appearance of the place conveyed a very good picture of the state of alarm and distrust in which the garrison perpetually lived—the effect of the lawless and unprofitable object in which they were engaged. Dampier tells a very ludicrous story to this effect:—While the captain of his ship and a passenger, with his wife, were entertained by the Dutch governor, in his house without the fort, an alarm was given of the appearance of Malays! His Excellency, without any warning to his guests, bolted out of one of the windows, and ran off to the fort, followed by all his servants and attendants. The feast was left standing, and the garrison began to fire the great guns, by way of giving the Malays to understand that they were prepared for them. The year after Dampier visited it, the garrison was cut off, nor have I heard that it was ever re-established. We discovered that the place had not been without some occasional European visitors, for on the plaster of the embrasures were carved the initials of several names, and in very plain figures, the years 1727, 1754, and 1821. This island, like others in these latitudes, affords a rich field for the botanist. Mr. Finlayson here discovered a new epidendron, of gigantic dimensions. The flowering stem was six feet long, and had from ninety to one hundred flowers upon it, each of which was two and a half inches broad, and four inches long, of a rich yellow colour, spotted with brown, and emitting a very agreeable fragrance. Deer and wild hogs seem to abound in the island; for we discovered many of their tracks in the sand.

As an European establishment, with which view it has been contemplated, this island, though the harbour be good, more easily accessible than any other which has been named for such a purpose, and far more in the direct track of active commerce than Penang, is certainly, upon the whole, unsuitable. It is, on the one hand, too far within the Straits for a place of resort and refreshment for our navy coming from the Bay of Bengal; and, on the other, much too far to the west, to be an emporium for the commerce of the nations to the eastward of the Straits of Malacca. Independent of these primary objections, there seems scarcely a spot in the island level enough for cultivation, or even for convenient and comfortable habitation. The prospect of deriving any benefit from the working of tin-mines in this island, even under an European Government, supposing the ore to exist in sufficient abundance, appears to me to be more than questionable. The whole island is an abrupt hard granite rock, from which ore could not be extracted with any profit in the state of skill and industry which exists among the natives of the country, or even among the Chinese themselves. In Banca, and other places where abundance of tin is produced, the ore is found in situations extremely different, that is, in streams through the soil of the low lands, from which it is easily extracted, readily smelted, and finally when smelted, affording a metal of superior value to what is obtained by the laborious process of mining in rocky districts.

Jan. 11.—We had now passed the territories of Perak and Salangore. Perak contains one hundred and five *mokims*, or petty parishes, and is said to be more populous than Queda. It extends about seventy-five miles along the coast, in by far the broadest part of the whole peninsula. This is the most productive part of the western coast in tin. I have never heard any exact statement of the quantity it yields, but of the 15,000 piculs, or about 2,000,000lbs, imported yearly into Penang, a very large share is from this country.* Perak, like Queda, is a vassal of Siam, and being refractory, about two years ago, was reduced to subjection by the Queda Chief, in consequence of orders from the Lord Paramount.

Salangore extends about ninety-six miles along the coast, where the peninsula begins to grow narrow. This is a very petty state, and inferior in population to Perak and Queda. The reigning family is Bugis of the Waju race that is of the most commercial and enterprising of the nations of Celebes. In this state, at a place called Lukot, situated immediately to the north of Cape Rachado, a valuable tin mine has lately been discovered, and is now worked.

Jan. 13.—Last night we came into the roads of Malacca, saluting a Dutch sloop of war and the fort; and this morning, about ten o'clock, we landed in the Dutch Governor's accommodation-boat, which had been politely sent for us. On landing, we were received on the wharf by the Governor's secretary, charged with an invitation from Mr. Timmerman Tysen, the Governor, whom I had had the pleasure of knowing some years before at Batavia. Such of our party as could be accommodated accepted the invitation, and the rest took up their residence in the town.

* Its produce is reckoned at 4000 piculs, of 133⅓lbs. of avoirdupois.

This morning I walked round the hill of Malacca, and surveyed those ruined fortifications which, under the Portuguese, had resisted twelve sieges. On the top of the hill, which is about a hundred feet high, are the ruins of the Portuguese church of St. Paul, still a conspicuous landmark in approaching the roads. It was built soon after the Portuguese conquest, and towards the beginning of the sixteenth century. The Dutch, after getting possession of Malacca, used it as a Protestant church and burying-ground; and hence the unusual spectacle which it presents of the tombs of conquerors and conquered, Catholics, and heretics, blended together in one spot. Without reading the inscriptions, the tombstones of the respective people are to be recognised by their age, and the different materials of which they consist. The Portuguese tombs are of granite from China, and the Dutch of a hard black trap rock from the Coromandel coast, for neither Malacca nor its vicinity afford either. Among the tombstones we read, in very distinct characters, and in the Latin language, the inscription on that of Dominus Petrus, second Bishop of Japan, who is stated to have died in the Straits of Singapore, in the year 1598. The body of St. Francis Xavier, the Apostle of the Indies, who died in China, once reposed here, but the sacred relic was disinterred and finally conveyed to Goa.

Jan. 14.—I called upon Mr. Milne this forenoon. This industrious and highly respectable character is an Englishman by birth, and the second in rank of the Protestant Mission to China, in connexion with the Malay, denominated the Ultra-Gangetic Mission. This fraternity has been established at Malacca since the year 1815, and since 1818 an Anglo-Chinese College has been established, the chief object of which institution is the cultivation of Chinese and English literature, and the diffusion of Christianity in the countries and islands lying to the eastward of Penang. Mr. Milne is one of the best Chinese scholars living, and the result of his indefatigable labours is, a version of the Scriptures, in great progress, a periodical work in the Chinese language, another in English, called "The Indo-Chinese Gleaner," and a little volume, entitled, "A Retrospect of the First Ten Years of the Protestant Mission to China," which last contains some excellent remarks on the manners and literature of the Indo-Chinese nations. These have all issued from the press of the seminary itself at Malacca. The labours of such men as Mr. Milne, Dr. Morrison, Dr. Carey, and Mr. Marchman, are of incalculable benefit to the cause of humanity and civilization, while it is acknowledged on every side, that their means and motives are equally unexceptionable and pure. Mr. Milne, in conversation, furnished us with some valuable hints respecting the objects of our Embassy to Cochin China, and with notes on the geography and commerce of that country; the result of his inquiries among the traders from thence, who have of late years visited the Straits of Malacca.

Jan. 16.—Last night Mr. Timmerman, the Governor, gave a ball and supper, in compliment to the departure of the military officers of the station, relieved by fresh troops from Batavia. Besides the inhabitants of the place, the party consisted of the officers of three Dutch men-of-war lying at the time in the Roads. This occasion gave us an opportunity of observing the manners and appearance of the colonists. Out of thirty-seven ladies, two or three only were Europeans, and the rest born in the country, with a large admixture of Asiatic blood. The female dress, of the younger part, was in the English fashion; and a very few only of the elderly ladies dressed in the Malay kabaya, a sort of loose gown, or wore the hair in the Malay fashion. The long residence of the English in the Dutch colonies,—the influence of the French, and lately, of their own more polished countrywomen,—have nearly banished these external marks of barbarism. Before the last ten years, the habits and costume of the female Dutch colonists partook more of the Asiatic than the European. Instead of Dutch, they spoke a barbarous dialect of Malay; they were habited, as I have described, in the dress of that people; they chewed the pawn-leaf publicly, and even in the ball-room each fair dame had before her an enormous brass ewer to receive the refuse of her mastication.

Jan. 17.—We re-embarked last evening, the Dutch Governor politely attending us to the wharf, and at eight at night, a fine sea-breeze having set in, we weighed and made sail towards Singapore, in company with a Dutch corvette.—The following is a short sketch of the place we had just left, the result of previous inquiry, as well as of examination on the spot. The territory of Malacca is forty miles in length along the sea, and extends thirty miles inland. The principality of Salangore bounds it to the north at Cape Rachado. Jehor bounds it to the south, at the river Mora, and the territory of Rumbo to the east. The largest mountain in the territory of Malacca is Ledang, which the Portuguese, and other Europeans in imitation of them, have denominated Mount Ophir. This is distant from Malacca twenty-four miles, in a straight direction, and thirty-two by the windings of a very bad road. Its height is about 4000 feet. Besides a number of petty streams, there are in the territory of Malacca two considerable rivers, namely, Mora, already named, and Lingituah, the embouchure of which is a little to the south of Cape Rachado. The granitic formation, which characterises the countries we have hitherto visited, partially disappears at Malacca; the whole territory of which, as far as we could learn, is one uniform mass of cellular iron-ore. The valuable minerals found within the territory of Malacca are gold and tin; but the first, nowhere in sufficient abundance to have fixed the imperfect industry of the native inhabitants; of the second, it is said to produce 4000 piculs. The soil must be considered as decidedly deficient in fertility, for at no period of its history does Malacca appear to have been capable of supplying its own scanty population with bread corn. Bad government must not be assigned as the sole cause, for Malacca has had various forms of European government; all of them, however bad or imperfect, generally superior to the native governments of several neighbouring countries, producing an abundant supply of grain. Fruits, the perfection of which depends more, in these latitudes, upon the culture they receive than upon the quality of the soil, and which are never skilfully cultivated but by Europeans, are produced in great excellence and variety at Malacca. Seventy-two species have been produced at once at a dessert; but, of course, the greater number very worthless. The mangustin and pine-apple are unrivalled at this place. The durian, the orange, the plantain, the shaddock, and the dukuh, are also very fine. Poultry and hogs are of good quality, and in abundance, but sheep do not exist, and horned cattle are scarce.

The present population of the town of Malacca and its territory is 22,000; a number which does not seem to have varied for at least the last six-and-twenty years; a fact which proclaims in intelligible language the decrease of wealth, or at least the absence of prosperity. A place which has been the seat of European commerce for three centuries, and was for more than two centuries and a half before in the possession of an active and commercial race of natives, and yet contains little more than eighteen inhabitants to a square mile, must be considered as labouring under some natural, and perhaps insuperable defects.*

The permanent inhabitants of Malacca are the Malays, a brown-coloured race of savages, with lank hair, called Benua and Jakong; a race of Hindu colonists from Telinga; the descendants of the Portuguese conquerors; and those of the Dutch. To this list may be added the usual admixture of Chinese, and of Mohammedans of the coast of Coromandel. To a brief account

* While we occupied Malacca, during the war, its population was estimated at 25,000. The Dutch estimated it, as stated in the text, at 22,000. By a census, or estimate, made in 1827, it is reduced to 16,000.

of these, I shall premise a short sketch of the history of Malacca.—About the middle of the twelfth century, when Europeans were as yet in ignorance of the existence of such a people, a colony of Malays, from Menangkabao, or perhaps more correctly from the north coast of Sumatra generally, are said to have settled at Singapura, at the extremity of the Malay peninsula, the very spot on which we ourselves have lately formed an establishment. After a residence short of a century at this place, they were driven from it by the Javanese, and retiring to the westward, founded Malacca in the year 1252. Four-and-twenty years after this event they were converted to the Mohammedan religion, and two hundred and fifty-nine years later they were conquered by the Portuguese, who, after one hundred and twenty-nine years possession, were expelled by the Dutch. The Malay population of Malacca are the reputed descendants of the first colonists from Sumatra. The Jakong and the Benua are wild races of men living in the deep forests of the interior of the peninsula, being spread over the territories of Malacca, Rumbo, and Jehor. They exist principally in the hunter state, some of the least uncivilized practising a little rude husbandry. Their persons are nearly naked, and their habitations extremely rude. A death happening in a tribe is always the signal for abandoning their habitations, and taking up a new encampment. They appear to practise no cruel rites, and in their manners to be altogether extremely inoffensive. What renders this wild people most remarkable, is their differing totally in language and physical form from the Negro races which inhabit the interior of the more northern parts of the peninsula. They are, in fact, Malays in the savage state. Doctor Leyden, who visited them in 1811, on our way to the conquest of Java, could discover in their language but seven-and-twenty words which differed from common Malay; and on examination of the specimens he gives, I find, that at least six or seven of these are extremely doubtful; while two or three appear original Malay words, for which Sanscrit ones have been substituted in the more modern dialect. Whether this rude people be the true original stock of the wide-spread race of the Malays, or a degenerated one from the colonists of Sumatra, before their conversion to Mohammedanism, is a matter not very easily determined. With respect to the Malays of the neighbouring state of Rumbo having emigrated from Sumatra, there is no question made. Other Malays denominate them "people of Menangkabao;" they speak the precise language of the people of this last country, ending their words always with a short *o* instead of a short *a*, as done by other Malays. A friendly intercourse is always maintained between the two states; Menangkabao being acknowledged the paramount one, and the Prince of Rumbo receiving a regular investiture from that country.

The Hindus of Malacca are the only ultramarine colonists of that people of whom I have heard. The popular notion of its being forbidden to Hindus to quit their country by sea, is sufficiently contradicted by their existence; and how indeed, without supposing such emigration, are we, in common sense, to account for the once wide spread of their religion among the distant islands of the Indian Ocean. The Malacca colony amounts at present to about two hundred and fifty families, and in the more prosperous days of the settlement, is said to have been far more numerous. The colonists are of the Telinga, or Kalinga nation, and at present composed only of the third and fourth, or mercantile and servile classes of the Hindu orders. Not a great many years ago, there were still a few Bramins and Chatrias among them. The Malacca Hindus practise all the ordinary rites of the Hindu worship; they refuse to eat with persons of other religions; and in their food reject beef and pork, but consume fish, goat's flesh, and fowls. Those of the mercantile order employ themselves as traders, accountants, and assayers of gold, in which last occupation they have a high reputation both for skill and fidelity. Persons of the lower order are employed in the usual occupations of the servile class, including agriculture. The family of Bisara Seti, the present chief of this tribe, from whom I derive my information, settled in Malacca one hundred and forty-three years ago; but he can give no information respecting the establishment of the first colonists. He states generally, however, that the greater number settled at Malacca during the Portuguese rule. When the Hindu settlers first came over, they were unattended by their families, and formed connexions with the women of the country, particularly with those of Celebes; they soon however abandoned this practice, as is evident enough from their preserving the genuine Hindu features, and a stature considerably beyond that of the islanders.

The Portuguese amount to 4000, and are all of the lowest order. Although with a great admixture of Asiatic blood, the European features are still strongly marked in them. I have no doubt there are among them many of the lineal descendants of the haughty, intolerant, and brave men, who fought by the side of Albuquerque; but they certainly inherit no part of the character of their ancestors, and are a timid, peaceable, and submissive race. They offer to us a spectacle not frequently presented in the East—that of men bearing the European name, and wearing the European garb, engaged in the humblest occupations of life, for we find them employed as domestic servants, as day labourers, and as fishermen.

Malacca is probably doomed to sink into still greater insignificance than that into which it has already fallen, but it is associated in our minds with one of the most interesting events in the history of our species—the discovery of a new route to the Indies, and the heroic achievements of the Portuguese which immediately followed it. We cannot, as Europeans, but survey with pride the spot on which stood the bridge by which Albuquerque, at the head of 700 Europeans, stormed walls and intrenchments that were guarded by 30,000 barbarians—an achievement superior to any of those of Pizarro, inasmuch as the Malays were a braver and even more civilized enemy than the Americans. An Englishman will see, with some mortification, the ruins of the fortification which the Portuguese constructed shortly after the conquest. It surrounded the little hill, on the top of which was the church of St. Paul's, already mentioned. The walls were of solid masonry, and of the iron-stone of the country. To the west it was protected by the sea, to the north by the river, and it had a moat to the other two sides. This specimen of the art of fortification in the beginning of the sixteenth century, the only one existing in these parts, and the pride and trust of the native inhabitants, was, by a piece of policy, equally barbarous and unnecessary, blown up by us in the year 1807.

The Dutch support at Malacca a most unnecessary civil and military establishment, which, independent of the revenue of the place itself, costs them three lacks of rupees, or near 30,000*l.* a-year. In a place remarkable for the peaceable character of its inhabitants, and without an enemy, European or native, they have an effective body of 400 troops, besides keeping on foot a militia or burgher corps. Fifty regular soldiers would have been quite adequate to the protection of the place, and a municipal establishment upon the humblest scale the most suitable for its good government.*

Malacca, in every stage of its history, owed its prosperity to its being the only port in the Straits of Malacca, where there was tolerable security for life and property. The Dutch themselves did much towards its ruin by the highly illiberal system of exclusive trade, which they long persevered in. The establishment of Penang, on different principles, brought the matter nearly to a crisis, and that of Singapore has com-

* Shortly after this passage was written, the Dutch judiciously reduced both their civil and military establishments. The place, as is sufficiently known, is now a British possession, and although not likely to be of much value, it may be rendered at least not burthensome to us, if its establishments be kept within the bounds of moderation. For taking an opposite course, it would be extremely difficult to find any pretext.

pleted its fall. The symptoms of decay are too striking to escape observation, and the traveller who has quitted either of those settlements, cannot fail to contrast their industry and activity with the lifeless dulness which reigns at Malacca.

Jan. 18.—At daylight this morning we had Pulo Pisang behind us, Pulo Kakab to our left, and the Carimons and other islands to our right, with Tanjung Bulus, (correctly, Buros,) the most southern extremity of the continent of Asia, in latitude 1° 15′ north, before us. We bore down upon the Carimons, with a view of making some inquiry respecting them; and at ten o'clock landed upon the Little Carimon, the latitude of the northern end of which is 1° 8½′ north. This island is about two miles long, and the highest part of it perhaps about 500 feet in height. The whole is high land, covered with a lofty forest, and the coast steep and rocky. The island is uninhabited, and indeed, from its formation and aspect, does not appear a fit residence for man in any stage of civilization. The Great Carimon is divided from the little one by a very narrow and deep gut. It is twelve miles in length, by five in breadth; has a great deal of low land, apparently suited for culture; and two peaked mountains about the centre, the highest of which did not appear to us to be less than 1800 or 2000 feet high. I am told there are a few Malay settlers upon it. To the west of the Carimons are distinctly visible many islands, the very names of which are unknown to Europeans.

We examined, with considerable attention, that side of the Little Carimon on which we landed. The rock of which it is composed is porphyritic hornstone, varying in appearance as the grain is larger or smaller: it is extremely hard and flinty, and exhibits a conchoidical fracture. The surface of the rock has every where a honeycombed appearance; and the hollows, when examined, are discovered to be drusy cavities, many of them containing portions of secondary limestone. One of these cavities I measured, and found to be four feet three inches long, two feet broad, and eighteen inches deep.*

Jan. 19.—At twelve o'clock to-day we passed the narrow channel of the Rabbit and Coney, the western entrance of the Straits of Singapore, and soon found ourselves surrounded in every direction by beautiful verdant islands. The sea was smooth, the sky clear, and the whole prospect equally novel and pleasing. From the

* In the autumn of 1825, while resident of Singapore, I visited the Carimon Island (correctly written Krimun); the hornstone mentioned in the text is confined to the coast, and is merely a partial and overlaying formation. The interior is composed of granite, with veins of white quartzl, and abounds in tin-ore. The inhabitants of the larger island amount to 400 in number.

deck there could be counted between fifty and sixty green and woody islands of various dimensions, and from the mast-head above seventy. I do not believe there is any part of the world which can afford a prospect, in its way, of superior beauty, and this indeed has been observed and confessed by all voyagers. At six o'clock we anchored in Singapore Roads.

Jan. 21.—Last night my old friend Colonel Farquhar, resident of Singapore, sent his staff, Captain Davies, on board to invite us on shore. We landed this morning; and Mr. Scott, a merchant of this new settlement, and the son of my respected friend, Mr. Robert Scott, an experienced and most intelligent merchant of Penang, hospitably and obligingly gave his house up for our accommodation. In the evening we dined with Colonel Farquhar, and went through the greater part of the new settlement. Notwithstanding the state of abeyance in which the political question regarding the settlement was involved, there was universally an air of animation and activity. Several miles of new road were already formed, and the habitations were so numerous, and the population so great, that we could hardly imagine that the whole was the creation of three short years.

Jan. 23.—We had to-day a visit from some individuals of the race of Malays, called Orăng-laut,—that is, "men of the sea." They have a rough exterior, and their speech is awkward and uncouth; but, in other respects, I could observe little essential difference between them and other Malays. These people have adopted the Mohammedan religion. They are divided into, at least, twenty tribes, distinguished usually by the straits or narrow seas they principally frequent. A few of them have habitations on shore, but by far the greater number live constantly in their boats, and nearly their sole occupation is fishing; those who are most civilized cultivating a few bananas. They are subjects of the King of Johore, and the same people who have been called *Orang Sallat*, or, "men of the straits;"—the straits here alluded to being, not the great Straits of Malacca, which are extensive beyond their comprehension, but the narrow guts running among the little islets that are so abundantly strewed over its eastern entrance. Under this appellation they have been notorious for their piracies, from the earliest knowledge of Europeans respecting these countries.

Jan. 27.—We went yesterday morning along the coast, to the westward, and visited the new harbour, or Sălat Panikam, as it is called by the Malays. This harbour is formed by Singapore and the islets which lie off the western limit of the roadstead. The entrance is narrow and difficult; but when a ship is once moored within it, she is secure from every danger,—from rocks, elements, and even from an enemy, for half a dozen guns would make it impregnable to any attack from sea. The prospect we had on entering it was beautiful and unexpected. We found ourselves completely landlocked, in every direction, by the green and woody shores of the islands surrounding us; and the sea, though considerably ruffled without, was here as smooth as glass. This is a favourite retreat of the Orăng-laut. On our arrival, their proas were lying along the shore; but as the flood-tide made, they advanced into the middle of the channel, and began to fish. Their principal mode of taking fish is by spearing, and hence the native name of the Strait, which has this meaning. The larger fish are followed by the proas, and easily traced through the water, which is perfectly clear and transparent. They are speared with a long trident, and with such dexterity as to be seldom missed. This mode of taking fish must be tedious and unproductive. It is suited, however, to the poverty of the people, who, perhaps, cannot afford the necessary supply of nets, and, I have no doubt, is strongly recommended to them by the pleasure they derive from the pursuit. They complain, I understand, of the numerous stake-nets erected by the industrious Chinese, in the harbour of Singapore, as detrimental to their employment, pretty much in the same way as European labourers complain of the introduction of new machinery, and with the same justice. The boats of the Orăng-laut are mere canoes, covered by a light shed of palm-leaves. We saw their whole families on board, men, women, and children; and both in their fishing and management of the boats, the women appeared to take as active a share as the men.

Feb. 2.—A junk which arrived a few days ago, had on board a native Cochin Chinese merchant, a man of respectability and intelligence, who paid us a visit to-day. According to his statement, the French are in considerable numbers in different parts of the Cochin Chinese empire, but they are mostly religious persons. He states that a French frigate came to the Port of Han, or Turan, in 1819, and made a demand for that place and its adjacent territory. The king replied, that he was not a petty Malay prince to barter his dominions for money, and ordered the ship to depart forthwith. Several French merchant-ships have also visited Cochin China since the peace; and two American ships have obtained full cargoes at the Port of Saigon, or Longnai, as it is called by the Chinese.

Feb. 3.—I walked this morning round the walls and limits of the ancient town of Singapore, for such in reality had been the site of our modern settlement. It was bounded to the east by the sea, to the north by a wall, and to the west by a salt creek or inlet of the sea. The inclosed space is a plain, ending in a hill of considerable extent, and a hundred and fifty feet in height. The whole is a kind of triangle, of which the base is the sea-side, about a mile in length. The wall, which is about sixteen feet in breadth at its base, and at present about eight or nine in height, runs very near a mile from the sea-coast to the base of the hill, until it meets a salt marsh. As long as it continues in the plain, it is skirted by a little rivulet running at the foot of it, and forming a kind of moat; and where it attains the elevated side of the hill, there are apparent the remains of a dry ditch. On the western side, which extends from the termination of the wall to the sea, the distance, like that of the northern side, is very near a mile. This last has the natural and strong defence of a salt marsh, overflown at high-water, and of a deep and broad creek. In the wall there are no traces of embrasures or loop-holes; and neither on the sea-side, nor on that skirted by the creek and marsh, is there any appearance whatever of artificial defences. We may conclude from these circumstances, that the works of Singapore were not intended against fire-arms, or an attack by sea; or that if the latter, the inhabitants considered themselves strong in their naval force, and therefore thought any other defences in that quarter superfluous.

Feb. 4.—On the stony point which forms the western side of the entrance of the salt creek, on which the modern town of Singapore is building, there was discovered, two years ago, a tolerably hard block of sand-stone, with an inscription upon it. This I examined early this morning. The stone, in shape, is a rude mass, and formed of the one-half of a great nodule broken into two nearly equal parts by artificial means; for the two portions now face each other, separated at the base by a distance of not more than two feet and a half, and reclining opposite to each other at an angle of about forty degrees. It is upon the inner surface of the stone that the inscription is engraved. The workmanship is far ruder than any thing of the kind that I have seen in Java or India; and the writing, perhaps from time, in some degree, but more from the natural decomposition of the rock, so much obliterated as to be quite illegible as a composition. Here and there, however, a few letters seem distinct enough. The character is rather round than square. It is probably the Pali, or religious character used by the followers of Buddha, and of which abundant examples are to be found in Java and Sumatra; while no monuments exist in these countries in their respective vernacular alphabets. The only remains of antiquity at Singapore, besides this stone, and the wall and moat before mentioned, are contained on the hill before alluded to. After being cleared by us of the extensive forest which covered it, it is now clothed with a fine grassy sward, and forms the principal beauty of the new settlement. The greater part of the west and northern side of the mountain is covered with the remains of the foundations of buildings, some composed of baked brick of good quality. Among these ruins, the most distinguished are those seated on a square terrace, of about forty feet to a side, near the summit of the hill. On the edge of this terrace, we find fourteen large blocks of sand-stone; which, from the hole in each, had probably been the pedestals of as many wooden-posts which supported the building. This shows us, at once, that the upper part of the structure was of perishable materials; an observation which, no doubt, applies to the rest of the buildings as well as to this. Within the square terrace is a circular inclosure, formed of rough sand-stones, in the centre of which is a well, or hollow, which very possibly contained an image; for I look upon the building to have been a place of worship, and, from its appearance, in all likelihood, a temple of Buddha. I venture farther to conjecture, that the other relics of antiquity on the hill, are the remains of monasteries of the priests of this religion. Another terrace, on the north declivity of the hill, nearly of the same size, is said to have been the burying-place of Iskandar Shah, King of Singapore. This is the prince whom tradition describes as having been driven from his throne by the Javanese, in the year 1252 of the Christian era, and who died at Malacca, not converted to the Mohammedan religion, in 1274; so that the story is probably apocryphal. Over the supposed tomb of Iskandar, a rude structure has been raised, since the formation of the new settlement, to which Mohammedans, Hindus, and Chinese, equally resort to do homage. It is remarkable, that many of the fruit-trees cultivated by the ancient inhabitants of Singapore are still existing, on the eastern side of the hill, after a supposed lapse of near six hundred years. Here we find the durian, the rambutan, the duku, the shaddock, and other fruit-trees of great size; and all so degenerated, except the two first, that the fruit is scarcely to be recognized.

Among the ruins are found various descriptions of pottery, some of which is Chinese, and some native. Fragments of this are in great abundance. In the same situation have been found Chinese brass coins of the tenth and eleventh centuries. The earliest is of the Emperor of Ching chung, of the dynasty of Sung-chao, who died in the year 967. Another is of the reign of Jin-chung, of the same dynasty, who died in 1067; and a third, of that of Shin-chung, his successor, who died in 1085. The discovery of these coins affords some confirmation of the relations which fix the establishment of the Malays at Singapore, in the twelfth century. It should be remarked, in reference to this subject, that the coins of China were in circulation among all the nations of the Indian islands before they adopted the Mohammedan religion, or had any intercourse with Europeans. They are dug up in numbers in Java, and are still the only money used by the unconverted natives of Bali.

Feb. 6.—We made an excursion yesterday to some coral banks lying among the islands which form the western boundary of the harbour of Singapore. These banks exhibit the strangest and most fantastic forms of organic life that can be imagined, in the various shapes of corallines, madrepores, asteria, and sponges. In still deeper water, and off the southern extremity of the island, there are found those gigantic sponges, which are peculiar to the coast of Singapore, and which Europeans have called Neptunian cups. The natives brought them to us in great numbers.

Feb. 7.—I had yesterday a farewell visit from the commander of the Siamese ship and his pilot, whom I had so often met at Calcutta, and more recently at Penang. They had arrived at this place before us, and had been waiting, like ourselves, for the abatement of the strength of the north-east monsoon to proceed. They were determined, if possible, to reach Siam before the vernal equinox;—the period of a great festival of the worshippers of Buddha, and which, by all accounts, is celebrated at Siam with much solemnity. Parts of their investment were intended for the celebration of the festival; and as they had been absent fourteen months, they had some apprehension of the bastinado, or something worse, if they did not arrive without farther loss of time. I had before obtained from them a great deal of useful information; but as we approached Siam they became much more shy and reserved, and now communicated nothing without a strict injunction to secrecy. They constantly resisted our solicitations to assist in translating the Governor-general's letter into Siamese, — observing, that the communication of his Majesty's titles would be considered as the divulgement of a state secret, which might cost them their lives. The commander, who spoke Hindustani imperfectly, passed his hand over his neck on such occasions, to represent the operation of a sword, that no doubt might be entertained of the nature of his apprehensions.

Feb. 10.—Mr. Finlayson and I visited, this morning, a Cochin Chinese, a Chin-chew, or Fo-kien, and a Siamese junk.* Our interpreter accompanied us, and we had therefore an opportunity of making some interesting observations regarding their internal economy, management, and trade. We were received by all with uncommon civility and attention; but the people of Fo-kien, who are least accustomed to Europeans, were remarkable for the earnestness of their hospitality, which much more than compensates for the rusticity and bluntness of their manners. They pressed us to sit down, to eat with them, to drink tea with them, and to smoke their pipes; and when we apologized for the number of our inquiries, the commander assured us, that we did them honour by taking an interest in their affairs. It is the custom, when persons of any respectability visit the Chinese junks, to beat the gongs at their arrival and departure; and this compliment was paid to us. The Cochin Chinese junk carried 4000 piculs, or was of the burthen of about 240 tons. Her crew consisted of the commander, two officers, and thirty-two men; and the sailors were paid for the voyage from Saigun to Singapore, calculated to last about three months, at the rate of twenty Spanish dollars a-head, which gives about seven Spanish

* Junk is apparently an European corruption of the Malay word *jung*, the common term for any large vessel.

dollars a-month, being equal to the wages of an able seaman in our country; whereas, the quantity of labour he performs, even in his own way, amounts numerically to only one half; twice the number of Chinese being required to the same amount of tonnage as there would of European mariners. The Chinese sailors are of course fed, and at sea receive salt pork, salt fish, occasionally poultry, with rice, and sour or salt krout; and when in harbour, they receive fresh animal food and fresh vegetables. The charge of feeding a sailor from Cochin China is reckoned at a dollar and a quarter a-month, but from Canton it amounts to full three dollars. The Fo-kien junk was a small vessel of 1600 piculs, or near ninety-five tons; and the Siamese junk was of 1500 piculs, or about ninety tons. The first, cost in the river of Kamboja, where she was built, 4000 dollars; and would have cost in Canton, had she been constructed there, 5000. The second was built in Fo-kien, and cost no less than 3000 dollars. The Siamese junk was built in the river of Siam, and cost only 1350 dollars. The cost of building per ton, according to this statement, is at the following rates:

	Dollars.	Cents.	
Siamese junk . .	15		per ton.
Cochin Chinese do. .	16	66	——
Canton do. . .	20	83	——
Fo-kien do. . .	30	58	——

It ought, however, to be remarked, that the Chinese junks are built of fir; whereas, the Siamese one has her upper works entirely of fine teak, and her lower of a hard, durable wood, the name of which I could not ascertain. Admitting, however, that the materials of both were of the same quality, we have here exhibited a fair comparative scale of the price of food, labour, and materials in the different countries in question; for the degree of skill must be supposed to be the same, the Chinese being, in all these cases, the architects and workmen. Labour and materials are cheapest in Siam and Kamboja; twenty-five per cent. dearer at Canton; and more than one hundred per cent. dearer in Fo-kien, which has, notwithstanding, by far the largest share of the foreign Asiatic trade of China.

All Chinese junks are, with trifling variation, built on one model, indescribably awkward and clumsy; but from which, notwithstanding, it is forbidden by law to deviate. In point of convenience of structure, they are much inferior to the trading craft of the rudest tribes of the Indian islands; a circumstance which, notwithstanding the superiority of the Chinese in industry, intelligence, and enterprise, proves a serious and indeed insuperable obstacle to any great success in their foreign commerce. The hold of a junk is, as is well known, divided into compartments, across the vessel's length. The number of these varies. The large Cochin Chinese junk which we had just inspected was divided into six compartments, and the small Fo-kien junk into no less than fifteen. All the compartments are separately waterproof, and their sole intention is to add strength to the ship, and, in case of leaking, to prevent the water from extending beyond the subdivision in which the leak actually takes place. The Chinese are ignorant of the use of the pump on board a ship, and have no means of discharging the water but by hand-buckets.

The only guide of the Chinese mariner appears to be the compass. Each of the junks we visited had a small one divided into twenty-four parts, as usual. This was placed close to the little temple near the stern of the ship, dedicated to the protecting deities of the winds and seas, which is invariably found in Chinese vessels. They have no instruments whatever for observing the heavenly bodies, nor any means even of determining a vessel's dead reckoning, and they keep no log or journal. When the wind is not tolerably fair, they can make little progress. When the wind is aft, however, they sail tolerably well. The commander of the Cochin Chinese junk told me, that at the height of the north-east monsoon, he sailed right before the wind from Pulo Kondor, on the coast of Kamboja, to Pulo Timun, on the coast of the Malay peninsula, in three days and a half, a distance of about four hundred and thirty miles, which is at the rate of one hundred and twenty-three miles a-day, or little more than five miles an hour. With the winds which he had, it is not improbable that an ordinary English merchant-ship would have sailed at least eight miles, and a good one perhaps twice the distance of the Chinese junk. By the same person's account, the ordinary rate at which money can be borrowed in Cochin China, for maritime adventure, is forty-eight per cent. and the expected rate of profits is proportional,—namely, from eighty to one hundred per cent.

The commander of a ship is usually part owner of her, and the goods are received on freight, the shippers commonly embarking with their own property, which, however, is always under charge of the commander during the voyage, the proprietors having no access to them. On the Cochin Chinese junk, the rate of freight paid for goods I found to be as follows: fine goods, as cottons and silk stuffs, five per cent.; tea, ten per cent.; sugar, twenty per cent.; and rice, forty per cent. In the Fo-kien junk, the freight paid for black tea was one dollar forty cents per picul; which, allowing nine and a half piculs for each ton, is at the rate of thirteen dollars thirty cents.

While on the subject of the trade and navigation of the Chinese, I may take the opportunity of mentioning the very singular species of adventure carried on by them in the Straits of Malacca, in large row-boats, commonly known by the native name of *prahu pukat.** One of these which I measured, was about sixty-five feet long, nine feet in the beam, and about four feet in depth, and carried a cargo of from one hundred and eighty to one hundred and ninety piculs, or near twenty tons. She was rowed by twelve oars and fourteen paddles, and had the occasional assistance of a sail with fair winds. She had a crew, consisting of the commander and twenty-six rowers. Such a boat is usually the property of the commander, and the cargo belongs to the crew, each according to the capital he has contributed to the joint adventure. There is not one idle person on board; for the commander steers, and each of the adventurers has his oar or his paddle. Their adventures are confined between the islands at the eastern extremity of the Straits of Malacca, and the town of that name, out of the influence of the monsoons, and under the protection of the variable winds which characterize these latitudes.† From the rapidity of their course, they are quite secure from the attack of pirates. The voyage backwards and for-

* Literally a seine-boat,—this description of vessel having probably been first used for fishing with a net of that description.

† In the westerly monsoon they often pass out of the Straits of Malacca, visiting the different trading ports on the eastern shore of the Malay Peninsula.

MALAY MAN.

MALAY WOMAN.

wards, may, of course, be performed at every season. In fair weather, one of them will sail between the Island of Linga and Singapore in two days; and in the least favourable weather, in six; performing the voyage, therefore, on an average, in four days. The distance is about one hundred and eighty miles; so that these boats go, under the most favourable circumstances, at the rate of ninety miles a-day, or close upon four knots an hour, and, at an average, forty-five miles a-day. Three voyages may be performed in a month, if the state of the markets do not occasion extraordinary delays. When pepper is the cargo, as very frequently happens, the adventurers are contented, I am told, with a profit of three-fourths of a dollar per picul, when the selling price of this commodity is ten dollars. This supposes a profit of $8\frac{1}{10}$ per cent. on each adventure.

During the last month I had many personal and favourable opportunities of inquiring into the manners and habits of the Orăng-laut. The term is used to characterize the race of Malays who have their habitations exclusively on the sea, in opposition to those who have fixed abodes on shore, — the Orăng-darat, or "men of dry land." They are sometimes called Orăng-sălat, or "men of the straits," under which appellation they have been stigmatized for their piracy as long ago as the time of John De Barros, whose work was composed in the sixteenth century. At other times we hear them called *Ryots,* or "Subjects;"—that is to say, subjects of the king of *Jehor;* but under this name, too, their reputation is no better, for the Western Malays use the term Jehor as synonymous with that of pirate or robber. I had no conception that any of the tribes bearing the Malay name were in so low a state of civilization as these people are. By far the greater number of them are born, live, and die in their miserable canoes, and the few who live occasionally on shore are scarcely more comfortably situated. These are ignorant of the culture of rice, and plant very few roots, neither do they cultivate the cocoa nut, a plant which conduces so much to the comfort of the other tribes of the eastern islands. The plantain, or *banana,* from the rapidity of its growth, and the volume of food which it supplies, is the great object of their attention in an agricultural view. Whether their habitation be on land or water, fishing is the great employment of the Orăng-laut; and what they do not consume themselves, forms the only fund from which they are supplied with the other common necessaries of life. In their general character, they are indolent, improvident, and defective in personal cleanliness. Like the other islanders, however, they are neither selfish, cunning, nor mendacious. In their external demeanour they are clownish, their manners unceremonious, and their dialect uncouth; but, withal, their behaviour is neither rude nor disrespectful. Of the character they exhibit in their predatory excursions, I am not competent to judge, but it is sufficiently bad.

A more accurate test, however, of this people's state in society than can be conveyed by a general description, is afforded by a short sketch of the actual expense of their mode of life. A house costs about five dollars, and the best seldom above twenty. A dwelling boat costs no more than six dollars, and a fishing canoe about four. The only furniture, if there is any at all, is a bedstead and pillows, worth four dollars, and a cast-iron cooking-pot, of Chinese or Siamese manufacture, worth about half a dollar. With the art of weaving these people are utterly unacquainted, and, as far as they are clothed at all, they are clothed in foreign manufactures. The *sarong*, or lower garment, of both sexes, is the manufacture of Celebes; it costs four dollars, and lasts four years. The turban, or rather handkerchief, which binds the head of the men, is the manufacture of the same country; it costs half a dollar, and lasts at least as long as the *sarong*. The vest of both sexes is white cloth of Coromandel, or at least what has once been white. The principal vegetable food of the Orăng-laut is crude sago, which is not the produce of their own country, but received by them from certain low islands on the north coast of Sumatra, where it is produced in great abundance. Rice is looked upon as a superior food, and even as a luxury; as much so, at least, as wheat would be considered by an Irish peasant. Sago is purchased on the coast of Sumatra, in cakes weighing about seventeen pounds each, at the rate of something less than half a dollar a picul of 133⅓ pounds, and is commonly consumed by the Orăng-laut, at the price of about two-thirds of a dollar for the same quantity. A moderate price for rice among the same people is 3⅓ dollars per picul; so that this grain is weight for weight five times the price of sago. It is however considered 2½ times more nutritious, or each portion of rice goes as far as 2½ portions of sago,—making the real cost of sago, considered simply as an article of nutrition, equal to 1⅔ dollar per picul. The difference of price beyond this is supposed to be made up by the superior agreeableness of rice as an article of diet. I have no doubt, the cheapness of sago, and the facility of obtaining fish, contribute materially to impede the progress of civilization among them. Did they not live in a state of great anarchy and disorder, it is probable that with such food they would become as numerous as abject. The aggregate expenses of one of these demi-savages, it may be inferred from the statement now given, will not exceed a dollar and half monthly; and this in a situation where the lowest description of vegetable food, on which he can exist, will alone cost him nearly three-fourths of this amount.*

* It is proper here to observe, that the establishment of the European settlements has produced a great and salutary change in the habits and manners of such of these people as reside near, or at our establishments. The change which a few years have effected at Singapore is very striking.

CHAPTER III.

Departure from Singapore Passage to the Coast of Borneo—Malayan Islands in the Channel.—Visit to Pulo-Ubi, and Description of it.—Numerous islands on the eastern coast of the Gulf of Siam.—Island of Phu-kok described.—Arrival in the roads of Siam.

Feb. 25.—THE violence of the easterly monsoon detained us at Singapore until this day; when, the weather becoming more moderate, we weighed anchor and sailed in prosecution of our voyage. At night, the ebb-tide failing, we anchored off the coast of Jehor, about thirty miles distant from the town of that name, where the Malays established their Government, when driven by the Portuguese from Malacca, in the beginning of the sixteenth century. That place is situated ten miles up a navigable river, the mouth of which is opposite to the east end of the Island of Singapore. It has been long abandoned as the seat of Government, and is at present no more than a poor village of fishermen.

Feb. 26.—We weighed anchor this morning,

and, in passing down, spoke the Topaze frigate, the ship which had an affray with the Chinese, in which some lives were lost, and which occasioned a considerable sensation, both in England and in India. She had been but eight days from Manilla; which afforded us, going in an opposite direction, no very favourable prospect of a speedy passage.

Feb. 27.—We anchored again last evening. Being close to the shore, Mr. Finlayson, Mr. Rutherford, and myself, landed. The spot was within a few miles of the extremity of the peninsula. Here the shore was bold, and the land elevated; but the chain of mountains which pervades the northern part of the peninsula, has long ceased, and the formation of the land is scarcely hilly. The same deep forest prevails as elsewhere, and, as far as the eye could see, no trace of human habitation was discoverable. On the coast, frequent ledges of rock ran into the sea, between which are small sandy bays, where it is easy to land. The wood was so close, that we found it difficult to penetrate; and we were dissuaded from persevering in the attempt, from observing on the sand the tracks of hog and deer, and of a leopard, or young tiger. The rocky formation is porphyritic hornstone, containing small grained crystals of felspar of a pink colour. From its hardness it would admit a fine polish, and is probably well fitted for statuary and ornamental architecture. The wild and desolate woods of this part of the peninsula are known to be inhabited by a few naked and wandering savages. The whole coast, from Johor to the extremity of the peninsula, affords good anchorage and shelter, and several situations not inferior, in convenience for a commercial emporium, to Singapore itself.

We weighed anchor early this morning, and at eleven o'clock passed Cape Romania and Pedro Branca. We had no sooner lost the shelter of the Malay coast, than we felt the full force of the monsoon. There was a heavy swell of the sea, and a strong southerly current. The course along the western shore of the Gulf of Siam was evidently difficult or impracticable. We therefore stood across for the coast of Borneo, intending to make our northing under shelter of that island, and then to stand across the China Sea for the Point of Kamboja, from whence an easy passage might be effected to the head of the Gulf of Siam.

Feb. 28.—The wind keeping well to the north, favoured our passage to Borneo. At noon, the little island called Victory in the charts, was visible from the mast-head, and at eight o'clock at night we passed close to windward of Saddle Island, which lies in latitude 1° 16′ north. This small island rises abruptly and precipitately from the sea to the height of four or five hundred feet.

We passed within three hundred yards of it, and observed the white surge breaking loud and high upon its rocky coast. Situated as we were, it would have been more prudent to have passed to leeward of it; for any trifling accident might have driven us upon its coast, and this, from the state of the weather, must have been attended with the total loss of the ship.

March 1.—Early this morning, the Island of Tambilan was visible on our lee-quarter. This is inhabited by true Malays, very poor and very inoffensive. It forms a portion of the territory of Jehor.

March 2.—The high land of Borneo was in sight yesterday afternoon, and at daybreak this morning we found ourselves within a few miles of the coast, opposite to three conical mountains of great elevation. Our meridian observation made us in 1° 33′ north; so that we were twenty miles to windward of the entrance of the great river of Sambas, between which and that of Pontiana lies the country so well known in these parts for its extensive production of gold. We had no sooner approached the coast of Borneo, than the water became smooth, the winds variable, and there was no longer a southerly current.

March 4.—High Island, or Sapata, so called in the maritime charts, and the most southern of the group denominated the Natunas, was visible yesterday, and we passed this morning within a few hundred yards of a small island lying off its coast. Sapata is the island called Sarasan by the Malays; and the great Natuna, a very large island, they denominate Bangoran. The name Natuna is not known in their language, and, it is probable, was imposed by the Portuguese. The Natunas, like Tambilan, are inhabited by true Malays, subject to Johor. As we passed close to Sarasan, we had a good opportunity of observing its general aspect. It is about seven or eight miles in length, with a bold coast, and it is high land throughout. A few fields of mountain-rice were discernible towards the south end.

Early this morning we passed a dangerous reef, two miles in length, which was not laid down in our charts. This part of the coast of Borneo has not been much frequented by European navigators. Off the north end of Sarasan, there are no less than six islands not delineated in the ordinary charts. The north-east monsoon having returned with considerable force, our progress was very slow.

March 7.—On the morning of the 6th, the sky was overcast, and the wind veering round to the south-west, with much thunder and rain, we were unable to stand our course; but to-day the monsoon, returning, blew so favourably as to enable us to stand at once for the Cape of Kamboja.

March 10.—The wind continuing favourable, we crossed the China Seas with clear, serene, and pleasant weather, the thermometer at noon being seldom above seventy-nine. At six o'clock this morning, Pulo Ubi was in sight, and at noon we saw the shore of Kamboja, the lowest land which it is possible to imagine; for the trees appear as if they were actually growing out of the water; and this indeed is no doubt the fact, those on the border of the sea probably consisting, as usual within the tropics, of the rhizophora, or mangrove. As we approached the land of Kamboja,—and the same appearance prevailed until we passed Pulo Ubi,—the water was as disturbed and muddy as at the mouth of the Ganges, in the westerly monsoon. This, as I afterwards understood, was occasioned by the river of Camao, called by the Kambojans, from the abundance of mud which it carries along with it, Takmao, or the "black stream." At three in the afternoon, we landed on Pulo Ubi, and spent two or three hours in rambling over the hills. In a little sheltered cove and valley, within a short distance of the place where the ship lay at anchor, we saw a single hut, with some persons moving round it, and we rowed towards the spot. As we approached the shore, a little elderly man, with a long grey beard, ran out upon a pier of stones close to the landing-place, and with many gesticulations, but in a language which none of our party understood, seemed to warn us not to land. We payed no attention to his remonstrances, but landed without hesitation. On observing this, he came up to us with an air of entire confidence, and invited us to his hut, earnestly pressing us to partake of his simple hospitality. After this first meeting, there was neither shyness nor distrust displayed by the poor inhabitants of Pulo Ubi. These proved to be eight Cochin Chinese, and two Chinese of the Island of Hainan. Through the latter we made ourselves intelligible. One of the party only was a woman, and there were two or three children, of whom she was the mother. In the little valley which surrounds the bay, there is a scanty cultivation of maize, sweet potatoes, and some coarse esculent greens; but all this was evidently inadequate to the subsistence of the inhabitants, who derived their chief supply from the charity or piety of the Chinese traders, who are in the habit of touching at the island to water, in their voyages up and down the Gulf of Siam. It is not improbable they may derive occasional assistance from the use of a species of *dioscorea*, with an enormous root, which grows wild in the woods. These weigh forty and fifty pounds each. The pits from which they had been dug out, were seen by us in several places as we walked through the woods. The only domestic animals which we saw were a few hogs. Some European writers have reported, that the inhabitants of Pulo Ubi are persons banished for their crimes; but there seems no foundation whatever for this opinion. The old man, our first acquaintance, turned out to be a priest. He had, by his own account, been twenty years on the island; and his business was to officiate at a small temple, dedicated to a certain deity, called Ma-cho-po, a sort of Chinese Amphitrite. Chinese mariners make votive offerings to this worthy, whose image we saw in the temple in question, with a wax taper burning on each side. Close to the image was suspended on strings twenty or thirty small painted boards, with inscriptions on them,—the offerings of as many junks which had touched at Pulo Ubi to water, or take a fresh departure, in the course of the season.

Pulo Ubi has several smaller islands lying off it, and is itself about two miles in length; bold elevated land every where, the highest hills appearing about eight hundred feet above the level of the sea. The thin soil seemed every where to rest upon an extremely hard, small grained, grey granite,—a circumstance which, taken together with the extreme steepness of the hills, seems naturally to account for the unsuitableness of the place for culture and occupation. The woods on the hills of Pulo Ubi are composed of trees of a dwarfish size, and there is no large timber. A species of banana, or plantain, the *musa troglodytarum*, was frequent in the forest. The only quadruped which these woods afford, according to the natives, is a small species of squirrel, of which we saw several individuals. Close to the sea-side were every where to be seen flying from tree to tree numbers of white pigeons, with the end of the wings and tail, to the depth of three or four inches, of a jet black. This bird is an inhabitant of the coasts of many of the smaller islands of the Indian Archipelago, and has been described under the name of *Colomba littoralis*. The name Pulo Ubi is Malay, and not improbably derived from the large species of dioscorea, or yam, to which I have above alluded;—the term meaning, in Malay, literally, the Island of Yams. From very early ages, an intercourse has existed between the Kambojans and the Malays; and considerable numbers of the latter are not only at present settled at Kamboja, but Malayan rovers still continue to infest its coast by their depredations. The island, in the language of Kamboja, is called Ko Tam-bung; in Cochin Chinese, Kon-gui; and in Siamese, Ko-Man;—all of which terms, I understand, have the same signification as the Malayan name.

We embarked in the afternoon, and the natives soon followed us on board; which gave us an opportunity of requiting their kindness, by presenting them with a little rice, tea, clothes, and some money.

March 11.—We sailed from Pulo Ubi last night, and this morning passed false Pulo Ubi, in the latitude of 8°, 56′, and longitude 104°, 38′ east. The land of Kamboja was still as low as when we first discovered it, but the water was no longer muddy and discoloured. We had now regular land and sea breezes, and the weather was remarkably fine.

March 12.—Having discovered, in the course of this day's sailing, that the coasts and islands, were, as indeed we expected, very erroneously laid down in the ordinary charts, we resolved not to proceed at night, but come to an anchor, which we did at ten o'clock in six fathoms. At day-break this morning we found ourselves surrounded by islands of various size, from mere rocks with a few trees upon them, to those that were five and six miles in length. The eastern coast of the Gulf of Siam was probably never much frequented by European navigators, and has not, that I know of, been visited by them at all within the last century. It is no wonder, therefore, that it should be erroneously delineated.

At six in the morning we weighed anchor, and were soon in sight of a very singular group of islands, consisting of one large island, about four miles in length, encircled by a ring of smaller islands, of which I counted twenty. This is the group called in the charts Hon-co-thron; but correctly, Hon-co-tre. The name is from the Anam, or Cochin Chinese language. At ten o'clock it fell calm, and we landed on a small island close to us. This, which was not a mile in circumference, was covered with low trees. The rocky formation was potstone, with compact feldspar: I found, however, a rolled piece of granite on the shore, although no vestige of this rock was discoverable in the interior, which we travelled over.

In the evening we again landed upon another islet not far from the last. This also was entirely composed of potstone. On both these islets we found, in great numbers, the same white pigeons which we saw at Pulo Ubi. Three sail of vessels were seen in the course of the day, which we took to be Chinese or Cochin Chinese junks.

March 13.—We came to an anchor again last night, being still surrounded by innumerable islands, respecting which, both our charts and directions were silent. We sailed this morning in the direction of a large island which lay north-west of us.

March 14.—We anchored close to the large island, and conjectured, from the number of fishing-boats which were sailing up and down the coast, that it was inhabited. Several of these boats came close to us this morning, and the people seemed anxious to pay us a visit; but, their fears being greater than their curiosity, they finally left us, without venturing to come on board. We were compelled at length to lower one of our boats, and on holding out a white flag from it, a few, at length, visited us. They proved to be Cochin Chinese; and through the few words of Siamese which they knew, they gave us to understand, that if we landed we should receive a hospitable reception.

A large party of us accordingly landed at one in the afternoon, purposely unaccompanied by any part of the military escort, that no alarm might be excited. Some of the natives waited our arrival on the beach, armed with long spears, and, by their gestures and vociferations, warned us to keep off. We took no manner of notice of these remonstrances, but leaped on shore, and walked up to them at once. They soon recognized among our party our Chinese interpreters and servants, and some of themselves being Chinese of the Island of Hai-nan, all was soon confidence and cordiality betwixt us. They informed us that our's was the first European ship which they had ever seen; and we learned, that upon our first appearance they had sent their women and valuables into the forest. The first surprise being over, they invited us to their houses, and offered us both food and betel. We gained their favour by offering them small specimens of English cutlery and other trifles. I observed that the women and children crowded round us as well as the men, and that the former betrayed no symptoms of Oriental reserve or fastidiousness. In their persons, these people, of both sexes, were short, squat, and ill-favoured. They paid small attention to cleanliness, either in their dress or habitations. They were evidently very poor, and, after they had experienced our little bounty, made no scruple in asking for every little trifle about our persons that excited their notice. After walking several miles along the coast, and looking at every thing we thought worth seeing, we returned on board in the evening, two of the principal people accompanying us. These persons were so well pleased with their reception, that they insisted upon passing the night on board. They partook heartily of our fare, and especially made free use of our brandy and liqueurs, to the neglect of tea and all other thin beverages. They were as communicative on the subject of the island, as our imperfect means of understanding each other would admit. This consisted in one of the Chiefs and our Chinese interpreter writing question and answer in the Chinese character, without attempting to exchange one syllable with each other orally. The

Chinese character is, as is well known, a language only to the eye, and understood by all the nations from the spot we were now in, to Japan and Corea eastward, who in this sort of pantomime can understand each other, however different their vernacular languages.

The place which we had now visited is called by the Cochin Chinese, Phu-kok, and by the Siamese Koh-dud, or the "far island;" the last name having reference to its relative distance, compared to other islands, from the coast of Kamboja. In the Kambojan language it is called Koh-trol, or "shuttle island," which is evidently the Quadrole of the old maps. It is the largest island on the east coast of the Gulf of Siam, being by our reckoning not less than thirty-four miles in length. It is commonly bold high land, the highest hills rising to seven or eight hundred feet. A few spots here and there on the coasts only are inhabited,—the rest being, as usual, covered with a great forest which, we were told, contained abundance of deer, hogs, wild buffaloes, and oxen, but no leopards or tigers. Its most valuable produce, however, is the lignum aloes, or agila. All the hilly countries and islands on this part of the coast of the Gulf of Siam abound in this production. We used every endeavour to obtain specimens of the tree in a fit state for botanical description, but without success. The lignum aloes, by the account of the natives, is a diseased portion of the wood. The tree, one of the tallest of the forest, is sufficiently common; but not so the individuals in a diseased state; and hence the high price of the odoriferous substance. They showed us several large portions of the timber in its ordinary state, and presented us also with pieces of the fragrant wood, recently extracted.*

The inhabitants of Phu-kok were described to us as amounting to from four to five thousand, all of the true Cochin Chinese race, with the exception of a few occasional Chinese sojourners. They grow no species of corn, and their husbandry is confined to a few coarse fruits, and esculent green vegetables, and farinaceous roots. Of the last, the best and most abundant was the Convolvulus Batata. They import their rice from Kang-kao, which lies opposite, and is an abundant grain country. The inhabitants of Phu-kok seemed to us to be all fishermen, and the eastern shore of the island had the appearance of a place well suited for their occupation. It was an extensive bank, having frequent overfalls. The fishing-boats were seen sailing, in considerable numbers, up and down the coast. These were managed with much dexterity, and were altogether the smartest vessels of the kind which I

* The tree is frequent in the woods of Singapore.

had seen in any part of India. Their rigging consisted of two shoulder-of-mutton sails, made of a very white mat, which had a neat appearance. The fishery of tripang, or bech-de-mar, was conducted near the shore in two and three feet water. This was carried on in small canoes, in which there was one person only, who stood up in the boat with a spear in his hand, and struck the animals as they presented themselves. Numbers of persons were thus employed as we came off in the evening.

March 15.—Our guests took leave of us this morning, and at eight o'clock we set sail with the intention of going round the southern extremity of the island. The natives had indeed informed us, (and we afterwards found, from good information, their statement to be perfectly correct,) that there was a good navigable channel between Phu-kok and the main; but we did not think it safe to place implicit reliance upon this account. We now sailed, therefore, in a southerly direction along the coast of Phu-kok, and in the evening, when it fell calm, we anchored off a small bay, close to the south end of the island. Several fishing-boats were seen, and at night the lights from a village in the bay were sufficiently distinct.

March 16.—At eleven o'clock last night, a stiff gale of wind came on from the south-east, making the island a lee-shore, and the ship dragged her anchor. This obliged us to get under weigh, which we effected with considerable difficulty. The heavy swell compelled us to wear the ship, in which manœuvre the water shoaled so rapidly, as to put us to considerable risk of suffering shipwreck. As we sailed along, we now saw that much of what we had hitherto considered as portion of the great island, was a chain of islets, twelve in number, extending from its southern extremity. The water, as we approached these, deepened so as to enable us to sail within two or three hundred yards of them, in twelve and thirteen fathoms. The gale of wind which we experienced through the night was of short continuance, and at one o'clock we had a dead calm; this gave us an opportunity of landing upon several of the small islets in question. The rocky formation here was sand-stone, with immense masses of imbedded conglomerate. We had no opportunity of making any geological remarks at Phu-kok itself, the coast where we landed consisting every where of a long sandy plain, in which no rock was exposed; and the hills in the interior being every where distant several miles, as well as rendered difficult of access by a deep forest. At the small islets, the rise and fall of the tide struck us to be remarkably great for so low a latitude. It appeared from the high-water mark on the rocks, not to be less than eighteen feet; whereas the usual rise in this part of the world, within a few degrees of the equator at least, seldom exceeds eight or nine feet. The botany of these islands proved extremely interesting. Among other forest plants we found the cashew-nut tree (*Anacardium*), which is commonly supposed to be exclusively a native of America, in full bearing. A greater quantity of sea-fowl than usual, so near the equator, were seen upon the rocks interspersed amongst the islands. They consisted of gulls (*Larus*), sea swallows (*Sterna*), and noddies (*Sterna stolida*). Several of the last, with their usual stupidity, lighted on the ship, and suffered themselves to be taken without difficulty. All these small islands seemed destitute of inhabitants.

My poor friend, Mr. Finlayson, caught, from the severe exertions he made to-day under a burning sun, the malady which afterwards proved fatal to him; and which, during the remainder of the voyage, unfortunately deprived me of the active exercise of his valuable talents.

March 17.—This morning we stood on our course to Siam, along the western side of the island of Phu-kok, with a favourable breeze from the east. Just as we were making sail, a very smart Chinese junk, which had lain at anchor close to us during the night, came down and spoke us with perfect confidence. She belonged to the island of Hai-nan, being one of the many junks which trade between that place and the capital of Siam, to which last port she was now bound like ourselves. We met two more junks in the course of the day. At three in the afternoon we had reached the northern extremity of Phu-kok, which is divided by a narrow channel from another island, the first of a chain running in a northerly direction to the distance of seventeen or eighteen miles. In the course of this day's sailing we saw a few fishing-boats. At dusk, a group of islands, seven in number, called, in the Siamese language, Hwi-su, distant about seventeen miles, was in sight. No notice whatever is taken of this group in the ordinary charts. Indeed, the whole of this coast is perhaps less known to European navigators than any portion of the globe of equal magnitude and importance. Our charts and maps, indeed, are thickly studded with islands; but they are without names, and put down at random, all that is known regarding them, being that they exist in great numbers.

March 18.—As every thing now appeared clear ahead of us, we did not anchor last night, as we had done for some days before, but proceeded without interruption. The Chinese junk which spoke us yesterday morning, was still close to us, although we had a seven-knot breeze during the night. This afforded us an opportunity of judging what this description of vessels is capable of doing, when going with a fair wind, as upon the present occasion. Some of them, it would appear, are nearly a match for an European vessel. On the other hand, from their flat construction, the Chinese junk is quite incapable of beating against a foul wind, and of course in the utmost danger when such a resource is called for.

March 20.—During the 18th and 19th we were out of sight of land, but to-day close in with the continent in the latitude of 12° 38′ and longitude 101° 30′ East. Two ranges of mountains, of considerable height, formed the background before us, between which and the sea was an extensive tract of lower land. The mountains which we now saw, were those which lie to the northward of Chan-ti-bon, one of the most productive and populous districts of the kingdom of Siam, abounding in rice, pepper, gamboge, and cardamums. This portion of the coast, in opposition to that which we had before passed, was open and unsheltered. One small rocky island was close to us, and upon this a party landed, while we waited for the sea-breeze. It was so surrounded by reefs that, although perfectly calm, it was difficult to find a place to land upon. Its shores had everywhere the appearance of a place much frequented by fish—the sea for miles in the neighbourhood being covered with spermatic animalculæ. There were numbers of sea-fowl on the rocks, and shoals of porpoises sporting about the shore. Some of the latter pursued their prey into such shallow water, that we were encouraged to make our boatmen wade out, with the hope of intercepting them and forcing them to run ashore, but in this expectation we did not succeed. Several fishing stakes were set on the shore of the island next to the continent, and the fresh footsteps of the fishermen were visible in the sand; but we saw nobody, and there were no habitations. This island is formed of granite and quartz rock, and is about five miles distant from the mainland.

March 21.—A numerous group of islands lay before us last evening, and we found it therefore prudent to come to an anchor for the night. We weighed at four this morning, and at ten came up with the islands in question. With the view of shortening our course, we passed the channel which divides them from a promontory on the main, called by the Siamese, Sam-me-san, and in our charts, Lyant. This channel, which is about a quarter of a mile wide, and about two miles in length, we passed with a light, but a leading wind, encountering no dangers, and never having less than four and a half fathoms water. Our boat went ahead of us all the way, sounding.

We found two small junks lying at anchor here, and we afterwards heard that the channel was a common route for the largest vessels of this description. The scene, as soon as we entered, was striking and picturesque. The shore on each side consisted of a series of sandy coves, and the country of a succession of hills, here and there bare of wood, pressing upon each other down to the sea. No habitations were to be seen, except those of a few fishermen on the coast, and the interior seemed to be an universal wilderness. We spoke one small vessel, with a Siamese crew, two days from Bang-kok, and from her we acquired the names of some of the principal islands and headlands. The group of islands now passed is much frequented by turtle, the collection of the eggs of which is a business of some importance, and is said to bring a considerable revenue into the Siamese treasury. We found the latitude of Cape Lyant to be 12° 36′ 30″, which is ten miles farther north than it is laid down in the charts, and its longitude, by two good chronometers, 101° 11′ East, being sixteen miles farther west than it is usually delineated.

March 22.—A great many islands were in sight last night, and we had them this morning on our starboard, for we did not think it safe to proceed during the night in the channel between them and the main. This, however, we afterwards learned is a common route of the largest Chinese junks, and is perfectly safe. Many of the largest islands in question are inhabited, such as Ko-kram and Ko-han. The inhabitants are a mixture of Siamese and Cochin Chinese, for the latter people, although the country be under the dominion of Siam, have penetrated thus far to the north. At noon we were in the latitude of 13° 8′. The high mountains of Bang-pa-soe were in sight to the eastward, but no land ahead. By our reckoning, however, we were within a few miles of the roads of Siam, and at five in the afternoon we came in sight of them, which we only ascertained by discovering three large Chinese junks lying at anchor, for the land at the head of the gulf was extremely low, and not yet visible. At seven o'clock we anchored in 3¾ fathoms water, close to the junks, having thus performed the voyage from the Straits of Malacca with ease in twenty-three days.

Front of the main Building of the King of Siam's Palace.

CHAPTER IV.

Communication of our Arrival made to the Court of Siam. —Entertainment given to the Mission.—Negotiation for proceeding to the Capital.—Ship ascends the River, appearance of its Banks.—Arrival at Bang-kok, appearance of the place.—Delivery of the Governor-general's Letter. —Visit to the Prah-klang, or Foreign Minister.—Delivery of the presents for the King.—The Mission lands.—Description of its Residence.—Visit to the Prince Krom-chiat, now King of Siam.—Arrangement of the Ceremonial for our Presentation to the King.—Second Visit to the Foreign Minister.—The Mission presented to the King.—Description of the Ceremony.—Inspection of the White Elephants, &c.—The Mission receives a visit, and is entertained by the Foreign Minister.

March 24.—As soon as we had come to an anchor, we prepared a letter for the Prah-klang,* or minister who conducts the affairs of strangers. In this we briefly informed him of our arrival, the number of our party, and such other particulars of the same nature, as we were given to understand would be expected. This was transmitted, early yesterday morning, by one of the officers of the ship to Pak-nam,† the first station in ascending the river. The officer returned this morning with a civil message from the Chief of Pak-nam, accompanied by a present of fruit, and he brought with him a pilot to conduct us over the bar.

March 25.—At seven o'clock this morning we weighed anchor, and attempted to cross the bar; but when about half-way over, the ship struck in the soft mud, in which, as the tide fell, she sunk four feet. We had, at the same time, not above four feet water. As the evening tide made, she floated, and we crossed the bar without sustaining any injury. A strong and favourable breeze soon carried us to the mouth of the Menam, a distance of not less than t n miles from the outer edge of the bar, ploughing almost all the way through the thin ooze; and at seven o'clock at night we anchored off the village of Pak-nam, about two miles and a half from the mouth of the river, upon its left bank.

* Literally, Lord or Master of the Warehouses.

† The word means mouth of the river, or rather water; it is applied to the *deboucheur* of any river.

March 26.—A Portuguese interpreter, dispatched from the Court, came on board this morning. He brought a message from the Chief of Pak-nam, the purport of which was, that he had received instructions from the Court to entertain us, and that a barge had been sent down to bring us to the Capital, but that before the ship proceeded it would be necessary to land our guns, according to invariable usage in such cases. We returned a civil answer, and sent the chief a small present, taking this occasion to remonstrate against the landing of our guns, as well as to signify to him that one boat was totally inadequate to the accommodation of so large a party as ours. In the forenoon his nephew came on board, to wait upon us. He stated that the orders of the governor on the subject of landing the cannon of foreign ships were peremptory, and could not be dispensed with, but that a reference would be made to the Court for instructions. On the subject of the barge, it was explained that the numbers of our party were not known, or more accommodation would have been furnished. This was not true, for we had stated the exact number of the party in the letter to the Prah-klang, and the circumstance of sending a single boat only, was evidently an early attempt to underrate the Mission and the authority by which it was sent. A temperate resistance therefore, however unpleasant, became necessary.

Our visitor had brought an invitation to our party to land in the evening, and partake of an entertainment which the chief had prepared for us. This, after some hesitation, was accepted, and at the landing-place we were met by the Governor's nephew, who escorted us to the chief's house. A crowd of men, women, and children, were collected out of curiosity, the greatest share of which seemed to be directed towards our Indian servants, whose neat, gay, and clean attire, formed a striking contrast to their own rude and slovenly semi-nudity. After passing a short way through mean lanes crowded with huts, we came upon the dwelling of his Excellency the Governor, formed of the same mean and perishable materials as the rest. We were ushered into a large apartment, raised a few feet from the ground, on a platform of split bamboos, which formed the floor. The thatch within was ill concealed by broken and soiled Chinese paper-hangings, and from the roof was suspended a motley collection of old Dutch chandeliers of miserable glass, and Siamese and Chinese lamps, covered with dust, with cobwebs, and with the smoke of oil, incense, and tobacco. The Governor civilly met us at the door, and shook hands with us very heartily in the European fashion. Chairs were placed for our accommodation. This chief was a man about forty-five years of age, of rugged features, but cheerful manners, and he seemed desirous to please. His nephew, who had ushered us in, and his secretary, sat upon a carpet before him. A messenger, who had just arrived from the Court, and who was deputed to conduct us thither, was also present. The name, or rather the title, of this person, with whom the Mission had afterwards a good deal of intercourse, was Luang kochai-asa-hak, formerly Nakhoda Ali. He was one of those Mohammedan adventurers whose ancestors had come several ages ago from the coast of Coromandel. He had visited Queda, Penang, and Calcutta, and spoke the Malayan language tolerably, for which reason it was that he was selected to attend us. In the centre of the apartment we found a table laid out in the European fashion, under the direction of the Portuguese interpreters, with plates, knives, forks, silver spoons, and some tolerable English glass-ware. It was loaded with viands, such as pork, fowls, ducks, egg, and rice, and with abundance of fruit, particularly mangoes, oranges, and lichis, all of which were in season.

A curtain, which was suspended across one end of the apartment, attracted our notice. We were told, to our surprise, that behind it lay in state the body of the late chief of Pak-nam. This person was brother to the present chief, and the father of the young person who had visited us in the forenoon. This last, indeed, had then informed us that his father had died five months ago; that his body was lying embalmed at Pak-nam, and that his funeral would take place on the 24th day of the present moon; but we had certainly no idea that we were to be favoured with the presence of the deceased during the repast to which we had been invited. Mr. Finlayson and Mr. Rutherfurd, when they landed the following morning, their curiosity being strongly excited on the subject of the body which was lying in state, ventured to make some inquiry concerning it. Their questions were by no means taken amiss by the son, to whom they were addressed, but considered rather complimentary; and he invited them without ceremony to view the body. It was lying in a coffin, which was covered with tinsel and white cloth, and the lid of which when removed exhibited the corpse wrapped up in a great many folds of cloth, like an Egyptian mummy, apparently quite dry, and covered with such a profusion of aromatics, that there was nothing offensive about it.

The chief alone sat down at table with us, but without partaking of our fare. He was assiduous in pressing us to the good things which were placed before us. My interpreter explained to me, that he requested us to "*eat heartily and not be abashed*"—a customary form of compliment, it appears, among the Siamese, in addressing a guest. No questions respecting the objects of the Mission were put to us during the entertainment, and I considered the visit as a matter of mere form and etiquette, but in this I was much deceived; for the repast was no sooner over, than question followed question with great vivacity. We were first bluntly asked what was the object of the Mission. We answered in general terms that the English and Siamese nations were neighbours, and that on our part we were desirous that a friendly and frequent intercourse should subsist between us, and that we were deputed to request such an intercourse. This did not satisfy the chief; he urged us over and over to state what particular request or demands we had to make of the Court upon the present occasion. We declined giving him the satisfaction he required; observing, that in proper time and place we should explain ourselves fully. We were next requested to state the quality and amount of the presents brought for the King, and a secretary placed himself behind the chief to take notes of what was said on this subject—one apparently of the first interest. We evaded giving any answer, except in very general terms, but were cross-questioned with dexterity and perseverance. I had noticed that among the presents there were some fire-arms. The chief begged to know their number. I said a few hundreds. He begged me to conjecture some approximation to the actual number. I added, probably three or four hundred. The answer was, "be good enough to say either the one or the other." I endeavoured to divert the chief's attention from the detail of muslins, broadcloths, crystal, looking-glasses, and such matters, by calling his attention to an English horse, which was one of the presents. He immediately requested to know his height, his age, his colour, the length of his tail, and finally, what fortunate or unfortunate marks he had about him. We put an end to all this importunity, by informing the Governor, that as soon as we returned to the ship, we would direct a clerk to make out a list of the presents for his satisfaction. This conversation afforded an early, but a good specimen of the indelicacy and rapacity which we afterwards found so characteristic of the Siamese Court and its officers, upon every question of a similar nature.

After the discussion respecting the presents, the chief reminded us of the compliment which his Siamese Majesty had paid the Mission, in so promptly dispatching an accommodation-boat to convey us to Bang-kok; and he entreated us to make no difficulty about accepting this gracious mark of royal attention, while he besought us also to comply with the established usage in landing the guns of the ship. We repeated what we had said before, of the total inadequacy of a single boat to accommodate our large party, which consisted of seventy-four persons. With respect to landing the cannon, we stated that a Portuguese man-of-war had, two years before, been permitted to visit the capital, and that a Mission from the British Government had a right to be treated with equal favour. Much pains were taken to convince us, that it would be proper to comply with the wishes of the Court, but we persevered in our objections. With this discussion our visit ended. It was a striking contrast to European usage, that the whole of this demi-official conversation passed in the presence and hearing of a great crowd of the lower orders, who occupied the entire area of the court, opposite to the place where we sat. The people indeed pressed up to the very door of the saloon. The chiefs by no means checked their curiosity, and on their part they listened to what passed with respectful attention.

What we saw in our visit to Pak-nam, was not calculated to impress us with a very exalted opinion of the progress of the Siamese nation in the arts which conduce to the comforts or reasonable enjoyments of life. The cottage of an English peasant, not on the brink of a workhouse, possesses more real comfort than did the mansion of the Governor of Pak-nam, who, as we were told, exercised an arbitrary authority over 50,000 people.

March 28.—As soon as I had returned to the ship after my visit to Pak-nam, I addressed a letter to the Prah-klang, recapitulating what I had urged to the chief of that place, on the subject of our conveyance to the capital and the landing of our guns. Yesterday no answer was received, but this morning Ko-chai-asa-hak, who, in the interval, had been at Bang-kok, came on board, to inform us that the Court had given us permission to ascend the river with our cannon, or, in case we preferred going in boats supplied by the Court, that a sufficient number would be sent down in a few days. We adopted the plan of going up in the ship, as the most independent, speedy, and commodious; and at ten o'clock we began to ascend the river against the tide, but with a strong breeze in our favour. The river at its mouth and up to Pak-nam is about a mile wide, but shortly after diminishes to one-half of this width,—a breadth which, with few exceptions, it preserves all the way to Bang-kok. Opposite to Pak-nam there is a sand-bank, bare at low-water,* and a few miles beyond it the

* Our contest with the Burmans so alarmed the Siamese, that during its progress they fortified Pak-nam with the sand-bank mentioned in the text. On these works there are said to be mounted about 200 pieces of heavy ordnance, some of which

ruins of a small brick fort, built by the Dutch, about a century and a half ago, when they carried on a trade with Siam. This last, by the encroachment of the river, is now within the stream, and covered at high-water. These two, and they are easily avoided, constitute the only dangers of the Menam, from its mouth to the capital. After passing them, a ship may range from side to side of the river, with from seven to ten fathoms water, approaching so near to the banks that her yards may literally overhang them. At one o'clock we reached a couple of forts, or redoubts, of masonry,—one on each side of the river,—which is here considerably contracted. The neighbourhood is occupied by a colony of the people of Pegue and Lao, refugees from the territory disputed between the Burmans and Siamese. A flag was hoisted from both forts, and we were serenaded by a Peguan band of music as we passed. A well-dressed chief, in the Burman or Pegue costume, came on board here, bringing us two boat loads of fruits and other refreshment.

Close to the river, and at least for twelve

are good English guns, but the greater number brass-cannon, cast at Bang-kok, and of the worst description. In the hands of a people of any courage or military skill, these fortifications would render the access to the capital impregnable. Such, however, is the ignorance and pusillanimity of the Siamese, that, in all likelihood, they would prove no serious impediment to an attack by European shipping.

miles up, the land appears to be unfit for culture, owing to the saltness of the water, which occasionally overflows it. All this tract is occupied by rhizophoras, and by the cocos-nypa, the leaf of which is so abundantly used by the inhabitants of tropical India as thatch. Beyond this again, and all the way to the capital, the banks of the river are more elevated, and the country as far as we could observe it, presented every where a rich extent of cultivation, consisting of rice-fields, interspersed with numerous villages, surrounded by orchards of palm and fruit-trees. The rice stubble was on the ground, for the crop had been reaped two months before, and among it were grazing numerous herds of buffaloes, the only description of cattle which were to be seen. This appearance of fertility and industry formed a pleasing contrast to the waste of rocks, mountains, and impenetrable and unprofitable forests, to which we had been accustomed for the last three months.

At four o'clock we came to an anchor for a couple of hours, waiting for the flood-tide, and took this opportunity to land. The fields afforded a great number of birds of different descriptions, and we were successful in adding several specimens to our collection. The natives, wherever we met them, received us with kindness, and betrayed no symptoms of distrust

Drawn by [illegible] Pub. by H. Colburn London 18[illegible]

VIEW OF THE CITY OF BANCKOK

or timidity. As soon as the flood-tide had made, we weighed, and at twelve o'clock at night reached the town of Bang-kok..

March 29.—The morning presented to us a very novel spectacle—the capital of Siam, situated on both sides of the Menam. Numerous temples of Buddha, with tall spires attached to them, frequently glittering with gilding, were conspicuous among the mean huts and hovels of the natives, throughout which were interspersed a profusion of palms, ordinary fruit-trees, and the sacred fig *(ficus religiosa)*. On each side of the river there was a row of floating habitations, resting on rafts of bamboos, moored to the shore. These appeared the neatest and best description of dwellings; they were occupied by good Chinese shops. Close to these aquatic habitations were anchored the largest description of native vessels, among which were many junks of great size, just arrived from China. The face of the river presented a busy scene, from the number of boats and canoes of every size and description which were passing to and fro. The number of these struck us as very great at the time, for we were not aware that there are few or no roads at Bang-kok, and that the river and canals form the common highways, not only for goods, but for passengers of every description. Many of the boats were shops containing earthenware, *blachang*,* dried fish, and fresh pork. Venders of these several commodities were hawking and crying them as in an European town. Among those who plied on the river, there was a large proportion of women, and of the priests of Buddha; the latter readily distinguished by their shaved and bare heads, and their yellow vestments. This was the hour in which they are accustomed to go in quest of alms, which accounted for the great number of them which we saw.

In the course of the morning, a boat was seen coming alongside with two persons of distinction in her. These were the son and nephew of the Minister, lads not above fourteen years of age, who were sent on board to compliment us on our arrival. They brought us a present of fruit and fine tea, and communicated a request from the Minister, that the ship would drop down a few hundred yards, and opposite to his own house, where a deputation would be sent on board to receive the letter of the Governor-general. The son of the Minister was a sprightly and intelligent lad, but seemed to have been greatly indulged. They were served with coffee and sweetmeats, and after this repast chewed betel, and smoked tobacco profusely, so as to give us ra-

* A fœtid condiment in very general use in the countries beyond the Ganges, and generally composed of bruised shrimps and other small fish.

ther an unfavourable impression of the education and habits of a young Siamese nobleman.

In the course of the day a secretary came on board well attended. He had his note-book and his pencil in his hand, and the object of his visit was to examine the English horse, which was one of the presents, and to take minutes for the information of his Majesty, from whom, and not the Minister, he took care to inform us, he was directly sent. His Majesty, it appears, had heard of the horse, and not being able to restrain his curiosity, had sent this person for the express purpose of drawing up a formal description of him.

In the evening, according to the intimation which had been given, a deputation came on board to receive the letter of the Governor-general. The principal member of it was Pia-pipat kosa, the deputy of the Foreign Minister, a fine-looking old man, above seventy years of age, of frank and pleasing manners. Siamese and European notions on the subject of foreign missions differ essentially. Among the Siamese, the principal honours are paid to the letter which is brought, and not to the envoy who brings it, and who is considered in little better light than that of an honourable messenger. In delivering the letter of the Governor-general, it was necessary to advert to this circumstance, and to see that every proper ceremony was attended to.

The chief of the deputation began by informing us, that according to Siamese etiquette, letters from foreign States must be delivered to the officers of Government before presentation to His Majesty, for the purpose of being authenticated and translated. We requested to know if a copy would not be sufficient. We were told, in reply, that the letter itself must be seen, that it might be ascertained that all necessary forms had been complied with. These forms have especial reference to the shape and quality of the paper, and envelope, titles, and such like matters. We then stated, that we expected the letter would be returned to us previous to our audience, in order that we might have the honour of presenting it personally to the King. We were informed that this was contrary to usage, but a pledge was given that the letter should be produced at the audience, and a Siamese translation of it read in our presence. The Governor-general's letter was now produced, and taken by the old chief in a gold vase brought for the purpose. It was received by the escort on the quarter-deck under a salute, and handed into the boat, where it was deposited under a state umbrella.

Ko-chai-asa-hak, who formed one of the deputation, stayed behind until the other members had gone away. His object was to deliver to us a message from the Minister, requesting I would favour him, in the evening, with a private interview. I agreed to this, with some hesitation; and Captain Dangerfield and I landed, accordingly, at six in the evening, and proceeded to the Minister's house, immediately on the river side. In compliment to us, he met us at the door, offering us his hand in the European fashion. He seated himself upon a silk cushion, and pointed to one opposite, which Captain Dangerfield and myself took possession of. None of his attendants or family came within several yards of him, but lay prostrate on their knees and elbows in an attitude particularly undignified and servile. The hall in which we were received was neat and well-furnished beyond our expectation. The window-curtains consisted of a handsome English chintz. The room was lighted by a pair of good cut-glass English chandeliers, and by several handsome Chinese lanterns.

Suri-wrung-kosa, for this was the Foreign Minister's name, was a man about thirty-eight years of age, rather a heavy figure, inclining to be corpulent, and of a complexion dark for a Siamese. His features were expressive of good sense, but there was an air of sullenness and reserve in them not calculated to gain confidence. His person was without ornaments, and, indeed, it may be said, nearly without dress; for he wore nothing, saving a piece of crimson silk, which was wrapped round his loins. Altogether, whether in person or manner, he had very much the appearance of a frugal Hindoo of the mercantile cast, in good circumstances. His questions, upon this occasion, were sensible and pertinent throughout, and evinced none of the troublesome importunity which I experienced from the Chief of Pak-nam. His principal inquiries were directed to the objects of the Mission; and he seemed satisfied with the explanations which were given. He requested us, as we had made a long voyage, to repose ourselves for a few days, when we should be presented to the King. It would, however, he added, according to the custom of the place, be requisite that we should be previously introduced to the Prince Kromchiat, the eldest son of the King, who superintended the foreign and commercial department. Our conversation was carried on in Malay, through the medium of Ko-chai-asa-hak; for our interpreters, although they accompanied us, were not allowed to act. Before we took our departure, a very neat dessert of choice fruits, sweetmeats, and tea, were served up to us.

The report made by the secretary, respecting the English horse, had so strongly excited the curiosity of His Siamese Majesty, that he was unable to repress it until the regular delivery of the presents; and a polite message was sent to request that he might be allowed to land. One of the boats employed to convey elephants, with a train of attendants, was sent to receive him, and he was safely landed last evening; the first of his race, I am sure, that ever reached the shores of Siam. He was a handsome thorough-bred entire horse, about fifteen hands high. Such an animal, in a country where horses are rare, and the few that exist mere ponies, was necessarily an object of much curiosity.

March 31.—In the morning, Seignor De Silveira, a gentleman who had been residing at Siam as Portuguese Consul during the last two years, sent his assistant, or secretary, to wait upon us; excusing himself from coming in person, as it was contrary to Siamese etiquette for a person in his situation to visit us before we had been honoured with an audience of the King.

We should now, after a long confinement on board of ship, have been glad to have gone abroad, and gratified ourselves with an inspection of the many novel objects which seemed to offer themselves, but this was contrary to etiquette. We were not indeed forbidden to go about, but it was stated to us, that to do so, before a public audience had placed us under the immediate protection of the Court, might expose us to be treated with rudeness by the populace.

April 1.—The presents for the King were landed this morning, at the particular request of the Court. The pretext for this, was to afford an opportunity of examining and registering them before they were presented at the audience, but I am afraid the real motive was no other than an anxious desire to be put in immediate possession. A trifling circumstance, which took place in delivering them, afforded a singular example of indelicacy on the part of the officers of the Siamese Government. Among a great many pieces of British muslin, which constituted an article of the presents, it was alleged that there was a short delivery of four, as the numbers did not correspond with the list given in at Pak-nam. This *serious* defalcation was communicated to me by a formal message, and a hope expressed that the deficiency would be made up. At the same time, no notice was taken of two pieces of fine Genoa velvet, which were delivered beyond the quantity expressed in the list, although of ten-times the value of the muslins! As soon as our clerk brought this last circumstance to the notice of the messengers, not another word was said about the alleged defalcation in the muslins!

In the course of the morning, two of the Court interpreters called upon us; the one a Christian and the other a Mohammedan. They dealt very freely with one another's character, and each assured us, in his turn, that the other was totally unworthy of confidence.

April 2.—Our party landed last night, and took possession of the dwelling allotted to us. It was a new house, of very coarse masonry, with a tiled roof, and consisting of four lower and as many upper apartments, all small and inconvenient. A house of a similar size and appearance was supplied, a few days afterwards, for the accommodation of such of our party as could not, upon the present occasion, find room. The Prah-klang had furnished our apartments after the Siamese taste; but so little to ours, that we soon discovered the necessity of landing our own furniture, and by this means made ourselves as comfortable as our situation would permit. Our new dwelling was within a few yards of the river, of which, as well as of the most populous part of the town, it afforded an extensive view to the front, while behind it overlooked the court-yard of the Prah-klang's house and his chamber of audience, so that, without exercising an impertinent curiosity, we were afforded an opportunity of witnessing, from time to time, a good deal of what passed. I had a message in the morning, to request that I would favour the Prah-klang with another visit. I declined doing so, as he had not returned the first visit paid to him; although he explained that his not doing so was in compliance with the etiquette of the Court, which forbade all open intercourse with foreign agents, until publicly recognized.

April 3.—The ceremony of our presentation to the Prince Krom-chiat was fixed for this night, and, as had been previously arranged, a twelve-oared barge came at eight in the evening to convey us. Mr. Rutherfurd alone accompanied me, the other gentlemen being indisposed and unable to attend. The Prince's palace is situated a little beyond that of the King, about two miles up the river. Upon our arrival, we were received in an anteroom by Pia-pipat-kosa, the aged officer whom I have described as coming on board to receive the Governor-general's letter. We were not long detained here, but soon summoned to the Prince's presence, by a message, conveyed to us in a few words of broken English, by the Intendant of the port, a native Christian, whom I had not before seen. We ascended the hall of audience by a flight of two or three awkward steps. Fronting the door of this apartment, was a large wooden skreen, to preserve the privacy of the interior. As soon as we had passed this skreen, we had a view of the Prince, sitting in full court, and offering a spectacle rather singular and imposing. The hall, which appeared about eighty feet long, and of a well-proportioned breadth, was covered with a profusion of gilding and vermilion. At the upper end of it there was a handsome altar-piece, which, we were informed, contained a small golden image of Gautama, but it was concealed from our view by a crimson satin curtain. To our left hand, and about the middle of the room, there was an elevated pulpit, and from this we were told that the Talapoins chant their hymns, and deliver their moral discourses, when the Prince is disposed to receive instruction, which frequently happens, for he has the reputation of being very devout. The hall was decorated with European lustres of cut-glass, with European and Chinese mirrors, and with a profusion of Chinese lanterns. The Prince, a heavy and corpulent figure, about thirty-eight years of age, but having the appearance of fifty, sat on a mat towards the upper part of the room, leaning against a pillar, which was one of a row that divided the hall by its whole length. His countenance was sensible and good-natured; but, destitute as he was of becoming attire, he had but a mean and undignified appearance. The courtiers kept at a great distance, crouching to the very ground, with their hands clasped before them. Among these were several Mohammedans of the sect of Ali, descendants of emigrants from the Coromandel coast. These people, who from education and circumstances are naturally subtle and intriguing, have considerable influence in the foreign department of the Siamese administration. Among the courtiers, the Prah-klang alone was a little in advance, but prostrate like the rest. Mr. Rutherfurd and I sat down upon a carpet which was pointed out to us, between the Prince and his courtiers. Near us we found the presents of the Governor-general to the Prince. We were no sooner seated than the Christian Intendant of the Port directed us, in a tone of authority bordering on rudeness, to make the customary obeisance. I felt under the necessity of rebuking him, by observing, that unless he could express himself with more propriety and decorum, he must not presume to address us at all. This had the desired effect, for we were not again importuned by him during the rest of the evening.

It had been provided that our interpreters should be admitted, but this was a promise which was by no means intended to be kept. To be admitted to the presence of the Prince, was considered too great an honour for persons of their condition, and besides a very inconvenient restraint upon the conversation which would ensue. Accordingly, when they attempted to follow us into the hall, they were jostled by the attendants and forced to withdraw. I even found that Ko-chai-asa-hak was not of sufficient rank to address the Prince directly. Another Mohammedan of superior rank, who was a little in advance for this purpose, received the Prince's words, and Ko-chai-asa-hak, who lay crouched behind us, rendered them to me in the Malay language. I was first asked if peace or war prevailed in Hindoostan, and then followed a number of questions, which were personal towards the Governor-general,—such as inquiries after his health; how long he had governed India, what was His Excellency's age, and whether or not he was brother to the King of England? When these inquiries were satisfactorily answered, the Prince observed, "I have heard of his reputation for justice and wisdom, from the merchants, of all nations, who have of late years resorted to this country."

The Prince after this referred to a subject of less dignity, but one which interested him more, —the fate of a ship, which, about fourteen months before, he had sent on a commercial speculation to Bengal. This was the vessel which we had seen at Calcutta, Penang, and Singapore, and which had left the latter place before ourselves, although she had not yet arrived. He asked whether we had seen her, when she might be expected, and whether or not she had an European pilot on board. After this last question, he wished to know whether we thought European or Indian mariners most skilful. The answer was not difficult; and he explained, in a tone of compliment, "When I speak of Europeans in general, I do not mean the English, for their superiority over all other people, in this respect, is well known." One question touching the subject now introduced was calculated to excite a smile. The Prince desired to know whether, during his residence at Calcutta, the commander of the Siamese ship had dressed in the English fashion, and conformed to the manners and customs of Europeans. The individual from whom this compliance with foreign manners was expected, was an unwieldly old Mohammedan of sixty, and of most uncompromising Oriental habits.

The next question put, touched slightly on the subject of European politics, and the Prince was especially solicitous to know, whether the British and Portuguese were at present at peace. It was readily answered, that the English and Portuguese nations had been friends and allies for many ages, and that there was every probability of their continuing so. The Siamese naturally form an undue estimate of the power of the Portuguese nation, from having at all times seen and heard more of them than of any other European people; and this accounts for the present questions.

We were asked after this, what objects we had in view after quitting Siam? This question afforded an opportunity of explaining the real objects of the Mission. The Prince observed upon this, in a strain of compliment, "It is wise in the

Governor-general of India, to seek friendship and commerce with distant nations."

Besides these, many trifling and unimportant questions were also put—such as the ages of the different gentlemen composing the Mission, the length and nature of their services, the number of European and Indian languages, which they had acquired, &c. The audience lasted nearly two hours, and was not over until between eleven and twelve o'clock at night. These late hours, as we afterwards found, are the favourite ones amongst the Siamese for the transaction of business. During this visit, no repast was served to us; but we had no sooner reached home, than we found eight large tubs of sweetmeats, sent to us as a present by the Prince.

April 5.—The 8th was appointed by the King for granting us an audience, and the ceremonial of our introduction was, in a good measure, arranged to-day. It was settled that a barge should be sent, to convey us from our residence to the landing-place opposite to the palace, and that from thence we should be conveyed in palanquins or litters. I had wished to stipulate for elephants; but we found that the use of these, so general in all other parts of the country, had been long discontinued at the modern capital, or, at least, interdicted to all but a few of the chief officers of Government. To ride on horseback, we found, was not considered respectable. We experienced, in the discussion of this question, a striking example of the singular and extravagant national vanity of the Siamese. This people, of half-naked and enslaved barbarians, have the hardihood to consider themselves the first nation in the world, and to view the performance of any servile office to a stranger, as an act of degradation. We had a hundred examples of this during our stay at Siam; and upon the present occasion, it was not without the greatest difficulty, and the utmost reluctance on the part of the chiefs, that they were at last brought to consent to allow us a few carriers to convey our litters.

I had apprehended much embarrassment about the nature of the obeisance which would be required of us at our presentation; but, upon the whole, this matter was arranged without any extraordinary difficulty. The Siamese officers, on their part, had great apprehensions that we should give offence by persisting in following our own customs in disparagement of their's. It was finally determined, that upon appearing in the presence, we should make a bow in the European fashion, seat ourselves in the place usually assigned to foreign missions, make an obeisance to His Majesty, when seated, by raising the two joined hands to the forehead, but, above all things, take care not to exhibit our feet, or any portion of the lower part of the body, to the sacred view of his Siamese Majesty.

April 7.—I had yesterday evening an urgent communication from the Prah-klang, intreating I would wave ceremony, and meet him at his house, as he had matters of considerable importance to communicate. I was extremely unwilling to throw any unnecessary obstacle in the way of the Mission, in the present stage of its progress; and therefore assented to his wish. I visited him this morning, in company with Mr. Finlayson. His desire was to discover, previous to the audience, what objects of Siamese ambition would be conceded on our parts, in return for such commercial advantages as might be granted to the British nation by the Siamese. With this view he asked pointedly, whether, if a treaty were made with the Governor-general of India, Siamese vessels would be permitted to purchase fire-arms and ammunition freely at British ports? The reply to this question was, that if the Siamese were at peace with the friends and neighbours of the British nation, they would certainly be permitted to purchase fire-arms and ammunition at our ports, but not otherwise. This pointed too plainly at the Burmans, and the interpreter hesitated to explain it;—informing me, in an under tone, that, according to Siamese notions, it was considered uncivil to make any allusion to the national enemy; an observation which shows the rancorous and irreconcilable temper with which those two nations view each other. This demand of supplying them with fire-arms, scarcely compatible with a strict neutrality, was that on which the Siamese set the greatest value throughout the negotiation, and I have to regret that I did not feel myself authorized to yield to it. The Minister began to discourse familiarly on the subject of trade, respecting which he evinced much shrewdness and intelligence; but his views were those of a keen trader, and not of a statesman. He complained that he had not found the trading adventures made to Bengal profitable; and it was no wonder, for the voyages had occupied eighteen months, and the goods had been consigned to native agents of indifferent character at Calcutta. He then dwelt upon the variety of productions which Siam afforded suited for foreign trade, and said, that the culture of coffee had been begun in consequence of the encouragement which the Americans had given him to grow this article. Before I took leave of him, he again reverted to the favourite subject of our supplying fire-arms, to which I gave the same answer as before.

We were informed this forenoon, whether truly or not I could not determine, that the Chinese had been very busy in misrepresenting the objects of the mission. They were stated to say, that the English came now with smooth words, pretending to want trade only—that in a little time they would ask for a factory—then for leave to build a wall round it—that on this wall they would soon plant cannon; and finally, that they would seize upon the country, as they had done upon many similar occasions. It was farther added, that as the English had no wars now on hand in Hindoostan, they had a large disposable army that wanted employment. It is not to be denied, but that the strange history of our Indian aggrandizement must always afford a subject of jealousy to the neighbouring nations, and ground to misrepresent even our most laudable views and enterprises.

April 8.—The ceremony of our introduction to the King having been fixed upon for this day, we left our dwelling at half-past eight in the morning for the palace. A twelve-oared barge, with the rowers dressed in scarlet uniforms, was furnished by the Court, for the conveyance of the gentlemen of the mission; another for our Indian attendants, about twenty in number; and the sepoys of the escort were conveyed in the ship's launch. It was made a particular request, that our servants, but especially the sepoys of the escort, should form part of the procession. About nine o'clock, we landed under the walls of the palace, where we found an immense concourse of people waiting to view the spectacle. The accommodation for conveying us to the palace consisted of net hammocks, suspended from poles, furnished with an embroidered carpet, and, according to the custom of the country, borne by two men only. The management of these unstable vehicles was a matter of some difficulty, and our awkwardness became a subject of some amusement to the crowd. The escort, after saluting us at the landing-place, fell in and formed part of the procession. After passing the first gate, we came to a very extensive market, crowded in every part with the populace. This led directly to the second gate, where a street of Siamese soldiers in single file was formed to receive us. These were of a most grotesque appearance, their costume being neither Asiatic nor European, but a strange mixture of both. Their uniforms consisted of a loose jacket of coarse scarlet broadcloth, buttoned in front; a pair of small loose trowsers barely reaching to the knee; and a hat with a small round crown and broad brim, which was coated with red paint or varnish, and composed of rhinoceros hide, a substance which is sabre-proof. Their arms consisted of muskets and bayonets, coated, like their hats, with a thick red varnish. Some of the muskets were without ramrods, and altogether in a very poor state in regard to efficiency.

At the second gateway we dismounted from our litters, and left the escort, which was not permitted to go farther. We were also compelled at this place to part with our side-arms, —no person whatever, we were told, being permitted to come armed within the immediate precincts of the royal residence. Passing through this gate, we went along an avenue having a line of sheds on both sides, under each of which was a cannon of enormous size. In this avenue also a street of Siamese military, similar to those just described, was formed to receive us. Turning a little aside from this avenue, we were conducted into an immense hall, which seemed to be not less than eighty or ninety feet long, and forty or fifty broad. This, I believe, was the principal hall of justice; but it did not seem to be much frequented, for pigeons, swallows, and sparrows, had nested in the roof—and were now flying about without fear or interruption, as it is a religious maxim not to disturb them. Close to this building, ten elephants, caparisoned, were drawn out; the first we had seen since our arrival.

Carpets were spread for us, and we were requested to wait a summons into the royal presence. We were not detained above twenty minutes when the summons arrived, and we proceeded to the hall of audience. This portion of the royal inclosure was, like the rest that we had passed, filled with a crowd of people who were curious and clamorous, but not rude. A number of officers, with white wands, attended to keep off the crowd; and two officers, after the manner of heralds, preceded us. We now reached the third and last gate, which contains the principal palace, a building with a tall spire, and roofed with tin; the hall of audience, distinct from the palace; and an extensive temple of Buddha. We were here requested to take off our shoes, and to leave behind us our Indian attendants. None of our party whatever, indeed, were permitted to go beyond this spot, except the four British officers of the mission. I had previously stipulated that our interpreters, although not admitted into the presence, should be within hearing; but in the hurry of the moment they were jostled, and hindered from following. As soon as we had entered the gate, we found a band of music, consisting of not less than a hundred persons, drawn up to form a street for our reception. The instruments consisted of gongs, drums, brass flutes, and flagolets.

Opposite to the door of the hall of audience there was an immense Chinese mirror, of many parts, which formed a screen, concealing the interior of the Court from our view. We had no sooner arrived at this spot than a loud flourish of wind instruments was heard, accompanied by a wild shout or yell, which announced, as we afterwards found, the arrival of his Majesty. We passed the screen to the right side, and, as had been agreed upon, taking off our hats, made a respectful bow in the European manner. Every foot of the great hall which we had now entered was literally so crowded with prostrate courtiers, that it was difficult to move without the risk of treading upon some officer of state. Precedence is decided, upon such occasions, by relative vicinity to the throne; the princes being near the foot of it, the principal officers of Government next to them, and thus in succession down to the lowest officer who is admitted into the presence. We seated ourselves a little in front of the screen, and made three obeisances to the throne, in unison with the courtiers. This obeisance consisted in raising the joined hands to the head three times, and at each touching the forehead. To have completed the Siamese obeisance, it would have been necessary to have bent the body to the ground, and touched the earth with the forehead at each prostration. I thought the place assigned to us, although not a very distinguished one, the highest it was intended to concede; but we had no sooner made our obeisances than we were requested to advance, and were finally settled about half-way towards the throne. The assigning to us the first place, and our advance afterwards to a more honourable one, was evidently an artifice of our conductors to exact a greater number of obeisances than we had pledged ourselves to make; for when we were seated the second time, the whole Court made three additional obeisances, in which we were compelled to join, to avoid the imputation of rudeness.

The hall of audience appeared a well-proportioned and spacious saloon, of about eighty feet in length, perhaps half this in breadth, and thirty feet in height. Two rows, each of ten handsome wooden pillars, formed an avenue from the door to the throne, which was situated at the upper end of the hall. The walls and ceiling were painted of a bright vermilion; the cornices of the former being gilded, and the latter thickly spangled throughout with stars in rich gilding. Between the pillars we observed several good lustres of English cut-glass. The apartment would have been altogether in good taste, but for the appearance, against the pillars, of some miserable lamps of tin-plate, which had been imported from Batavia, and which were in all likelihood prized only because they were foreign.

The throne and its appendages occupied the whole of the upper end of the hall. The first was gilded all over, and about fifteen feet high. It had much the shape and look of a handsome pulpit. A pair of curtains, of gold tissue upon a yellow ground, concealed the whole of the upper part of the room, except the throne; and they were intended to be drawn over this also, except when used. In front of the throne, and rising from the floor, were to be seen a number of gilded umbrellas of various sizes. These consisted of a series of canopies, decreasing in size upwards, and sometimes amounting to as many as seventeen tiers. The King, as he appeared seated on his throne, had more the appearance of a statue in a niche, than of a living being. He wore a loose gown of gold tissue, with very wide sleeves. His head was bare, for he wore neither crown nor any other ornament on it. Close to him was a golden baton, or sceptre.

The general appearance of the hall of audience, the prostrate attitude of the courtiers, the situation of the King, and the silence which prevailed, presented a very imposing spectacle, and reminded us much more of a temple crowded with votaries engaged in the performance of some solemn rite of religion, than the audience-chamber of a temporal monarch.

The King seemed a man between fifty and sixty years of age, rather short in person, and disposed to corpulency. His features were very ordinary, and appeared to bespeak the known indolence and imbecility of his character; but upon this subject it was not easy to form any correct opinion, owing to the distance we were at from the throne, and the sort of *chiaro scuro* cast upon it, evidently for effect.

To the left of the throne we saw exhibited the portable part of the presents from the Governor-general; a secretary proceeded to read a list of them; and I make no doubt they were represented as tribute, or offering, although of this it was impossible to obtain proof. The letter of the Governor-general was neither read nor exhibited, notwithstanding the distinct pledge which had been given to that effect.

The words which His Siamese Majesty condescended to address to us, were delivered in a grave, measured, and oracular manner. One of the first officers of state delivered them to a person of inferior rank, and this person to Ko-chai-sahak, who was behind us, and explained them in the Malay language. The questions put, as they were rendered to us, were as follows: "The Governor-general of India (literally, in Siamese, The Lord, or Governor, of Bengal) has sent you to Siam—what is your business?" A short explanation of the objects of the mission was given in reply. "Have you been sent with the knowledge of the King of England?" It was here explained, that, from the great distance of England, the political intercourse with the distant nations of the East was commonly entrusted to the management of the Governor-general of India. "Is the Governor-general of India brother to the King of England?" To this question it was replied, that the Governor-general of India had been the personal friend of his sovereign from early life, but that he was not his brother. The following questions were successively put: "What difference is there in the ages of the King and Governor-general?"—"Was the Governor-general of India in good health when you left Bengal?"—"Where do you intend to go, after leaving Siam?"—"Is peace your object in all the countries you mean to visit?"—"Do you intend to travel by land or water, from Sai-gun to Turan?"—"Is it your intention to visit Hué, the capital of Cochin China?" After receiving replies to these different questions, His Majesty concluded with the following sentence: "I am glad to see an envoy here from the Governor-general of India. Whatever you have to say, communicate to the minister, Suri-wung-kosa. What we chiefly want from you are fire-arms."

His Majesty had no sooner pronounced these last words, than we heard a loud stroke, as if given by a wand against a piece of wainscoting; upon which the curtains on each side of the throne, moved by some concealed agency, closed upon it. This was followed by the same flourish of wind instruments, and the same wild shout which accompanied our entrance; and the courtiers, falling upon their faces to the ground, made six successive prostrations. We made three obeisances, sitting upright, as had been agreed upon.

As soon as the curtain was drawn upon His Majesty, the courtiers, for the first time, sat upright, and we were requested to be at our ease,—freely to look round us, and *admire the splendour and magnificence* of the Court—such being nearly the words made use of by the interpreter in making this communication to us.

During the audience, a heavy shower had fallen, and it was still raining. His Majesty took this opportunity of presenting us each with a small umbrella, and sent a message to desire that we would view the curiosities of the palace at our leisure. When we arrived at the threshold of the hall of audience, we perceived the courtyard and the roads extremely wet and dirty from the fall of rain. We naturally demanded our shoes, which we had left at the last gate. This was a favour which could not be yielded, and we were informed that the first princes of the blood could not wear shoes within the sacred enclosure in which we now were. It would have been impolitic to have evinced ill-humour, or attempted remonstrance; and therefore we feigned a cheerful compliance with this inconvenient usage, and proceeded to gratify our curiosity.

The greatest of the curiosities to which our attention was directed were the white elephants, well known in Europe to be objects of veneration, if not of worship, in all the countries where the religion of Buddha prevails. The present King has no less than six of these, a larger number than ever was possessed by any Siamese monarch; and this circumstance is considered peculiarly auspicious to his reign. Four of them were shown to us. They approached much nearer to a true white colour than I had expected: they had, indeed, all of them more or less of a flesh-coloured tinge; but this arose from the exposure of the skin, owing to the small quantity of hair with which the elephant is naturally covered. They showed no signs of disease, debility, or imperfection; and as to size, they were of the ordinary stature, the smallest being not less than six feet six inches high. Upon inquiring into their history, we found that they were all either from the kingdom of Lao or Kamboja, and none from Siam itself, nor from the Malay countries tributary to it, which last, indeed, had never been known to afford a white elephant.

The rareness of the white elephant is, no doubt, the origin of the consideration in which it is held. The countries in which it is found, and in which, indeed, the elephant in general exists in greatest perfection, and is most regarded, are those in which the worship of Buddh and the doctrine of the metempsychosis prevail. It was natural, therefore, to imagine that the body of so rare an object as a white elephant must be the temporary habitation of the soul of some mighty personage in its progress to perfection. This is the current belief, and accordingly every white elephant has the rank and title of a king, with an appropriate name expressing this dignity—such as the "pure king," the "wonderful king," and so forth. One of the Jesuits, writing upon this subject, informs us with some *naïveté*, that his Majesty of Siam does not ride the white elephant, because he, the white elephant, is as great a king as himself!

Each of those which we saw had a separate stable, and no less than ten keepers to wait upon it. The tusks of the males, for there were some of both sexes, were ornamented with gold rings. On the head they had all a gold chain net, and on the back a small embroidered velvet cushion.

Notwithstanding the veneration with which the white elephants are considered in some respects, it does not seem to be carried so far in Siam as to emancipate them from occasional correction. Two of them were described as so vicious, that it was considered unsafe to exhibit them. A keeper pricked the foot of one, in our presence, with a sharp iron until blood came, although his majesty's only offence was stealing a bunch of bananas; or rather, snatching it before he had received permission!

In the stables of the white elephants, we were shown two monkies, whose presence, the keepers insisted, preserved their royal charges from sickness. These were of a perfectly pure white colour, of considerable size, and of the tribe of monkies with long tails. They were in perfect health, and had been long caught; but we were advised not to play with them, as they were of a sullen and mischievous disposition. These were both taken in the forest of Pisiluk, about ten days' journey up the Menam.

From the white elephants we were taken to the crowd of their brethren which had the ill luck to be born black, and were therefore doomed to toil, or harsh usage. They did not appear to us to be remarkable either for size or beauty; but some of our Indian servants, who were better judges than ourselves, considered them as possessing, in an eminent degree, all those points which are admired by amateurs, and which distinguish the noblest race of this animal.

We were struck with the great number which were partly white, principally about the head and trunk. One of these, which was kept in a separate stable, had the whole head and trunk white: it was eight feet high, and in point of symmetry quite perfect. This, like some of the white elephants, was caught in the forests of Lao. The elephant usually rode by his Majesty was exhibited among the rest; it was tall and very docile, but not remarkable for beauty.

A glance at his Siamese Majesty's stud of horses was quite sufficient to satisfy our curiosity. It consisted of a few ponies imported from the Eastern Islands, and of a small breed of horses, said to be brought from the Chinese province of Yu-nan. There were a few horses from Western

India, old and miserable. One of these, we were informed, had been presented by Mr. Light, the first Governor of Prince of Wales's Island.

As we passed along, we were requested to examine the large cannon which we had seen on entering. They consisted of seven or eight pieces lying on beds, and were mere objects of curiosity. Some of them were eighteen feet long, the walls of enormous thickness, but the calibre not exceeding nine inches. They appeared to have been perfectly well cast. Each had an inscription upon it, inlaid in silver, which, as we were told, described its charge of powder, but, from what we could understand, in very exaggerated terms. These guns bore no comparison in point of size to some of those cast by the Mohammedan princes of Hindostan, and neither in size nor workmanship, to several which we afterwards saw in Cochin China.

We were now conducted to the great temple of Gautama. This consisted, like all other Siamese temples, of an immense square inclosure, and contained one principal temple, with several inferior ones. There was a colonnade and covered passage all round, and here the walls were covered with Siamese paper, the paintings upon which represented the Adventures of Rama, a favourite subject with the Buddhist nations. The principal temple was a spacious square chamber, at one end of which was a kind of altar, about eight feet high, containing a number of gilded figures of Buddh, in the sitting posture in which he is most commonly represented. In the middle of these gilded figures was one of the same deity, of a green-coloured stone, and about eighteen inches high. This, our conductors assured us, was made of emerald; but the material had not the least appearance either of that or any other gem, being, although highly polished, dull and opaque. It was not within reach of examination, but it is not improbable that it was a light-coloured malachite, imported from China.

Our examination of this temple was but cursory, and I shall not attempt any detailed account of it, as we had afterwards much better opportunities afforded us of examining and describing other Siamese temples of the same character, but upon a much larger scale. I ought, however, to observe that the first appearance of a Siamese temple made a forcible impression upon us. It was impossible to see the extent of the buildings, and the laboriousness and costliness of the workmanship and materials, without feeling that we were amongst a numerous people, who had made considerable advances in civilization, and who were ruled by a despotic government and a superstitious priesthood.

After having thus viewed such of the royal curiosities as were exhibited to us, we were led back to the hall where we had first rested, before our presentation. There was here prepared for us a repast, consisting of abundance of dried fruits and Siamese confectionary, served up with great neatness and propriety.

After partaking of this repast, we bent our way back, receiving the same compliments and marks of attention as when we entered, and we reached home about noon, so that the whole affair did not occupy above three hours and a half.

We had scarcely arrived at home when officers came to us from the King with a civil message, bringing a large supply of Siamese confectionary, and from twenty to thirty tubs of Chinese dried fruits and sweetmeats. By the same opportunity, we were informed that the Minister, Suri-wung-kosa, would visit us in the course of the afternoon, having received directions to furnish us with an entertainment at our own house, and there to do the honours of the feast.

This visit afforded an opportunity of observing one of the most singular and whimsical prejudices of the Siamese. This people have an extreme horror of permitting any thing to pass over the head, or having the head touched, or in short bringing themselves into any situation in which their persons are liable to be brought into a situation of physical inferiority to that of others, such as going under a bridge, or entering the lower apartment of a house when the upper one is inhabited. For this sufficient reason, their houses are all of one story. The dwelling which we occupied, however, had been intended for a warehouse, and consisted, as already mentioned, of two stories, while there was no access to the upper apartments except by an awkward stair and trapdoor, from the corresponding lower ones. This occasioned a serious dilemma to the minister. A man of his rank and condition, it was gravely insisted upon, could not subject himself to have strangers walk over his head, without suffering seriously in public estimation.

To get over this weighty objection, a ladder was at last erected against the side of the house, by which his Excellency, although neither a light nor active figure suited for such enterprises, safely effected his ascent about three o'clock in the afternoon. The native Christians, of Portuguese descent, had prepared an abundant entertainment after the European manner, which was now served up. The minister sat at table, but without eating. His son and nephew, the youths whom I have before mentioned, also sat down, and partook heartily of the good things which were placed before them. No oriental antipathies were discoverable in the selection of the viands. Pork, beef, venison, and poultry, were served up in profusion, and there was certainly nothing to indicate that we were in a country where the destruction of animal life is viewed with horror, and punished as a crime. The fact is, that in practice the Siamese eat whatever animal food is presented to them without scruple, and discreetly put no questions, being quite satisfied, as they openly avow, if the blood be not upon their own heads.

The minister put several questions of a public nature to us while we sat at table. He asked, If an account of the present mission would be transmitted to the King of England? I replied to this, That circumstantial accounts of every transaction of the Indian Government were regularly transmitted to England. Upon hearing this explanation, he asked pointedly, Whether the King of England, when he heard the result of the present mission, would address a letter to the King of Siam? I replied, That his Majesty the King of England had generally delegated his authority to the Governor-general of India, but that, if it were particularly wished for by the King of Siam, I made no question but a letter would be immediately addressed to him. There can be no doubt but that these and the similar questions put during the audience, were dictated by the pride of the Siamese Government, which was evidently reluctant to maintain an equal intercourse with the delegated Government of India, and courted a direct one with the Sovereign. With respect to the East India Company, it is absolutely unknown as such by the princes of the further East, who could not, were it right to attempt an explanation, be made capable of comprehending the delegation of a vast political power to a body of merchants. Even the natives of Hindustan, who frequently use the English word "Company," attach no other meaning to it than the governing power, or supreme political authority as exercised by the English.

In reference to the reception which we had received in the morning, Suri-wung-kosa observed, That he trusted we were now well pleased that we had visited Siam, after the reception which his Majesty had given us in the morning; and he added, "You are about to visit other countries, and from the reception you get there, you will have an opportunity of appreciating the honours which have been conferred upon you by the Court of Siam." The minister now begged to inform us that his Majesty would in future discharge the expenses of the mission; and a silver bowl, containing 240 ticals,* was, with considerable ostentation, placed upon the table, and I was requested to accept of this money, as a month's allowance for our whole party. The paltriness of this sum, which was scarcely adequate to forty-eight hours' ordinary consumption of the persons attached to the mission, I am convinced never struck the Siamese officers:—I have no

* The tical is worth about half-a-crown.

doubt, on the contrary, that they thought they were acquitting themselves handsomely,—such is the sordid and pitiful manner in which the Government is accustomed to reward its own officers, even those exercising the highest trusts; and such, in a word, is the real poverty both of Government and people! I endeavoured to explain that we were all amply and liberally remunerated by our own Government, and that it was forbidden to persons in public employment to accept of money from strangers, or for the discharge of a public duty. It was necessary, however, in the sequel, to accept of his Siamese Majesty's bounty, in compliance with immemorial usage, and to prevent giving umbrage; for a gift by his Majesty, whatever its amount or nature, is considered to confer so great an honour upon the person who receives it, that to reject it would be viewed by his subjects as little better than an act of sacrilege.

The demeanour of Suri-wung-kosa during this visit, was not peculiarly prepossessing. His manner was cold, without being well-bred or dignified. To the inferior persons who accompanied him, he was coarse and familiar. These individuals consisted chiefly of Christians and Mohammedans, whose situation was not very enviable; for the first, consisting of the Portuguese interpreters, and even the Intendant of the port, waited upon us at table as footmen, and the last were compelled to feign to relish his Excellency's bad jokes respecting their prejudice against pork and wine, which he pressed them to partake of.

White Monkey in the Elephant stables.

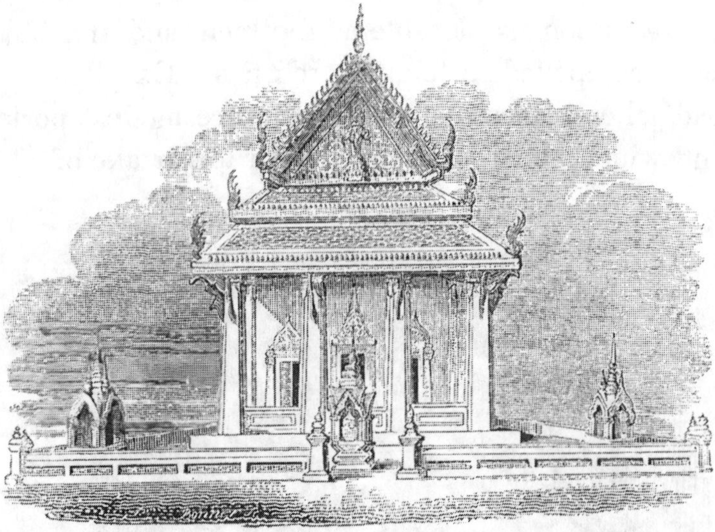

Siamese Temple.

CHAPTER V.

Mission visited by the Portuguese Consul.—Rapacity of the Court.—Visit to the Portuguese Consul.—Visit to Siamese Temples.—Number and Variety of the Votaries.—Visit to the town of Bang-kok.—Buddhist Temple.—Hindu Temple.—Ancient Ruins. — Commencement of the Negotiation.—Relics of Gautama.—Despatches sent by the Mission across the Peninsula.—Visit to the Prince Krom-chiat.—Opinion entertained by the Siamese respecting our Indian Conquests.—Funeral of a Siamese.—Excursion to the Neighbourhood of Bang-kok.—Religious Regard of the Siamese for Animal Life. — Splendid Temple constructing by the Prince Krom-chiat. —Negotiation renewed.—King's Character and Employments.—Annual Ceremony of the King's holding the Plough. — Punishment of a Christian Interpreter.—Arrival of a Portuguese and an English Merchant Vessel.

April 9.—We received this morning a visit from Mr. De Silveiro. This gentleman had come to Siam about two years before, with the title of Consul from the Viceroy of Goa. The Siamese Government had given him a small piece of ground to build a factory upon, and he had also commenced the building of a large ship. Mr. de Silveiro, whom we frequently saw during our residence in Siam, was a native of the Brazils. He spoke French and English with facility, and made many communications to us with frankness, from the respectable stock of local information which he had already collected.

In the evening Ko-chai-sahak called, and took care to remind us that we had dropped some hints respecting certain small presents which we intended to present to the King and the Prince Krom-chiat. These consisted of some spectacles, and a few specimens of English cutlery. Such was the anxiety even for these trifles, that the officers of Government had not the decorum to wait until they were regularly offered. In this visit, Ko-chai-sahak made various attempts to extract from us the object of our visit to Cochin China; but, above all, to ascertain the nature and value of the presents intended for that Court. He received no satisfaction upon these points; not because concealment was of any advantage to us, but because explanation was not due to a conduct that was obviously indelicate and improper.

April 10.—I had a message from the Prah-klang to know which of the princes or chief officers of Government we wished to visit; and hints at the same time were thrown out, with a view of ascertaining what presents we intended to offer to each. I replied, that I would wait upon any of the princes whom he would point out as proper to visit; but considering the hints respecting presents indecorous, I took no notice of them. It was evident, however, that our visits were chiefly requested on account of the presents expected, and that our acquaintance was not considered of any value without them. There were, at this time, two parties at the Court of Siam: at the head of one of which, was the Prince Krom-chiat and the then Prah-klang; and at that of the other, the Prince Chao-fa,* the eldest legitimate son of the King, and his maternal uncles. The Prah-klang, therefore, was perhaps glad, on this occasion, to avail himself of any excuse to prevent an intercourse between us and his rivals.

April 11.—The Chinese festival of Lanterns commenced to-day, an occasion which seems to be equally respected by the Siamese. No business whatever was transacted, and the time was devoted to amusements, to religious ceremonies, to feasting, and to making presents to the Talapoins. At night the Chinese vessels in the river were

* Literally, Lord of the heavens, or sky.

decked with lanterns, presenting a fanciful and striking appearance. The Siamese call this festival Sung-kran, which is probably the corruption of some Sanscrit or Bali term.

In the afternoon we returned the visit of Mr. de Silveiro, at the Portuguese factory, which was about two miles farther down the river than our own dwelling. The Menam exhibited a scene of considerable activity, and afforded evidence of the existence of a respectable trade. We counted seventy junks, large and small, engaged in foreign trade. There were five or six of the largest description on the stocks, and, besides these, there was a numerous small craft engaged in the internal trade, as well as many rafts conveying merchandize. Mr. Silveiro showed us the ship which he was building, and which was a vessel of between three and four hundred tons burthen, entirely of Siamese teak.

April 12.—We were now at full liberty to go abroad, and, in consequence, this morning passed several hours in examining some Siamese temples. A temple, or monastery—for they are nearly inseparable, called in the language of the country, Wat or Wata,—is always a large square enclosure, consisting of the following parts—a place of worship, with the images of Gautama, an extensive area, a library, and the dwellings of the Talapoins. The largest temple which we visited on this occasion is called, in Siamese, Prah-chettăp-pon, or the "temple of the people," because accessible to every one. A sketch of this building will suffice to convey a notion of all Siamese temples. Each side of the wall which surrounds it measures a hundred Siamese fathoms, or six hundred and fifty English feet. The central building is in the form of a parallelogram, and contains a single sitting figure of Buddha, of gigantic proportions. The walls of the fane are hung with painted paper, containing mythological representations, and the gilding, carving, and other decorations are highly laboured.

Around this central temple, and upon a terrace, was a series of small pyramidal pagodas surmounted by a spire. Each of these contained a stone not unlike in form to a bishop's mitre; on which very solid ground it was, that some of the early Roman missionaries fancied that Christianity and prelacy must have been established in Siam in remote times. These stones are considered essential to every temple, but no one can tell either their origin or object.

Surrounding the main temple, and after the intervention of an area of considerable extent, there was a triple square-formed range of buildings, each row of which was connected with the other at the angles. Each of these angles again consisted of three distinct temples, one belonging to each row, so as to make the whole amount to twelve in number. They were connected with each other by long galleries of about half their own height. Several of the twelve fanes now alluded to contained gigantic statues of Gautama, and the galleries an endless series of images of the same deity, smaller, but all much above the human size.

The first of the distinct fanes of this portion of the building to which we were introduced, contained a figure of Buddha in an erect posture, of the enormous height of five fathoms and a half Siamese, which is equal to thirty-five feet and three quarters English. The breadth of the image at the shoulders was six cubits, and the length of each foot two cubits and two inches. This idol was principally composed of brass, but some portion of the drapery was of wood—a circumstance, however, which we should not have discovered, without being told of it, for the figure is richly gilt all over, so as completely to conceal the nature of the materials of which it is composed. In the wall of the chamber which contained this image was a stone tablet, with an inscription in the mixed Bali and Siamese character. This was explained to us by the chief lay-attendant; and its purport was, that the temple was built in the year 2338, of the sacred era of the Siamese, corresponding with the year 1795. The most curious portion of the inscription is the estimate which it gives of the cost of the whole temple. The single item of clearing the ground on which it stands, and making provision for the original occupants, who were turned out, is reckoned at 16,400 ticals, and the total charge is stated to have amounted to 465,440 ticals. These sums in sterling money, valuing the tical at *2s. 6d.*, are equivalent to 58,180*l.* A second chamber exhibited Gautama sitting under a fig-tree (*ficus religiosa*). The tree, with its branches, leaves, and fruit, were tolerably well imitated. It was of considerable height. The paper-hangings of this chamber represented the war of the Ramayana.

A third chamber represented the god, with two votaries, or disciples, in an attitude of supplication before him. The figures of Gautama, in these two last chambers, represented him in the usual sitting attitude, with the legs crossed, and the soles of the feet turned up.

In a fourth chamber he is represented sitting on a secluded mountain. At his feet are an elephant presenting a cup of water, and an ape offering him a honeycomb from the branch of a tree. The figures of these animals are of brass, and not gilded,—being, indeed, the only ones that are not so, throughout the temple. The walls of this chamber contain representations of the Hindoo creation, and full-sized figures of natives of Lao, Pegue, China, Tartary, Hindustan, and Persia. The objects thus represented, we were told, were considered matters of indifference, as they were purely ornamental, and not of a religious character. There appeared, indeed, no question respecting this point; for the wall of the same chamber was also decorated with several Chinese copies of French and English prints, by no means according with the character of the building—such, for example, as the portrait of an English lady—"*la pensive Anglaise!*"

A fifth chamber contained Gautama, again sitting under a fig-tree, upon the coils of a seven-headed and hooded snake, the heads forming a canopy over him. This idol, including the pedestal, or, in other words, the coils of the snake, measured twenty-four feet high. The representations on the walls here, exhibited sketches of the modern city of Bang-kok. The river is shown, with Chinese junks and European shipping; and among the most prominent figures are several Europeans, in the grotesque costume of the end of the seventeenth and beginning of the eighteenth centuries.

In a sixth chamber, the god is represented with five votaries before him, and a minister at his feet publishing his orders. Here the paper-hangings represented Gautama preaching to the assembled deities of the Hindoo Pantheon.

The long galleries which connected these chambers were occupied, without interruption, with the images of Gautama,—all in a sitting attitude, ranged in regular order, and of an uniform size in each gallery. The area, which intervenes between this central temple and the quadrangular range, contains at each corner a tall pyramid of masonry, with an iron trident at its apex. These, although I am not acquainted with their intention, seem to be inseparable from every Siamese temple.

Between the quadrangular portion of the building now described, and the outer wall, is an extensive area, in which are several scattered and detached buildings. The first of these which we entered was a long arcade, which contained no images; but on the walls of which were daubed many human figures, thrown into attitudes the most whimsical, distorted, and unnatural that can well be conceived. Under these figures were inscriptions in the vernacular language, giving directions how to assume the attitudes in question, and recommending them as infallible remedies for the cure of certain diseases. In many of the cases which we saw, the remedy, if practicable, would certainly be worse than the disease, whatever that might be.

We were next conducted to certain dark and gloomy galleries, corresponding in number and position with the sides of the quadrangle. These contained a great number of figures of Buddha, remarkable for the variety of attitudes in which they were exhibited, when compared to the general uniformity which prevails on this subject. A few were in the usual sitting posture, a great many were standing; some were upon their knees, with the body thrown backward; and some were reclining at full length, supported by pillows and cushions. One figure of Gautama, but one only, was exhibited as dead, in a wooden coffin, the lid and front side of which were left open, and a votary was seen embracing the feet.

The chapel was the next object shown. This was an oblong square building, which contained a large figure of Gautama, with a smaller one on each side, and two pulpits very richly carved and gilded. Close to the chapel, but distinct from it, was the library, which seemed to be viewed as the most sacred portion of the whole building. This alone was in the immediate charge of the priests, of whom we scarcely saw one in the body of the temple. They hesitated to admit us into the interior; but we offered, of our own accord, to pull off our shoes before entering—and this little civility induced them to open the doors at once, without insisting upon any inconvenient ceremony on our part. The library was as rich in decoration, as carving, gilding, and bright vermilion could make it; and this was not confined to the inside only, but extended also to parts exposed to the weather. The platform on which it stood, however, was composed of rough planks ill-joined, and so was the flight of stairs which formed the ascent to it—these parts affording a contrast truly barbarian, with the building itself. The centre of the library contained a sort of ark, or sanctuary, composed of a dome surmounted by a spire. The workmanship of this was rich and elaborate beyond the rest. The doors were thrown open to permit us to inspect from a distance the sacred volumes, which, we were told, were fifty in number. To gratify our curiosity, one was taken out; it consisted, like all other books of the same description in this country, of long narrow slips of palm-leaf, filed at both ends on a cord. The writing, which was in the Bali, or religious character, seemed to be neatly executed. The edges of the volume were richly gilded, and the manuscript had in all respects a neat and handsome appearance.

Between the library and chapel there was a small pond, which contained a considerable quantity of fish, and a single alligator, which the priests were in the habit of feeding.

One or more tall spires would appear to be a necessary and inseparable portion of every Siamese temple. The area which I am now describing contained no less than twenty-one—a group, consisting of one large and four small ones, being distributed at each corner of the square. Besides these, there was one remarkable spire close to one of the gateways; this measured ninety-seven feet to a side at the base, which was square, and its height was described to us to be one hundred and sixty-two English feet. These spires are called, by the Siamese, Prah-chă-di, and are the same which are known in Ceylon by the name of a Dagoba.

Towards each of the four gateways of the enclosure, are a pair of monstrous and gigantic statues, representing warders. This is an enumeration of all that is contained within the walls of the temple; the entrances to which are by four arched gateways, of laboured architecture, each surmounted by the favourite spire.

After passing the walls of the temple, we still meet several detached objects connected with the establishment. The principal of these are the cells of the Talapoins; for every Siamese temple is not only a place of worship, but also a monastery. The cells of the monastery now described were wooden structures, raised on pillars, and extending in a regular range along one whole face of the square.

As we passed towards these, and close to one of the gates of the temple, we perceived a handsome belfry, and near to it an enormous urn, full twenty feet high, formed of brick and mortar. Here are deposited the ashes of all the high-priests of this temple. There is no door or other entry to it, and an aperture must therefore be made whenever there is occasion to make a fresh deposit. Not far from this spot we saw the chief-priest, seemingly no pattern of humility or moderation. He was conveyed in a crimson silk litter by inferior priests, and had over him a yellow umbrella, an emblem of high honour and distinction. We would willingly have held some conversation with this dignitary, and sent him a message to that effect, but he did not seem to be desirous of our acquaintance.

The temple which we had now visited contained, as we were informed, no less than fifteen hundred images, large and small, four hundred of which were of gigantic proportions. This statement is most probably an exaggeration; but certainly, situated as we were, I can safely say they were too numerous for us to count. The number of regular Talapoins attached to the temple, or, as we should express it, on the foundation, we were told was five hundred, and the number of noviciates, or pupils, seven hundred and fifty.

Having recrossed the river, we visited another temple, much smaller than the one now described, but neater and in better order: its general plan resembled the last. There was a quadrangular wall, with four gates; a wide area, containing the chapel, library, and other detached buildings, with the sacred spires or Prah-chă-dis, a single quadrangular range of buildings;

and finally, after the intervention of a small area, one great, central temple. In this case, the quadrangular range was a colonnade, open towards the temple; and, as we had an opportunity ourselves of ascertaining, for we counted them, contained one hundred and twenty sitting figures of Gautama, all gilt, and of gigantic proportions. The central temple contained three great figures of Gautama. Among its ornaments were some English and Chinese mirrors, several of them in handsome gold-burnished frames. There were also several lustres of cut-glass of English manufacture. During our visit, two large and costly Chinese mirrors arrived at the temple, as a present from the King. They were in standing frames, and on pedestals, and intended as screens to be placed before the principal idols. The workmen began to put them up while we were present.

All around the inner temple, there were handsome earthen jars, with some plants of the Indian lotus (*Nelumbo Indica*) growing in each; which had a very pretty effect. The area between it and the colonnade was paved with slabs of Chinese granite.

All the temples of Siam are constructed of brick and mortar; the roof is made of timber, covered with red tiles;—and all the principal structures are of a square form, with gable-ends. The arch and dome seem nearly unknown to Siamese architecture. All the buildings are of one story only, in consequence of the prejudice to which I have already alluded, —the strange horror which every man entertains, confining the expression to its literal sense, of suffering his neighbour to pass over his head. That portion of the building which is of masonry, is thickly coated over with plaster, in which there is no dearth of rude ornament, but the materials are coarse, and this part of the workmanship is not skilfully finished. The greatest skill, labour, and expense, are bestowed upon that portion of the buildings which is of wood, in which are comprehended the gable-ends, eaves, doors, window-frames, and shutters, and the whole inside of the roof. These are painted, varnished, gilt, and carved in the most profuse and laborious manner—all this decoration being equally bestowed upon what is exposed to the open air, as upon what is under cover. Of the images, the greater number were a composition of mortar and plaster; but, whether of this coarser material or of metal, they were invariably and throughout richly gilt.

With all this labour and expense, a Siamese temple seems far from being calculated to excite those feelings of reverence and solemnity which should belong to a place of worship. The want of magnitude in any one part, the want of height every where, and the mean and perishable nature of some portion of the materials, with the gaudy meretriciousness of others, are far from being calculated, according to European notions, to excite sentiments either of respect or veneration. Although, perhaps, not less costly and more ostentatious, they are greatly inferior in grandeur, and even in taste, to the Hindoo and Mohammedan monuments of Western India, as well as to the ancient monuments of Java, consecrated to the same form of worship as themselves.

This character of the temples of Siam may be accounted for without difficulty. The alluvial tract of the Menam affords no materials for a substantial and durable architecture; and thus what would have been expended on solid materials, is wasted upon gilding, carving, and other temporary embellishments. The frame of society, perhaps, greatly contributes to the same effect. Every temple is built and endowed by some one in power, from personal motives of piety or ostentation. He can leave behind him, from the character of the Government, no secure funds for the maintenance of the establishment, and no successor capable of supporting it. The absence of a hereditary priesthood interested in maintaining the honour and character of particular temples, most probably conduces to the same result. The motives, therefore, to construct lasting monuments do not exist.

There are scarcely, I am told, any ancient monuments in Siam, notwithstanding the religious zeal, which is evidently predominant. Several of the temples of Bang-kok, although the place is little more than forty years old, are already in a state of decay and neglect; and many of the splendid temples of the old capital, described to us by the European writers of the close of the seventeenth century, are at present abandoned and in a state of ruin, the principal images having been transported to the present seat of Government.*

During the visit which I have just described, all the temples, but particularly the larger one, were, on account of the holidays, crowded with visitors, and this incident afforded us a striking picture of the manners and habits of the people. The votaries were of all ages and sexes, and the women were not less numerous than the men. The bulk were Siamese, but there were also Cochin Chinese, Cambojans, people of Loo and Pegue, and a great number of Chinese. Instead of the gravity and decorum which might have been looked for in a temple, the demeanour of the

* Another cause, beyond those referred to in the text, is, that the great religious merit consists in building a temple; whereas, there is little or none in repairing or keeping it up. This accounts, in a great measure, both for the great number of temples which exist, and the want of durability in their materials.

visitors was noisy, clamorous, and playful. They were at one moment prostrate before the idols, and at another engaged in some frolic, or singing an idle song. One man, for example, coolly lighted his segar at an incense-rod which a devotee had just placed as an offering before one of the idols, and another deliberately sat down before an image and played a merry air on a flageolet, while many were engaged at the same shrine in performing their devotions.

The women mixed in the crowd, unveiled, as indeed they always are, and were neither shy nor timid; on the contrary, there was considerable familiarity between the sexes; and our conductors, Mohammedans, hinted to us, although I cannot pretend to say with how much truth, that the temples were frequent places of assignation. All this levity certainly formed a very striking contrast to the decent and reverencial devotion of a Christian, or even of a Mohammedan people, and struck us with surprise.

The women were the most decorous in the performance of their religious duties, and also the most assiduous. They went about sprinkling the images with perfumes, and making offerings to them. The oblations were of various descriptions—such as lighted incense-rods; fresh lotus, and other flowers; chaplets of artificial flowers, and cloths of various descriptions. There were, indeed, few of the many idols which I have mentioned, that were not decked with a scarf of silk or cotton cloth, commonly of a yellow colour, the offering of some votary. The Chinese, on their part, burned sacrificial paper, and hung up, as votive offerings, from the roofs of the temples, banners of cloth or paper with Chinese inscriptions upon them.

No officiating priests were to be seen; and, in truth, as I have already mentioned, there was not a Talapoin within the precincts of the temple, except the few whom we met in the library, and these were distant from the crowd, and appeared to take no share whatever in what was passing.

I should mention, that those who frequented the temple were not confined to the lower classes. One group of well-dressed females was pointed out to us, consisting of above thirty persons. These were one of the concubines, and an infant-child of the Prince Krom-chiat, with their attendants. The infant, apparently not above three years of age, appeared to have been well-tutored, for he went through his prostrations with great composure before the principal image in the central temple. Several of the followers were young and handsome; and we were somewhat surprised, at hearing our conductors request us to point out any amongst them that we might desire to form a matrimonial connexion with during our stay in Siam.

Our appearance in the crowd excited a degree

of curiosity, which stopped short only of rudeness. —We were followed wherever we went. Our presence was sometimes announced by shouts, and a hundred idle questions were put to us, which either our interpreters would not explain to us, or we had no time or inclination to answer. A strong inclination was also felt to ascertain, by personal examination, the quality and texture of our dress, and the nature and use of the trinkets which we had about our persons. In all this, the ludicrous importance and vanity of the Siamese character was conspicuous, even among the lowest persons whom we encountered.

April 13.—We made an excursion this morning through the town of Bang-kok. The ground on which it is built is a rich tract of alluvial land, low, but not marshy, and intersected by numerous winding creeks and canals. We crossed the river, from our dwelling, towards the palace, which lies along the western bank of the river. A kind of canal surrounds it, and this, which was navigable, and communicated with the river, we entered in our boats at the southern angle of the fortification, passing under the walls, which had some mean bastions, with small embrasures, but no cannon. The canal was crowded with merchant-boats, loaded with rice, salt, cotton, dried fish, oil, dye-woods, &c. As we passed along, there was pointed out to us, on our right-hand, the residence of the fugitive prince who, under countenance of the Siamese Government, lays claim to the throne of Kamboja: it was a very poor dwelling, indeed.

In our progress, we had to pass under a bridge, which, after the profusion of expense which we had lately witnessed in the temples, afforded a surprising example of the stupid inattention of a despotic Government and a superstitious people to all objects of public convenience and utility. The value of a very few of the brass images which we saw yesterday, would have been sufficient to build a noble bridge at this place, where it was so much required; but the one which we now saw, consisted of a single plank, and was elevated to the giddy height of at least thirty feet. The passengers, for safety, took hold of each other's hand as they passed along it. Out of politeness to us, and in deference to the prejudice which I have already alluded to, that makes it a dishonour to have others pass over our heads, those who intended to go over, halted until our boat had gone through.

After passing on between two and three miles behind the palace, we came to a spacious temple, which was commenced by the present King about two years before, and was not yet finished. This was of the same general form as those I have already described, but in costliness and magnificence far excelled them. The doors and window-shutters, and the capitals and pedestals of the wooden columns, were curiously and laboriously carved almost throughout, exhibiting figures of flowers, trees, and animals: this carved work was again richly gilt. The central temple, which, in this case, was raised on a very elevated terrace, consisted but of one chamber, or fane, measuring fifty-eight and a half English feet in height, seventy-one and a half in length, with a breadth equal to the height. A single brass statue of Gautama occupies this noble chamber, for such it unquestionably is. The image, exclusive of the pedestal, measures, in its sitting posture, twenty-nine and a quarter feet: from the point of one knee to that of the other is twenty-two feet nine inches. This was an ancient statue, lately brought down the river, from the town of Sokotai, by order of the King. The minor images in the gallery of the quadrangular inclosure of this temple were one hundred and sixty in number, all of plaster, and most of them in an unfinished state.

At the temple we found that the festivities of the season were celebrating with deafening tumult and discord. The principal chamber was crowded with people, and a noisy band of music was playing before the idol. In the same situation there was a set of comedians, who excited the mirth of the crowd by their extravagant and ludicrous buffoonery.

The Praḥ-cha-di, or "tall thin spire," with a

broad base, appears to be a favourite emblem of the Buddhist religion. Accordingly we noticed that the whole loose earth of the area of the temple now visited, was here and there raised into little temporary conical mounds, on the top of each of which a rod was fixed, containing a slip of paper, on which was written the name of the votary who had taken the trouble of erecting it. In the course of the day we frequently observed floating along the river and canals, on the stems of banana-trees, numerous little mimic temples, which contained similar mounds of sand or earth with those I have just described.

Close to this temple of Gautama our conductors showed us a Hindoo place of worship—a novelty in this part of the world, and therefore calculated to excite our curiosity. There were three temples within one inclosure, each consisting of a long brick building, with an ordinary tiled roof. Access to them was from one end, while the altar and images were at the opposite one. They were dreary and comfortless-looking places, destitute of all ornament, and their poverty and simplicity afforded a remarkable contrast to the wealth and magnificence of the Buddhist establishment in their neighbourhood. There was no mistaking the religion which had the countenance and protection of the State. One of the three buildings contained fifteen large handsome images, all in a standing posture, of brass, with their crowns, amulets, and drapery gilded. The most distinguished was a figure of Mahadewa, nine feet high. There were several smaller ones of the same deity, with figures of Prawati, Padmi, and Vishnu, and one statue of Brahma. A second building appeared to be dedicated to Ganesa, whose statue was the most conspicuous. Here were also four statues of Mahadewa. The third building appeared to be dedicated to the worship of the Linga, of which there was a large gilded figure in the centre of the altar, surrounded by forty or fifty small brass images—such as those of Siwa, Ganesa, Naraina, Hanuman, the Bull Nandi, &c. &c. We were told that all these images had been brought, at different times, from Western India.

There was no one in attendance at the temples, but the priests attached to it lived at no great distance, and one of them came at our request. He was an elderly person, of slender form, and still retained much of the peculiar features of the Hindoo. He had a white scarf over his shoulders, and, in opposition to the cropped heads of the Siamese, he wore his long hair tied in a knot behind. He informed us, through our interpreter, that he was a Brahmin, and the fifth in descent from his ancestor who had first settled in Siam, and who, according to his statement, came from the sacred Island of Ramiseram, between Ceylon and the Main. He was gratified at the slender acquaintance which we displayed respecting the Hindoo religion, and took a pleasure in continuing the conversation with us on this subject.

Not far from this temple were erected two enormous wooden-posts, or pillars, joined at the top by a cross-beam. Each of these pillars was certainly not less than seventy feet high, and in size equal to the main-mast of a ship of four or five hundred tons. Certain ceremonies of the Buddhist worship, the nature of which I could not ascertain, are annually performed at this spot.

The tide having retired and left the creek, by which we had reached the temples which we now visited, dry, our boats were previously sent round to a convenient wharf, higher up the main river, and we walked to where they were. This led us to a very extensive bazaar, paved throughout with brick, and with a row of very good shops on each side, chiefly in the occupation of the Chinese. Among the articles exposed for sale, were large quantities of Chinese crapes, which are much worn by the Siamese women, principally in the form of scarfs. These shops also contained considerable quantities of Indian printed goods, and English chintz and broadcloths.

Quitting the bazaar, we passed under the walls of the Fort or Palace. This has no ditch, the curtain no embrasures; and the bastions, although having embrasures, are without cannon. As a place of strength it is too contemptible to deserve any notice.

As we passed along, the gunpowder manufactory, which is extensive, and the public prison, where the Burman captives are confined, were pointed out to us. We could not ask, however, to inspect these, for fear of exciting suspicion.

April 16.—We were now at perfect liberty to go about the town as we pleased,—a privilege of which we availed ourselves, by making frequent excursions on the river. In one of these, in the course of this forenoon, I passed the ruins of the old Portuguese fort. These lie on the western bank of the river. The dilapidated brick walls are now patched up, and within it is the palace of Krom-a-lŭăng, one of the principal ministers of the Siamese Government, and a great favourite of the King. Opposite to it was situated the fort occupied by the French, at the close of the seventeenth century, in the extraordinary attempt made by Louis XIV. for the civil and religious conquest of Siam. Farther up the river, on its right bank, we came to the extensive ruins of the palace of the Chinese King, whose power was overthrown by the father of the reigning monarch. Although this event took place only forty years before, the ruins might be supposed, from their appearance, to be centuries old.

April 17.—The occurrence of the holidays, the loved procrastination of the Siamese in every thing, and, I have no doubt, also the reluctance of the Court to enter upon the subject, delayed the commencement of the negotiation until yesterday, when we had our first conference with the Prah-klang. This, as well as all the succeeding ones, took place at the Minister's house, and always between the hours of eight and ten at night, the customary time for transacting all public affairs in Siam. The Minister stated that the King perfectly understood the nature of the request made by the Governor-general of India, but he wished us specifically to state the extent of the demands which we had to make. The answer to this was, that the wishes of the Governor-general of India, generally, were to see the imposts upon European commerce at Siam lightened, and the intercourse rendered, in all respects, so free and fair as to make it agreeable to both parties.

This sentiment was by no means conformable to the wishes of the Siamese negotiator, and he immediately gave the conversation another direction. He said, that undoubtedly the more English ships that visited Siam the better; and he was so anxious upon the subject, that he wished for a specific engagement, that not less than four should come yearly. I said, that it would be difficult to specify any particular number; but I was thoroughly convinced that many more than the number to which he alluded would come, if the intercourse was put upon a fair and easy footing.

In justification of the demand now made, the Prah-klang observed, that two years ago the Siamese had made a commercial treaty with the Portuguese, and reduced the import duties from eight to six per cent. No Portuguese ships, however, had come to Siam since; and it was therefore a matter of some scandal to the Siamese Government, that it had made a treaty, as it were, about nothing. I explained, that the Siamese were not unaware of the commercial resources of the English nation, and that there could be no possible risk on this account.

The Prah-klang now stated that a letter would be prepared, in reply to that of the Governor-general of India, in which it would be stated, that the concessions granted to the English commerce in Siam had been fully explained in person to his agent, and he trusted this would answer every purpose—an observation which showed at once the reluctance which the Court felt to enter into any specific arrangements, or fetter itself by a written treaty. I answered, that matters of this nature, according to our customs, would not be considered satisfactory unless committed to writing. The answer to this was:—"The Governor-general, in his letter to the King, has stated that you are his representative, and therefore whatever is told to you is the same thing as if told to himself." I, of course, persevered in my objection; and he concluded by saying, that such a written document as I required would be furnished.

After the public discussion was over, the Minister entered freely into a great deal of private conversation. The subjects introduced upon such occasions had always some personal and interested object in view. He mentioned that the Island of Ceylon now belonged to the English, and that it was full of relics of Gautama; adding, that there was one relic in particular highly venerated by the Siamese, a certain elephant's tooth, which his Majesty the King of Siam was extremely desirous to be put in possession of through the good offices of the Governor-general. I replied, that as the relic in question was also venerated in Ceylon, and in the custody of the Cingalese priests, this would be impracticable; as it was an invariable rule with the British, wherever they were masters, never to violate the religious feelings of the native inhabitants.

The Prah-klang observed, that the relic in question had two years ago been shown to some Siamese priests by an English gentleman at Candy, and of whose learning, on subjects connected with their own religion, as well as politeness, they spoke in high terms. This, I believe, was the late Sir John Doyle, at the time Commissioner of the Candian Provinces.

The Prah-klang, and those who sat with him,

perceiving that we took an interest in the subject of the Siamese religion, put a number of questions to us respecting it. He said, that a country called Magada was the birth-place of Gautama—asked whether it was a British possession—how far it was from Calcutta—whether there were any worshippers of Gautama in the country—whether the present language of the people was Pali, and whether there were any relics of the god. He was also particularly anxious to ascertain whether the British Government would permit Siamese pilgrims to visit Magada. I need scarcely add, that the country alluded to is the British province of Bahar, and more especially that portion of it called Buddha Gya. We were enabled to give satisfactory answers to most of these questions, and with respect to the last, in particular, I gave an assurance that every facility would be afforded.

About this time the Prah-klang sent us word that a dispatch-boat was about to be sent to Ligor, from whence there was an easy communication with Queda and Penang. We availed ourselves of this opportunity to forward letters to Bengal and England, which we found afterwards had arrived safely.

April 18.—We had last night an audience of the Prince Krom-chiat. The avowed object of it was to renew the public discussion; but the subject was never once touched upon, and was in all probability purposely evaded. We had, however, a great deal of desultory conversation upon a variety of topics, the most striking parts of which I shall now relate.

We reached his Royal Highness's palace about half-past eight o'clock at night, and were detained at least an hour in the anteroom before we were introduced, for his Highness was engaged in his devotions. During the whole of this time, indeed, we heard the voices of a crowd of Talapoins, chanting prayers, or Buddhist hymns, in a loud, drawling, and monotonous tone. When they had done, they departed, without waiting for the audience, and passed through the anteroom where we sat, without taking the slightest notice of us or of any one else, for it is their duty to feign the most absolute indifference towards every temporal concern.

This was a private audience, and the Prince was surrounded only by a few of his personal friends. The interpreters, upon this occasion, were allowed to enter. The Prince began by making civil inquiries after our healths, and the nature of our occupations and amusements since our arrival in Siam, and was particularly desirous to have our opinion of the temples which we had visited, in comparison with similar buildings in other countries. He had heard of our conversation with the Prah-klang respecting Ceylon, and renewed it. With the assistance of Mr. Finlayson, who had resided several years on that island, satisfactory answers were given to many of his inquiries. He asked if the whole island of Ceylon belonged to the English, and then, whether it was subject to the authority of the Governor-general of India. To this last question it was answered, that Ceylon had a governor of its own, not subject to the authority of the Governor-general, and that it was the only part of our Indian dominions so circumstanced. He observed, that no doubt the King of England had made this distinction because Ceylon was *holy ground!* He asked whether the Governor of Ceylon was equal in rank to the Governor-general—what was the amount of the revenue of Ceylon, and whether it was remitted to England. It was explained, that the revenue of Ceylon, although considerable, was inadequate to the maintenance of the island, and that it was necessary to remit large sums from England for this purpose. He immediately said, "If this be the case, it can be of no use to you; and for what purpose was it conquered and is it now retained?" We endeavoured to explain, that during the wars in which we were lately engaged with our European enemies who occupied the coast of the island, they harassed our commerce from its ports, and therefore, in self-defence, there was a necessity for taking possession of it.

Our power and our conquests in the East, of whatever nature and description, never fail to excite the alarm and jealousy of the nations of India, and hence the origin of such questions as the present. In several conversations which we held with the Siamese chiefs, they displayed a degree of knowledge and acuteness on the subject of our Indian power, which were scarcely to be looked for in their situation. A striking example of this was afforded in a conversation which a gentleman, attached to the mission, held with the Prah-klang. The gentleman in question described our nation as now at peace with all the world, but, perhaps a little indiscreetly, dwelt upon the strength and numbers of our navy. The Siamese chief coolly observed, "If you are at peace with all the world, why do you keep up so great a navy as that which you now describe?"

The Prince, after his questions respecting Ceylon, turned the conversation to a subject of a different nature. He inquired what profession Mr. Finlayson followed. It was answered that he was a physician and a naturalist. He then asked whether he had studied medicine for amusement or for utility; how many diseases the human frame was liable to; if Mr. Finlayson knew all their names, and could cure them all; how many races of men there existed in the world; with a number of questions of the same nature. He said that he had heard that the English were acquainted with an antidote against the small-pox. In answer to this, we took considerable pains in explaining the discovery of the cow-pox and its value. His Highness wished to know whether the Governor-general of India would, if requested, send a skilful person to Siam, to instruct the Siamese in the use of this antidote.

During this conversation, the behaviour of the Prince to those about him was affable, and even familiar. Among them were several Shias, or Mohammedans of the sect of Ali, whom he condescended to rally, by asking us whether, in any part of Hindustan, there were practised such fantastic and extravagant ceremonies as those observed by the Mohammedans residing in Siam during the festival of the Mohorrum. The impression which his conversation throughout the night made upon us was favourable, and he seemed certainly to maintain the character assigned to him in public estimation, of being the most intelligent of all the princes and chiefs of the Siamese Court. The Portuguese Consul afterwards told me an anecdote respecting him, which showed that he was not insensible to deeds of high renown, or unacquainted with the great events which had recently passed in Europe. Mr. De Silveiro stated that the Prince had frequently expressed to him his admiration of the great achievements of the Emperor Napoleon; and that he had at last offered him a handsome sum of money, if he would translate from the French into the Portuguese language a history of his wars, for the purpose of being rendered into Siamese through the Christian interpreters. Our audience lasted until near twelve o'clock at night.

April 20.—We had heard much of the singular ceremonies practised at the funeral of a Siamese, and yesterday a party of us passed the principal portion of the forenoon in witnessing the forms of one. The bodies of Siamese of all ranks are with few exceptions burned upon a funeral pile, and the spot chosen for this purpose is always the court of one of the temples. Some of the temples are more frequented with this view than others; and we were assured that if we went to the temple called Tan-le-na, on the left bank of the river, and some way down the stream, we might be quite certain of seeing funeral rites performed between the hours of twelve and three. We accordingly proceeded thither yesterday, and arrived on the spot at about twelve o'clock. The ceremonies of a funeral were just about to commence. The body, in a coffin which rested upon a bier, was lying under some fig-trees, of which there were numbers in the court or gardens surrounding the temple. These are highly venerated by the Siamese, who hold it to be as great a sacrilege to lop off one of their branches, as to slay one of the nobler animals, also a high offence against religion. Yet in Siam the sacred fig is not a handsome, spreading, or shady tree, "the benefit of it," as Knox says of the same tree in Ceylon, "consisting principally in the holiness of it."

The coffin and bier together were at least seven feet high, and, instead of having a dismal funereal look, had a gay and lightsome air. The bier was covered with white cloth, and the coffin itself with a gold tissue on a red ground, while its lid was decorated with tinsel ornaments. Over the coffin there was a canopy of white cloth, ornamented all round with festoons of fresh jessamine flowers. Both bier and coffin, besides these ornaments, were decorated with cornices of fresh plantain stem fancifully carved.

The different parts of the ceremony were ushered in by the discordant music of a brass flageolet, a gong, and two drums. The first part of the ceremony in order was the reading of prayers This was done by a priest of twenty-three or twenty-four years of age, from a pulpit under a wooden shed in the court-yard. The prayers were in the Bali language, and read from slips of palm-leaf. A small circle of persons, chiefly females, sat on a platform underneath the pulpit, with a taper before each. They were neither serious nor attentive, and most probably did not understand one word of what was said. The prayers lasted about half an hour.

While this part of the ceremony was going forward, the court of the temple was crowded with Talapoins of all ages, who, however, paid no attention to the solemnities which were passing within a few yards of them. On the contrary, they escaped from them, and flocked round our party, exhibiting a degree of curiosity, familiarity, and confidence beyond any thing we had yet witnessed, or rather any thing we had yet been subjected to. There was, however, no absolute rudeness, or, at least, no apparent intention of giving offence.

After the ceremony of reading prayers, the priests were called upon to act their part. To the head of the coffin there was attached a piece of white cloth, at least twenty feet long, of which they laid hold, ranging themselves on each side. In this situation they muttered three short prayers. This being over, the coffin and bier were dismantled, and the cloth which covered them distributed as presents among the Talapoins.

The next part of the ceremony was that of washing the body. This was performed by one of the secular attendants of the temple, whose fee for each funeral is one tical. Upon the present occasion he certainly earned it well, for the body had been kept for four days, with the thermometer often above ninety-six, and was therefore in a most offensive state.

The deceased had been a man about sixty years of age, and considerably above the lowest rank in life. His sons, daughters, and relatives, attended the funeral, and indeed took an active share in the performance of the different rites. Their demeanour was grave and decent; but no symptom of grief escaped from any of them, with the exception of one individual, who might well be called the chief mourner. This was a young woman, about eighteen or twenty years of age, and, as we were told, the favourite daughter of the deceased. She was in mourning,—that is, had her head shaved, and was dressed in white. She sat down before the bier, and, at sight of the body, began weeping and sobbing bitterly, and appeared to be in real distress.

The bier, with a layer of wet earth laid upon it, upon which was placed a heap of dried fuel, constituted the funeral pile. This circumstance distinguished the funeral from a more ordinary one; for on common occasions the bodies are simply burned upon a low earthen terrace, which was close at hand, and on which were still lying several heaps of vulgar and neglected ashes.

The pile being thus prepared, the body was replaced in the coffin, and carried three successive times round it, borne by the sons and sons-in-law of the deceased, and followed by the favourite daughter, uttering loud lamentations. It was then deposited upon the pile. A number of wax tapers and little incense rods were now distributed to the by-standers. A priest, ejaculating a prayer, set the first fire to the pile, and was followed by the rest, and among others, by ourselves, for we had been offered tapers, and particularly requested to join in the ceremony. As soon as the first flame had ascended, the daughter began to distribute small pieces of money to some beggars who were present, and who consisted chiefly of elderly women, dressed in white, who reside in the temple, and who perform menial services for the priests. The male relations of the deceased at the same time went through a most fantastic ceremony. They tied their clothes in a bundle, and standing on each side of the pile tossed them over it six successive times, taking great care not to allow them to fall to the ground. The object of this formality we could not learn, nor was it, probably, capable of any rational explanation. This ended the ceremony—the relations, however, continuing by the pile until the body was consumed.

April 22.—Continuing our excursions through the town and its vicinity, we made a very long one yesterday, which occupied us six hours. After ascending the river, for a short way, we entered a large branch called Ban-kok Yai, nearly opposite to the palace, and on the right bank. We proceeded upon this in a westerly course, for about two miles, and then entered a smaller ramification, which connects the three great branches of the Me-nam with each other. This last, which runs in a southerly direction, is known by the name of Bang Luang. On the principal branch there was the appearance of a brisk internal trade, for this is the principal channel by which salt, teak, and Sapan-wood are brought to the capital.

The first singular object that struck us in ascending the principal branch, was a pair of neat wooden pillars painted white, one being on each side of the stream. Upon arriving near these, our conductor, who was a Mohammedan, observed, That beyond these posts one might "sin" without danger, but that all within them was sacred. He meant by this that the space within the pillars in question, was considered as an asylum for the lower animals, but that beyond them they might be slain with impunity. In truth, it is not only forbidden to kill the larger animals within a certain distance of the King's palace, but it is even forbidden to fish in the river, within the boundaries which are marked by the pillars which we now saw.

We proceeded in all about five miles, having on each side of us a low rich country, universally cultivated, and thickly inhabited. In our route, we counted no less than twenty-two temples; some very large, and all of considerable size. Our visit terminated at that which was constructing by the Prince Krom-chiat, and which he had called "Wat-chan-tong," or, "the temple of the golden sandal tree." This, for style and neatness, far exceeded the temples which we had before visited. It was still in an unfinished state, thus exhibiting to us, in an interesting manner, the progress of the different parts of the work. The casting of the principal image was the first thing that attracted our notice. The different portions of it were lying about under an extensive shed, preparatory to being joined. The metal of which it was composed, was an alloy of tin, zinc, and copper, without much regard to proportions, which, indeed, would have been a matter of some difficulty; for we were informed, that when an image of this description is founding, it is the practice of the pious to contribute to it, and that no contribution, however trifling or incongruous, is rejected. The metal was, of course, a mere case about two inches in thickness. The casts, as they came from the moulds, were very imperfect, and there was a great deal of patchwork, occasioned by filling up crevices. These defects would be of little consequence when the work was completed, as the whole image would be covered over, as in other cases, with a rich coat of gilding. The image was to be a sitting one, and from one knee to the other measured ten feet, which would have made it equal in size to a standing figure of about twenty-two feet.

The plan of the temple was generally similar to that of others, and consisted of a quadrangular enclosure. The central temple which was intended for the reception of the principal image, composed but a single apartment, and formed a noble and spacious room. The pedestal for the image was already constructed, and was extremely handsome, being cased all over with Chinese marble, upon which was carved in relief devices of plants and animals. The roof of the temple had a singular, but not unhandsome appearance, being covered with green tiles, which colour we were told was communicated to them by a kind of varnish. The usual area, or court of the temple, in this case was a neat garden, planted with ornamental and fruit-trees. The dwellings of the priests were altogether in a new style—for, instead of the wooden cells which accommodated the Talapoins at other temples, these were constructed of brick and mortar, and neatly tiled and whitewashed. Their individual appearance put us, in fact, in mind of neat English cottages, in spite of the situation and the opposite character of their tenants. They amounted to fifty in number, and were confined to one side of the square. At each end of the row there was a building much more spacious than the rest. These were the houses of the prior and abbot; for in a monastery of Talapoins there are dignities corresponding to these titles. This temple, I have no doubt, owed its existence and superior splendour to the wealth acquired by the Prince in his superintendance of the extensive foreign trade, which Siam has lately been conducting. We went into the prior's house by invitation. He received us with politeness, but the pride of his order would not allow him to pay us much personal attention. He however directed a dessert of fruits to be placed before us. Here we saw a number of priests assembled, and engaged in their studies. For this purpose they were seated upon the ground, each with his book before him placed on a neat reading-desk. Every thing exhibited an appearance of cleanliness, comfort, and abundance. We were permitted to go over the different apartments without any difficulty. Some portion of the ornaments of that of the prior himself, struck us as odd, if not out of place. These were stiff Chinese copies of English pictures in gilt frames. One, for example, exhibited a fox chase, another the charms of a country life, and the third and fourth were portraits of celebrated English beauties.

Many of these are copies of our best prints, and the Chinese, by extraordinary cheapness of price, have contrived to disseminate them widely. In Siam they are very frequent, and I have no doubt a traveller would also discover them in the heart of Kamboja, Lao, or Chinese Tartary. We may see from this example, that in the intercourse of nations, it is impossible to discover beforehand, whether or not the productions of one be suited to the taste of the other, until the price be rendered low enough to meet the consumer's means of purchasing.

Sitting amongst the priests, we observed a man of intelligent appearance, and about forty years of age, in a secular habit. Our conductor informed us that he was a person of great learning, and that in his younger days he had been a priest; but falling desperately in love with a young woman in the neighbourhood, he had quitted holy orders to marry her; and although courted for his acquirements, and requested to resume the monastic life, he had ever since refused to quit his family. He was now employed in instructing some of the young priests. He entered freely into conversation with us, readily answered such questions as we put to him, and supplied us, on the spot, with a short vocabulary of the Bali language. With all his frankness, however, he was extremely desirous to be assured that we had a sufficient respect for his religion, and not satisfied with our assertions to this effect, he would have us attest our sincerity by making an obeisance to an image of Buddha, which was in the apartment where we were sitting.

On our return home, we visited a temple, which contained a relic of Gautama. This was the impression of a foot, or as such relics are called by the Siamese, a Prah-bat, or "holy foot." This was deposited in a small temple on the top of an artificial mount, which lay behind an ordinary Buddhist temple. The mount was of masonry, and of a quadrangular form. The extent of each face was about twenty-seven paces, and the height of the whole about twenty-two, exclusive of the little temple which contained the relic. Underneath it were many dark and winding passages, in imitation of caverns; for the object of this monument was to represent one of those mountains to which Gautama in his life-time had retired as an ascetic. The doors of the little temple were shut, and owing to the accidental absence of the keeper, but not to any reluctance to exhibit it, we had no opportunity of examining the relic.

April 23.—We had a conference with the minister last night, which lasted from nine to twelve o'clock. On this occasion, I explained at length the nature of the commercial arrangements which we were anxious to make, and for this purpose took with me notes for a treaty, which provided generally for a free and fair trade; for the determination of the export and import duties, and of all fees and charges; providing at the same time security for the persons and properties of British subjects resorting to Siam. The Portuguese having obtained permission for the residence of a commercial agent, and a promise to a similar effect having, as was understood, been made to the Americans, we hinted at a like arrangement for the British Government. In general, no negative was put upon these various requisitions at the time, with the exception of that which provided security for the person and properties of British subjects. In answer to this proposition, the Prahklang distinctly stated, that the King of Siam would make no alteration in the established laws of the country in favour of strangers. This indeed was a point which could not be insisted upon. If the subjects of a free and civilized government resort to a barbarous and despotic country, there is no remedy but submission to its laws, however absurd or arbitrary, so impossible is it in all respects to reconcile the fair and equal commerce of nations in opposite states of civilization with the freedom of conduct which must be supposed vested in every independent government, whatever its nature. It could scarcely be hoped, although it has sometimes happened, that an arbitrary government should concede to strangers a degree of liberty and security which it denied to its own subjects. Before parting, it was agreed upon that the conference should be renewed on the following night.

April 24.—I had a sudden and unexpected visit this morning from the Prah-klang, who came, as upon the former occasion, by scrambling over the gable-end of the house into the corridor. I thought this visit was intended to prevent or anticipate the conference which was agreed upon in the evening, but he came with very different views. He told us that he had come for the purpose of requesting assistance in recovering two pairs of ordinary glass lamps, which he alleged had been offered to the King by an individual belonging to the mission-ship, but afterwards sold to some one else. He said that his Majesty had set his heart on the lamps, that he was highly indignant at any one else presuming to purchase them, and that he had threatened half his courtiers with corporal punishment on account of his disappointment. I promised to inquire into the transaction, but could not help informing him that amongst us, the person who gave the best price for a commodity was generally considered as establishing the first claim to it.

In the evening I had an apology from the minister, and a request that the conference might be put off to another time. The excuse made was a singular one, that his father-in-law, or at least, one of the numerous persons who stood in that relation to him, had broken a favourite mirror, at which the minister was in such distress that he was utterly incapable of attending to public business.

April 26.—We were awakened in the night by the cries of some one suffering corporal punishment in the court-yard of the Prah-klang's house, immediately under our windows, and in the morning we heard that this was the Christian interpreter, attached to the mission-ship. He had failed to report the sale of the four lamps, of which the King had become so unaccountably enamoured, and this was the offence for which he had received castigation. He called upon us in the course of the day, and when we expressed our sympathy for the unmerited chastisement he had received, he only answered, that "he and the other Christians had nothing but patience to support them in the country where their lot had been cast." These men are, notwithstanding, the descendants of the Portuguese conquerors of India, and, possibly, some of them may have in their veins the blood of a Di Gama, or an Albuquerque; men whose very names made the monarchs of the East tremble.

April 27.—This was a day of some celebrity in the Siamese calendar, being that on which the kings of Siam, in former times, were wont to hold the plough, like the Emperors of China, either as a religious ceremony, or as an example of agricultural industry to their subjects. This rite has long fallen into disuse, and given place to one which, to say the least of it, is of less dignity. The ceremony took place about two miles from Bang-kok, and, I am sorry to say, we were not apprised of it in time enough to be present. A Siamese, however, who had often witnessed it, gave me the following description :—A person is chosen, for this occasion, to represent the King. This monarch of a day is known by the name of Piya-Pun-li-teb, or King of the Husbandmen. He stands in the midst of a rice-field, on one foot only, it being incumbent on him to continue in this uneasy attitude during the time that a common peasant takes in ploughing once round him in a circle. Dropping the other foot, until the circle is completed, is looked upon as a most unlucky omen ; and the penalty to "the King of the Husbandmen" is said to be not only the loss of his ephemeral dignity, but also of his permanent rank, whatever that may be, with what is more serious—the confiscation of his property. The nominal authority of this person lasts from morning to night. During the whole of this day the shops are shut ; nothing is allowed to be bought or sold ; and whatever is disposed of, in contravention of this interdict, is forfeited, and becomes the perquisite of the King of the Husbandmen.

Another ceremony, we were told, accompanies

the ploughing. Specimens of all the principal fruits of the earth are collected together in a field, and an ox is turned loose amongst them, and the particular product which he selects to feed upon, is, on the authority of this experiment, to be considered as the scarcest fruit of the ensuing season, and therefore entitled to the especial care of the husbandman.

The circumstance which led to the punishment of the Christian interpreter was fully explained to us this morning, and was such as to exhibit the Siamese Monarch and his Court in a very ludicrous if not disgusting light. Suri-wung-kosa, the Prah-klang, had shown his Majesty nine pairs of small globe lamps which were offered for sale, and of which his Majesty approved; but it so happened, that before the bargain was finally concluded, two pairs had been disposed of to some other person. The King missed the lamps, flew into an ungovernable passion at his disappointment, and threatened the Ministers all round with the bastinado if they were not produced. Our acquaintance, the Prah-klang, was to have had for his share a hundred blows; and the King informed him, in good earnest, that his being a relation (which he was) should not screen him. In fact, we were told, that he finally escaped only by keeping out of the way until the royal anger had abated. The Ministers thought proper to consider Mr. Silveira, the Portuguese Consul, who was under pecuniary obligations to the Court, as implicated in the transaction. He was accordingly sent for, put under an arrest, and treated with indignity; one of the Ministers informing him that he was liable to corporal punishment. All Bang-kok was in a state of agitation for two days respecting these lamps, the intrinsic value of which might be about four pounds sterling! They were at last discovered in the possession of an old woman, who hastened to the Palace and offered them as a present, pretending that it was with this intention she had purchased them.

The monarch, who was liable to these gusts of anger, was the unbounded lord of the lives and fortunes of perhaps not less than five millions of people. It is but justice to him, however, to observe, that the country prospered under his administration—that he was rarely guilty of acts of atrocity, and that upon the whole he was admitted to be one of the mildest sovereigns that had ruled Siam for at least a century and a half.

April 29.—At rather an unseasonable hour last night, a messenger came to us from the King. He had with him a puppet near three feet high, not ill executed, and purporting to represent an European. The object of the message was the singular request, that any of us who were skilled in such matters, would give the necessary directions for having the figure attired, so as to represent the late Emperor Napoleon; or if this was a matter of difficulty, that the puppet might be put into the costume of a young Englishman. Four tailors and two shoemakers accordingly made their appearance this morning, with a supply of cloth, velvet, gold lace, and leather; and as an Indian tailor was one of our attendants, he received directions for carrying his Majesty's wishes into effect. The King of Siam has a taste for such amusements as these, and is besides a very pious Prince. Every day he is said to gild with his own hands a small image of Gautama, which he presents as an offering to some temple, thus at once combining the indulgence of a favourite passion with a religious duty. In every matter of moment he is entirely in the hands of his ministers, but upon certain small occasions, he now and then, and somewhat outrageously too, asserts his prerogative, if not his dignity; as, for example, in such an affair as that of the four glass lamps.

May 1.—A Portuguese brig arrived to-day from Macao, and brought an account of the favourable termination of the quarrel which we had with the Chinese authorities at Canton, in consequence of the affair of the Topaze frigate. This transaction was already well known in Siam, and the Prah-klang had put several questions respecting it to some of our gentlemen.

May 2.—We received to-day accounts of the arrival of the English brig Phœnix, from Calcutta. This vessel brought us public and private letters, and files of English and Indian newspapers. We felt secure from all violence, and therefore could read with indifference, or with a smile, the assurance which one of the Calcutta editors gave his readers, on the authority "of authentic letters kindly handed to him," that "the King of Siam was to seize our persons, until the Raja of Queda, who had taken refuge at Penang, was delivered up to him."

A PRAUCHIDI, OR SACRED SPIRE.

SPIRE OF THE TEMPLE CALLED WATA-NAGA.

CHAPTER VI.

Negociation put off, owing to his Majesty's changing his Residence.—Acquaintance made with a Siamese Priest.—Arrival of a Ship belonging to the King of Siam from Bengal.—Anecdote illustrative of the Character of the Siamese Government.—Visit to a singular Temple.—Renewal of the Negociation.—Arrival of Ambassadors from Cochin China, and their Reception.—Second Visit to the Siamese Priest, and Conversation.—Practice of kidnapping Strangers, and selling them in Siam for Slaves.—Death of a Princess from Cholera Morbus.—Visit from some Brahmins, and an account of them.—Account of a Siamese Ceremony.—A Conference with the Prah-klang, or Foreign Minister.—Siamese Letter-writing.—Visit from a Chief of Lao.—Setting in of the South-West Monsoon.—Siamese Reptiles.—Arrival of an American Ship.—Another Conference.—Cochin Chinese Ambassadors visit the Prah-klang.—Visit to the Catholic Bishop of Siam, and Conversation with him.—Another Conference with the Minister.—Final Conference with the Prah-klang.—Answer to the Letter of the Governor-general, and Commercial Engagements.

May 5.—THE negociation was now again interrupted, and the important cause alleged was the King's changing his residence from one portion of the palace to another, a matter which was said to give occupation day and night to all his ministers. The benediction of the Talapoins was necessary to the King's new residence, and a few days ago we were told that several thousands were assembled to bestow it, who, in return for prayers, were well fed, and presented with new garments.

The right bank of the Menam, where our residence was, had only a narrow strip of dwellings along the river-side. Behind these, the country, which is extremely fertile, is intersected with narrow and inconvenient foot-paths, and frequent canals, over which there are no other bridges than single narrow planks or trunks of trees. There is no cultivation of grain to be seen any where near Bang-kok, but the whole of the land in question is occupied by fine orchards—for the culture of fruit-trees seems to be the most advantageous that can be followed so near the capital. Among these orchards here and there occur a temple. For want of a more convenient promenade, several of our party were in the habit of strolling over this quarter in the evening. In one of these excursions, I found an agreeable and instructive acquaintance, in the person of the chief priest of a new temple, which the Prah-klang was constructing. I had several interviews with the same person afterwards, and invariably found him kind in his manners, and cheerful in his behaviour. In point of intelligence, he was greatly superior to any other Siamese with whom I had conversed;

and he was always ready to communicate his knowledge without reserve or ostentation. In my first visit, we entered freely into conversation respecting the history and tenets of his religion. In the course of it, he informed me that the Buddhists gladly received converts, but did not go about seeking for them; and he mentioned that four proselytes had been recently made from among the Christian inhabitants of Bang-kok, and many more from the Mohammedan population. He exhibited to us the library of the temple, which was seemingly composed of about a hundred handsome volumes. Several of these were produced for our inspection. They consisted, like those I had before seen, of smooth slips of palm-leaf, about two inches broad, and a foot and a half long, filed at both ends, on a silken cord. They were all gilt at the edges, and some of them handsomely illuminated. Upon this, as on all future occasions, we were presented by this respectable individual with tea and betel.

May 6.—The arrival of his Majesty's ship, which had been to Calcutta, was announced two days ago. She took eighteen months to perform this voyage. The Prah-klang estimates the loss which the King would sustain from this adventure at three piculs of silver, or twenty-four thousand ticals; and it is most probable that the Siamese will not soon again attempt a project so much beyond their skill and strength as a voyage to

Bengal. The Siamese ship left Singapore ten days before we did. Attempting a direct passage up the Gulf, she was tossed to and fro for six weeks at the entrance of the Straits of Malacca, and finally falling to leeward, she ran aground near the Dutch settlement of Rhio. Here the local officers of the Dutch Government took the opportunity of settling an old account with the Siamese Government, by making the commander pay a balance said to be due, on account of certain arbitrary transactions of the latter at Bang-kok, relating to three Dutch ships which had come to Siam in 1824 for cargoes of salt, for the supply of Java in a season of scarcity.

Every day brought to light some new occurrence calculated to display the ceaseless jealousy and suspicious character of the Siamese Government. A government so arbitrary and unjust, can place no reasonable reliance upon its own subjects, and seems to be in perpetual dread that they are to be excited to insurrection or rebellion by the example of strangers. This is unquestionably the true explanation of the hectic alarm and distrust which it entertains of all foreigners. One of the interpreters of the Mission reported to-day the circumstances of a conversation which he held the day before with one of the brothers of the Prah-klang, who was much in the minister's confidence. This person said, that "the English were a dangerous people to have any connexion with, for that they were not only the ablest, but the most ambitious of the European nations who frequented the East." The Interpreter answered, that it was impossible the English could have any ambitious views on Siam, "for what," said he, "could they, who have so much already, and are accustomed to convenient countries, do with such a one as yours, in which there are neither roads nor bridges, and where you are ankle-deep in mire at every step. The reply, according to the Interpreter's report was, "Do not speak so; these people are clever and active, and the country would not be long in their possession, before they made it such that you might sleep in the streets and rice-fields." It may be necessary to mention that the person who made this communication was by birth a Siamese, and by disposition very talkative and communicative.

May 7.—We rowed several miles up the river yesterday morning. On the right bank, and opposite to the most northerly angle of the palace-walls, there are a great number of long sheds, under which are placed the war-boats, and the King's barges of state. One of the latter description, I am told, is a great curiosity, on account of its enormous length;—its being hollowed out of the single trunk of a tree, and the richness of the gilding and carving by which it is ornamented. We had no opportunity, however, of gratifying our curiosity, by inspecting "the royal navy," for the tide was low, and an intervening bank of deep mud prevented our approach.

The town, with its floating houses, continues along both banks of the river as far as we could see; and such of the Siamese who now accompanied us as had visited the old capital, stated that both sides of the river were well-peopled all the way to that place. The distance cannot be less than sixty miles.

In returning home we visited the temple, called by the Siamese Watnak, or in Pali Wata-naga, or "the temple of the snake," which has a singular spire and belfry attached to it. This remarkable object is, within, of ordinary masonry, but externally exhibits an odd and fantastic species of Mosaic; being overlaid throughout with pieces of small china-ware of every hue and colour. The figures carved upon this motley fabric consisted of many snakes of monstrous size, from which it takes its name,—of figures of elephants, of lions, and of monstrous human forms, male and female.

The temple to which this belfry is attached had nothing remarkable about it. The central fane contained a great figure of Gautama in brass, with a group of disciples at his feet, all gilded in the usual manner. The priests who ushered us in would have us pull off our shoes, but this we declined to do, as the same demand had not formerly been made by persons of more respectability. What we saw on entering was not calculated to excite our peculiar respect. Several Talapoins were lying fast asleep and stretched on the floor before the altar, and a priest and a layman were playing chess close to the feet of the God; whilst a crowd of idle fellows, both lay and clerical, were looking on. The players stopped to explain to us the nature of the game, which is nearly the same as our own, the powers of the pieces being, however, more restricted. The same curiosity was displayed to-day, as upon all former occasions, when we came into contact with large numbers of the people, but there was no rudeness nor ill-humour.

May 8.—I succeeded, after many difficulties, in renewing the conference, and last night had a long discussion with the minister. This chief had within the last few days been raised to the permanent post of Prah-klang, in which he had before only officiated, and now obtained the name and title of Suri-wung-kosa, instead of Suri-wung-muntri, which he had formerly borne. Every advance in rank or station is in a similar manner marked by some alteration in the title.

From what I had observed of the temper and character of the Siamese Government, and particularly the specimen of their conduct towards the Portuguese Consul, which had come under our observation since the last conference, the prudence of forbearing from urging the proposal for a resident British agent became obvious, although, indeed, such an appointment had been first suggested by the Siamese themselves, the year before, to an English merchant of Singapore, who was the bearer of letters from the Resident of that place, as well as from the Governor of Prince of Wales's Island. No direct negative was now put upon it, but there was, notwithstanding, an evident reluctance to it; and I therefore resolved to drop the subject altogether, lest it might interfere with objects which promised to be more attainable. There is no question, at the same time, but that such an officer is extremely desirable, and will ultimately afford the only means of giving security, respectability, and extension to our commercial interest at Siam. In the present state of our acquaintance with the Siamese, however, such an appointment might lead to difficulties. An indignity offered on their part could not be overlooked—a quarrel might be the consequence, and such a quarrel might involve, in spite of ourselves, a breach of that neutral policy which we have long made it a rule to pursue in reference to the continental nations beyond the Ganges.*

A Siamese translation of the sketch of the treaty which I proposed, had been furnished to the Prah-klang since the last conference, and the Siamese Court was, of course, now fully

* This passage was written before the Burmese war.

aware of the nature and extent of our demands. No objections were made to the greater number of the detailed arrangements which we proposed, but a very decided one to a free and unrestrained trade. The Prah-klang insisted upon the King's right of preemption, stating that it was a prerogative which had existed from time immemorial, and could not be surrendered. He well knew, that as long as this was maintained, all the minor arrangements might readily be defeated. The mode of carrying on the foreign trade at Siam, is, in short, this: when a ship arrives, the officers of Government, under pretext of serving the King, select a large share of the most vendible part of the goods, and put their own price upon them. No private merchant, under penalty of heavy fine, or severe corporal punishment, is allowed to make an offer for the goods until the agents of the Court are satisfied. A large portion, and often the whole, of the export cargo is supplied to the foreign merchant upon the same principle. The officers of Government purchase the commodities at the lowest market rate, and sell them to the exporter at an arbitrary valuation. The resident Chinese alone, from their numbers and influence, have got over this difficulty, and of course are carrying on a very large and valuable commerce. This pernicious and ruinous practice is the only real obstacle to the European trade in Siam, for neither the duties on merchandize or tonnage are excessive, property is sufficiently secure, and the country is fertile, abounding in productions suited for foreign trade beyond any other with which I am acquainted. A stout resistance was made to the exercise of this right, and the freedom from official interference which existed, not only at all our own Indian ports, but in China and elsewhere, was particularly urged. I addressed myself, however, to a party deeply interested in maintaining the present order of things—to the individuals, in short, whose emoluments arose from the very source of corruption which was complained of, and who were not therefore likely to be convinced by any arguments. The injustice of the principle was too apparent to be openly maintained, and the Prah-klang only attempted to palliate it by urging the moderation with which it was exercised, and the security which the interference of Government afforded to the foreign merchant in realizing his returns.

At this interview the Prah-klang asked whether the British Government would enter into a contract with that of Siam, for the supply of salt for Bengal; a commodity, he said, which Siam afforded, of an excellent quality and in great abundance. He observed that the King of Siam would contract at once to supply 400,000 piculs, or about 24,000 tons, and a larger quantity afterwards, if required. I was unprepared for the discussion of this point at the time, but resolved to renew it at a future interview, hoping that some advantage might be drawn from it.

May 9.—On the 28th or 29th of April, the arrival, at the mouth of the Menam, of an Embassy from the new King of Cochin China was announced. The Siamese Court received this mission with much respect and attention. Great preparations were made all the way from Pak-nam to the capital for its accommodation and reception, which were in all respects as magnificent as the Court could contrive. The Ambassadors were feasted on the way, serenaded with Siamese music, and amused with gymnastic and theatrical exhibitions, wherever they rested. The preparations took so long a time that it was only last night that the Mission arrived at Bang-kok. About five o'clock in the afternoon, the procession passed, and we had a full and near view of it from our windows. It had certainly a very gay and imposing appearance. There were not less than twelve or thirteen gilded barges, each rowed, or rather paddled, by from twenty-five to fifty boatmen, who were uniformly dressed in scarlet, and who pulled with great animation, keeping time to a Siamese song. This equipage was entirely furnished by the Siamese Government; for the three small junks in which the Embassy had arrived, were still at the entrance of the river. The Cochin Chinese Ambassadors took up their residence on the opposite side of the Menam to us, and within the enclosure of the Palace.

I had some days ago sent the Mission-ship down the river, with directions, if possible, to cross the bar, that no delay might take place in quitting Siam, as soon as the negociation should be brought to a close. Both the commander and Siamese pilots reported, upon this occasion, that it would not be practicable to get over the bar with less than thirteen and a half feet water, and that at present, at the highest flood-tide, there was not above twelve. This proved, in our situation, a serious disappointment; for the delay which it occasioned, threatened to defeat some of the subsequent objects of the Mission, and, what was still worse, to bring us in the mean time into an unpleasant state of collision with the Siamese authorities.

May 12.—The Cochin Chinese Ambassadors were yesterday presented to the King. They were received, I am told, without much ceremony,—the intercourse being considered of so friendly and familiar a nature, as not to call for extraordinary formalities.

We were now permitted to go abroad freely, and at all hours, but our visits never extended beyond a few miles of the town. The jealousy of the Siamese Government was sufficiently apparent, and every precaution was necessary to prevent its taking alarm; a matter indeed, which, after all, was nearly impossible. I once made a proposition to visit the old capital, which would have shown us a good deal of a country not for many years visited by Europeans; but it was received with so much coldness that I took care not to renew it.

Frequent engagements to renew the conference were as often put off, and for several days to come the Prah-klang had an apology in the affair of his eldest son's tonsure, one of the most important events in the life of a Siamese.

May 14.—I paid another visit to the old Prior of the Prah-klang's monastery. He was extremely communicative on every subject respecting morals or religion, but upon matters of a temporal nature he refused to speak, showing above all a strong reluctance to touch upon any thing that was in the remotest degree of a political character. For example, he would make no communication whatever on the subject of the civil history of the country. In the course of the conversation he repeated to us the ten commandments of the Buddhist system of morals. The fifth of these says, "You shall not drink wine or the juice of the palm." The old man thought this a fitting occasion to address a lecture to us, and, pausing, he besought us, as we valued our happiness, to desist from drinking wine, for that the punishment of that crime in another state of existence was to have a stream of melted copper perpetually poured down the throat! We assured him of our moderation, but this did not satisfy him; for he seemed to consider the most trifling violation of the precept as scarcely a less offence than the sin of drunkenness itself.

In reference to the commandment which forbids the destruction of animal life, we brought to his notice the practice of the Jains of India, who often wore a cloth over the mouth, to prevent even the accidental ingress of insects—who always looked before they trod the ground, and who made it a practice to strain the water before drinking—all out of tenderness for animal life. He seemed to consider all this as highly meritorious, and said it was a degree of piety which the priests of Siam had not attained, and that they might reasonably be ashamed of their inferiority.

Returning home after it was dusk, we met two persons conversing together in the Javanese language. Its accents, in this remote place, excited our curiosity, and we entered into a conversation with the strangers. One of them recognized me as an old acquaintance, and described himself as one of a party, consisting of seven young men and six young women, who had been kidnapped at Samarang, in Java, about three years before, by the Commander of a Chinese junk, and sold as slaves to the Siamese.

The Siamese Government has encouraged this nefarious practice. I am told, that of late years upwards of four hundred young Chinese have been kidnapped by their countrymen, and brought to Siam, and sold as slaves. Notwithstanding the vigilance which prevails on this subject in our own ports, the King of Siam's ship contrived to carry off from Calcutta, and Prince of Wales's Island, five young African negroes. They were presented as curiosities to the Prince Krom-chiat and the Prah-klang, and we had frequent opportunities of seeing several of them.

May 15.—The epidemic *cholera morbus* which, two years ago, committed dreadful ravages in Siam and the neighbouring countries, broke out afresh at Bang-kok, with considerable activity about this period. About twelve o'clock last night I was awakened by a message from the Palace, informing me that one of the Princesses, sister to the King, was attacked by the epidemic, and requesting that Mr. Finlayson might prescribe for her. Although at the time suffering severely from the effects of the malady, which afterwards proved fatal to him, Mr. Finlayson went without hesitation. He was not, however, permitted to see his patient, but kept waiting in the Palace of the Prince Krom-chiat for upwards of three hours, with the view of obtaining an opinion upon the symptoms and progress of her complaint, as they were reported by her attendants. The Prince kept him company all the time. His conversation was chiefly upon medical questions; and, according to Mr. Finlayson's account, he put many extraordinary ones.

The Princess died a few hours after Mr. Finlayson left the Palace. She was a young woman of about sixteen years of age, and unmarried. The event seemed to create much affliction among her relatives. The more joyous parts of the festivities now going on at the Prah-klang's house, were in consequence, for a time, interrupted. Not knowing of her death, and thinking it an act of civility, I sent a messenger to inquire after her health. The person to whom it was delivered, the brother of the Prah-klang, returned for answer, that the subject was one which he dared not even speak of. All the other Siamese to whom I introduced the subject, spoke of it in the same mysterious manner, as if persons of the royal blood were exempted from the common law of mortality, or that at least it did not belong to the vulgar to imagine otherwise.

May 16.—The Prah-klang sent to wait upon us this morning the Brahmins who were acting as astrologers at the ceremony of his son's tonsure. Among these was the person with whom I had formerly conversed at the Hindu temple; but the principal man, and the chief of all the

Hindus at Bang-kok, was a person whose name, or rather, I suppose, title, was Prah-maha-raja-kro-putra-guru. The first of these words means Lord, and is the common appellative of the priests of Buddha in Siam; and the two last, which are Sanskrit, "the son of the spiritual guide;" for his father, by the account he rendered to us, was the first of his family that came to Siam about seventy years ago. Putra-guru was a tall slender old man, with much of the Hindu form of features, although born of a Siamese mother. The account he gave of himself, and of the rest of the Hindus of Bang-kok, was, that their forefathers were all emigrants from the sacred isle of Ramiseram; that they came without their families, and intermarried with the women of the country; that they were all of the two first Hindu classes, or priests and soldiers, and of the sect of Siwa. We had an opportunity of observing, upon the present occasion, that they painted the forehead according to the type of that sect, and that they wore the cord which marks the higher orders of the Hindus. They told us that they had lost the use of the vernacular language of their forefathers, but that they had writings amongst them in the Sanskrit language, and in the provincial character of their original country. They honour Buddha not as a God, but as a saint of great reputation. Their learning appears to be small, and they live upon the reputation of their astrological knowledge, being constantly consulted by the Court, and by persons of rank, to give prognostications; for astrology, as an art, is forbidden to the Talapoins. I am not aware that they possess any astronomical knowledge, although it was from the predecessors of these people that La Loubere obtained the first Indian astronomical tables brought to Europe, and which afterwards excited so great a share of curiosity.

Some questions put to our visitors upon the present occasion, respecting the origin of the Hindu images we saw in the temple, elucidated a point of some consequence in the history of Hindu emigration. They stated that the images in question were brought to Siam from Western India in the year 765 of the vulgar era of the Siamese, which corresponds with the year 1406 of our time. This fact, if correct, proves that an intercourse subsisted between Western India and Siam a full century before Europeans had found their way to the latter country.

We made the Brahmins, before parting, a present of some white Indian cloth, which is their only wear, and upon which they set a high value. They thanked us, and were about to depart; but recollecting themselves they returned, and said, that if we had no objections they would make a short prayer for us on the spot, as the country was threatened with a visitation of sickness. They accordingly seated themselves once more, and chanted a brief prayer for our health and prosperity, and then retired, apparently satisfied with having performed their duty, and discharged their obligation for the present which had been made to them.

May 17.—The ceremonies attending the tonsure of the Prah-klang's eldest son, which commenced on the 13th, ended only to-day. The whole took place immediately under our windows, and we had an opportunity, at all hours, of observing what was going forward. These festivities appear to me to afford both an interesting and striking picture of the religion, manners, and opinions of the Siamese, and I shall therefore offer a sketch of them. The Brahmins, acting as astrologers, had divined that the fortunate day and hour for commencing the ceremonies were the 9th of the dark half of the moon, and the 3d watch of the day. The ceremony began with a feast, and as the guests sat down, the music, consisting of two full bands of not less than fourteen or fifteen musicians, struck up. About four o'clock in the afternoon, the young chief made his appearance, and although thirteen or fourteen years of age, he was carried upon the shoulders of an attendant. He was gorgeously decked out with a load of gold and jewels. Seven Brahmins dressed in white preceded him, and led him to a seat in the centre of the open saloon, the same in which the Prah-klang was accustomed to receive ourselves when we visited him. A crowd of Talapoins had by this time assembled. These keeping at a distance from the guests who were still feasting, as well as from the procession, began to chant prayers or hymns in a loud but not harmonious strain. This lasted for two hours. Several heaps of yellow cloth in ready-made dresses, were displayed upon the floor, and from these a dress was distributed to each Talapoin, as soon as the prayers were over. They received and put them on on the spot without any acknowledgment, for this is beneath the dignity of a priest of Gautama, however high the rank of the donor, or valuable the gift. Slender attention was paid to the prayers. Most of the auditors were eating, and some were smiling or laughing, others yawning. These prayers being in the Bali language, must have been unintelligible to most of them; but independently of this, the Siamese laity make a complete surrender of all spiritual concerns to the Talapoins, being of opinion that when they pay them sufficiently well, they discharge every necessary religious duty, and it may be presumed most of their moral obligations also. During all this time the music continued playing, the musicians seemingly striving with each other, not for melody, but for noise.

At night the saloon was brilliantly and even

tastefully lighted up, for this is an art which the Siamese understand very well. At one end of it there was a fancy altar-piece, decorated with coloured lamps, and artificial and natural flowers. On the top of it was displayed the Prah-klang's library of sacred books, consisting of thirty or forty very handsome volumes. In the court-yard, and before the saloon, a pulpit was erected, having over it a canopy of white muslin. From this the priests delivered discourses almost all night, relieving each other at intervals. Songs, some of them, as we were told, of a licentious and indecent character, were occasionally introduced; but what gave most satisfaction were the jests and mimicry of a professed buffoon, who set the company in a roar. This singular medley of feasting, praying, singing, and buffoonery, went on with little interruption, leaving only a few hours in the morning for the inmates of the house to repose. From the third day, indeed, the more joyful parts of the ceremony were in some measure interrupted, owing to the death of the princess already mentioned. From that time there were no more songs or buffoonery, and the gymnastic and dramatic exhibitions which were promised were not exhibited.

Early on the morning of the fourth day of the ceremony the actual tonsure of the head took place. On this occasion the Brahmins, as before, had predicted the fortunate moment. They ushered the young man, still on the shoulders of an attendant, but dressed in a suit of white, into the saloon. The Talapoins repeated hymns, and the tonsure was effected by the hands of two Siamese of considerable rank, as no person of an inferior condition could presume to touch so sacred and inviolable a part of the young chief as his head, without dishonouring him. After this operation, which consisted in shaving the whole head, he was placed under a canopy erected in the court-yard, and here a quantity of water was poured over him. He was then dressed in a new suit, and furnished with a sword. Thus habited he walked back to the saloon without being carried; all this part of the ceremony being intended to express his emancipation from childhood, and his entering upon the condition of manhood. The Prince Kromachiat honoured this part of the ceremony with his presence.

After the ceremony was so far concluded, a vast quantity of ready-dressed food was served to persons of all descriptions and denominations; the better sort of people feasting within the saloon, and the crowd in the court-yard. The Talapoins alone, to whom it is unlawful to eat out of their monasteries, had between thirty and forty huge Chinese jars of dressed victuals and sweetmeats, apparently containing a meal for several thousand persons, sent to them. We could discover no vestige of religious antipathy on the part of the motley guests, who consisted of lay Siamese, Kambojans, Chinese, Christians, Mohammedans, and Brahmins. The latter not only eat food dressed by Siamese cooks, but made a hearty meal in the same apartment where the other guests were consuming beef, eggs, and such other articles as their forefathers would have deemed an abomination. But the Hindus, like other men, notwithstanding their stubborn pretensions, yield in this, as in many other things, to the force of necessity, and learn the wisdom of accommodating themselves to their situation.

May 18.—Yesterday being the fifth and last day of the ceremony, the Prah-klang, in compliment to us, gave an entertainment, and the Portuguese Consul, with his secretary, and the commanders and officers of the English vessels in the river, were invited to meet us. The party consisted of fourteen Europeans, most probably the greatest assemblage which had met together in Siam since the visitation of the French, 130 years before. The dinner was in the European fashion, the Christian interpreters acting as *footmen*, and the Christian Intendant of the Port as *maître-d'hotel*, for the Siamese chiefs are reckless how they use or abuse these poor people. The table was abundantly furnished with viands, dressed in a cleanly way, not offensive to the European palate, as is most commonly the case with Indian cookery. Among the viands there were beef, venison, and abundance of poultry. The Prah-klang, observing that we were somewhat surprised at this, smiled, and begged us to put no questions, but eat heartily, and that this was the principle upon which he himself acted in similar cases. During the entertainment he sat near us, doing the honours of the feast, without however partaking of it. His son and nephew sat down as upon a former occasion, and eat heartily and indiscriminately of every description of animal food, refraining scrupulously, however, from wine. The Prah-klang, who, from the frequent resort of European and American vessels of late years, has acquired some knowledge of our customs, proposed to us to drink the following toasts, in the order in which I now mention them. "The King of Siam," "the King of England," "the King of Portugal," "the Prince Kroma-chiat," "the Governor-general of India," and "the Viceroy of Goa." He noticed that we did not drink the health of the King of Siam with three cheers, as he had observed Europeans and Americans do on similar occasions. It was explained that this tumultuous mark of consideration was omitted out of respect to his grief for the melancholy event which had recently taken place in the Palace. He replied with vivacity, and in the true strain of an Eastern courtier, "If this house should fall on my head, let no mark of respect to the King (literally the owner of heads) be omitted, for the greatest misfortune befalling me or any one else, is not to be put in comparison with the most trifling honour which is due to my King." We got up from the entertainment between eight and nine o'clock, serenaded by a Siamese band of music as we departed.

May 19.—Upon the occasion of a young man's tonsure, friends and relations are in the practice of making presents. The Prince Kroma-chiat had given the young chief five catties of silver, or 400 ticals, and I took the opportunity of presenting him with seven or 560 ticals, in the name of the Marquis of Hastings.

The conference was renewed to-day at twelve o'clock. I urged the necessity of unrestricted trade, and the advantage which would accrue from foregoing the claim of preemption. The Prah-klang feigned to be of my opinion, but said, that after due deliberation, he and the rest of the ministers had decided, that the proposal implied so great an innovation upon the established customs of the country, that they dare not mention it to the King, and that I must propose it personally, at an audience, which would be granted in a few days for this purpose. I was much surprised at this unexpected offer, and although its sincerity was suspicious, I gladly closed with it.

The subject of supplying salt to Bengal was introduced, and I stated the terms upon which it could be admitted, consistently with the fiscal regulations of the Indian Government. The subject excited a strong interest—Chinese accountants and *sanpans* were put in requisition, and the necessary calculations were made on the spot. It was declared as the result, that no profit could be made by these speculations, and the project was therefore abandoned. An open trade in this article with the Bengal provinces, would probably add great facilities to the establishment of an extensive intercourse between them and Siam; for salt, which is produced in such excellence and abundance in the latter country, must always form a great part of the cargoes exported to other Indian countries, where there is a scarcity of that commodity. It is chiefly by means of it that Siam maintains, at present, so considerable a traffic with Palembang, the Straits of Malacca, and other portions of the Malay country.

At this meeting the Prah-klang requested me, as a favour, to afford my assistance in rendering an intelligible translation into Siamese, through the Malay language of a letter which he had received from one of the secretaries of the Indian Government. I undertook this, and as soon as I had reached home was waited upon by the Christian Intendant of the Port, accompanied by three Siamese secretaries. It was an extremely difficult matter to satisfy them. They cavilled at and discussed every sentence as my Malayan interpreter proceeded. When they came to the conclusion of the letter, they pointed out some broken lines in the original, of which they desired a literal translation. This was nothing more or less than the European complimentary form which precedes the subscription. No possible translation could have been given of this, which the vanity of the Siamese would not have construed into an acknowledgment of inferiority on the part of the writer and his Government. Eastern ideas may be rendered, without difficulty, into the copious and flexible languages of Europe; but to render the peculiar idioms and formalities of the languages of Europe into the meagre and obdurate dialects of India is altogether impracticable, except when we write with an express view to future translation, which is the safest course to pursue in our intercourse with the Eastern nations. When, about two years before our arrival, the Governor of Macao addressed a letter to the King of Siam, he expressed the deep regret which he felt at not being able to repair in person to Siam, that there he might have "the honour of kissing his Majesty's royal hand." If the Governor of Macao had really been at Siam, he would not have been permitted to approach within twenty yards of the King's person. His proposal, therefore, which was intended for respect and civility, was considered by the Siamese as highly offensive, and was expunged by the ministers before they would venture to explain the contents of the letter to the King.

In the afternoon I had a visit from a native chief; a circumstance which did not often take place, for our vicinity to the Prah-klang's house, and the fear of exciting the jealousy of the Government, prevented many persons from calling upon us, who were otherwise well disposed to do so. The manners of this individual, who was a native of Lao, were singular. When he entered the room, I begged him to be seated; but before complying, he made three obeisances towards the palace, then three towards the residence of the Prah-klang, and three more to the company before him. His conversation was frank and intelligent, and he appeared well-informed respecting his own country, which forms so interesting and considerable, but to Europeans so little known, a portion of the present Siamese Empire.

May 20.—Within the last two or three days the rains, which had hitherto been moderate, set in with great violence. It blew fresh every day from the south-west, and this description of weather lasted until the beginning of July, a period of about six weeks, constituting the only tempestuous season in the Gulf of Siam, which is fortunately free from the violent equinoctial gales, which are a scourge to many other portions of the Indian seas. These heavy rains tempered the weather, which had been before sultry and oppressive, the thermometer in the shade rising almost every day to ninety-five and ninety-six between the hours of twelve and four o'clock in the afternoon. These advantages, however, were counterbalanced by inconveniences of a different description. Our ill-constructed house leaked every where, and the rains brought from their hiding-places swarms of insects and reptiles. Among the most troublesome of the latter, was the Gecko, or Tokai of the Malays, correctly pronounced Tăkke, a large species of lizard from six to nine inches long, marked with red and green spots, and frequent tubercles.* These are much more frequent in Siam than in Java or any other country of the Indian Archipelago, and in the evening deafened us with their singular, loud, and monotonous cry. Snakes of different descriptions were also very numerous, and some of them from ten to fourteen feet long. These last were Pythons, erroneously called Boa Constrictor. One of this description, about eleven feet long, was taken alive last night in our kitchen during a heavy fall of rain. It had come to prey upon some fowls, and was very active. Although severely beaten over the head, it recovered, and after a month's confinement, effected its escape from a large chest, in which it was kept,

* Le Gecko de Siam, Cuvier.

although the lid was pressed down by several large stones. Two more were seen on board the vessels in the river, and one of them, about fourteen feet long, killed. How they got into these situations it is not very easy to understand, but it is most probable they crept up the cable.

In the forenoon, the commander of the American ship, Aurora, arrived in Bang-kok, having left his vessel off the bar of the river. He stated that he had come for a small quantity of sugar to fill up his cargo, and unacquainted with the modes of transacting business in Siam, and the difficulties he had to encounter, he promised himself that he would be detained no more than four or five days, as would be the case in an American or European port.

May 21.—The reappearance of the epidemic *cholera* spread great alarm amongst the people, a matter which was apparent enough from the precautions which they took against its attacks. The King, under some superstitious imagination, which I am unable to explain, directed the people to keep at home, and abstain from all work for seven days. The temples at this time were more frequented than usual, and numbers of persons were to be seen wearing shreds of white cotton yarn round the neck as amulets, whilst others endeavoured to recommend themselves to the good will of the gods by purchasing fowls and other animals from strangers, with a view of giving them their liberty and saving them from slaughter. The secular superintendent of the great temple, which was the first we visited, called upon us in the course of the day, and said that he had no fear of the *cholera morbus*, as he made frequent prostrations before the idols, and wore a skein of cotton thread round his neck as a charm. As he spoke, he pointed to this potent amulet!

I had another long conference last night with the Prah-klang. Thanmun, an officer of some rank, was present, and took an active share in the conversation. The commander of the American ship came in while the discussion was going forward. The Prah-klang seeing him, introduced the subject of the American trade, and said, "These people bring us what we are most anxious to receive, plenty of fire-arms and ready money, and take away large cargoes of sugar, and other produce of the country." He added, although evidently without any ground for the assertion, that he expected this year eight or ten of their ships. The Siamese Government had indeed found the American trade hitherto a very lucrative matter, because they had made their own terms with the few vessels which had visited the place; but the advantages were all on one side, and the Prah-klang was disappointed as to the return of the Americans, for few or none have visited Siam since.

At this conference, the subject of the invasion of the Malay state of Quedah by the Siamese, and the flight of the Rajah to Prince of Wales's Island, which I had hitherto carefully avoided, that it might interfere as little as possible with the principal object of the Mission, was at length introduced. The Siamese negociators stated, that they knew nothing more of this matter, than that the Rajah of Quedah, a tributary of Siam, had abandoned his own country, and fled to a foreign one for protection. They said, that instead of seeking an asylum at Prince of Wales's Island, he should have come to the capital, and represented his grievances to the King, and they added, that if he would still come, ample justice would be done to him. They proceeded to enumerate the offences with which the Malay Prince was charged by the Siamese Governor of Ligor, the officer who superintends the affairs of all the Malayan tributaries. They stated that this officer had received an order from the Court to invade the Burman territories; that for this purpose, he had assembled an army, and making the usual demand for contributions from the Rajah of Quedah, the latter had contumaciously refused them; the consequence of which was, that the Siamese chief had marched upon Quedah to enforce his demand. I endeavoured to extenuate the conduct of the Malay chief, dwelling upon the poverty of his country, and the frequent exactions by which it was harassed by the Rajah of Ligor. I now felt myself obliged to bring to the notice of the negociators the overbearing and intemperate letters which the latter Chief had addressed to the Governor of Prince of Wales's Island; for this individual, as before stated, had written with great presumption, claiming the instant surrender of the Rajah of Quedah's person, and *threatening with punishment whoever* should *venture to detain him.* They feigned entire ignorance of this last circumstance; but on my return home, I sent them copies of the original correspondence.

I hinted at various proposals for our mediation in restoring the Rajah of Quedah to his principality; but the only alternative which would be admitted was this Prince's repairing to the Court in person, and submitting his cause to the justice of the King. From what passed at this conference, there could be no question, indeed, but his having sought an asylum at Prince of Wales's Island had wounded the Siamese pride exceedingly, and given rise to much irritation.

It was remarkable that neither at this, or any subsequent conference, was our right in Prince of Wales's Island, or the right of the Rajah of Quedah to dismember his fief, questioned. This possession was obtained by us in a period of great weakness and anarchy on the part of the Siamese Government, and when its tributary

States had rendered themselves nearly independent. Six-and-thirty years undisputed occupancy may be considered as having given us a strong prescriptive claim to it; but still the Siamese Court could not be unaware of our defective title, or of the legal incapacity of the Malayan chief, then as now a tributary, to alienate a portion of his territory. Its silence, therefore, could only be accounted for by its fears, which prudently induced it to abstain from making a claim which it had not the power to enforce. This is corroborated by what took place afterwards, with respect to the quit-rent which had been paid for the island to the Malay prince. The Siamese, upon taking possession of Quedah, laid claim to this; but, upon its being once disallowed, it was never afterwards renewed.

The Prah-klang gave, last night, a formal audience to the Cochin Chinese Ambassadors. As always happened upon such occasions, we saw the whole ceremony from our windows. The Ambassadors landed at the wharf near our house, between nine and ten o'clock at night, and walked up the short avenue to the Prah-klang's house, which was lined on both sides with torches in compliment to them. The present, consisting of two large cases of silk, went before; then came the Ambassadors, four in number, moving with that slow, measured, and solemn step which with us is confined to funeral processions, but which the Chinese, and the nations who imitate them, consider so peculiarly dignified upon all occasions. They were themselves dressed in long silk robes, and wore caps of ceremony. They were preceded by four men, each carrying a sword in one hand, and a flambeau in the other. These persons wore a frock of scarlet broad-cloth, and had caps on their heads with a plume of cock's feathers at the top. They were, in fact, the first specimens that we had seen of Cochin Chinese soldiers. The Prah-klang received his visitors with much formality. He sat on a velvet cushion at the upper end of the hall, surrounded by all the inferior chiefs of his department. The Ambassadors on their part seemed, as far as could be observed, to conduct themselves with dignity. The first Ambassador, as soon as he entered, demanded with a motion of his hand the place intended for him; and when it was pointed out, assumed it, after making a slight bow to the Prah-klang, which the latter did not return. The others followed his example. There were no prostrations after the Siamese fashion, nor even such as a Cochin Chinese would have performed to a superior of his own nation.

May 23.—In one of my excursions yesterday, being near the residence of the Catholic Bishop of Siam, I took the opportunity of paying him a visit. The extreme jealousy with which all strangers, and especially Europeans, are watched in

Siam, had rendered this, on my part, a matter of difficulty; nor was it at any time possible for the Bishop to visit us, so guarded was the conduct which he found it necessary, upon all such occasions, to observe. I had a long and interesting conversation with this dignitary, who is a native of Avignon, and whose titular dignity is Bishop of Sozopolis. He had lived either in Siam or Cochin China for the long period of thirty-four years, having left France the year before the Revolution; of the wonderful scenes of which, as well as the changes to which they have given rise, he scarcely knew any thing but by rumour. He had passed his long sojourn in a singular manner for an educated European, and, above all, for a sprightly Frenchman, which the Bishop still was, notwithstanding that he bordered on sixty, and had passed the prime of life under circumstances apparently so depressing. He has lived for years together without an European within a thousand miles of him—without scarcely ever hearing the accents of his native language; and finally, among a race of barbarians, who treat the followers of the religion of which he is the pastor, with contumely.

M. Sozopolis is of the order of Dominicans, and the successor of the first Bishop appointed for Siam by the See of Rome, as early as the year 1659, and who arrived in the country about three years thereafter. His spiritual authority extends over all the Catholic Christians of Siam and the Malay peninsula. Those of Siam alone amount to three thousand, of whom a thousand are at the capital. These are the whole fruits of a hundred and sixty years' labour, not to mention the earlier efforts of the Portuguese, and the occasional assistance of the Jesuits.

The Bishop informed us that there were three Christian churches in the town of Bang-kok—Santa-Cruz, Santa-Anna, and Santa-Asomption. The last is a new church close to the residence of the Bishop, and which, for want of funds, is not yet finished. We now visited it; it had a sorry appearance indeed, in comparison to the gorgeous temples of the heathen. At the old capital, I am told, is still standing the chapel which was built by the Greek adventurer, Constantine Phaulcon. It is said to be a handsome piece of architecture, and the Siamese, being of this opinion, have converted it into a temple of Buddh.

The person whom the Bishop sent with us to point out the new church was a native Christian priest, who had lived long in the Malay countries, and spoke the language with perfect fluency. The restraint of an interpreter being removed, he spoke upon various points with great freedom. He praised the facility with which converts were made at Prince of Wales's Island, and assured us that in Siam the Christian priests seldom or ever made a proselyte, for the Siamese were a very untractable people in this respect. We wished to know what objections the Siamese had against the Catholic religion. His reply was, "They consider it too difficult and troublesome a road to Heaven,"—an observation which perfectly agrees with the religious apathy and loose morality of the Siamese.

On our return from the visit to the new church we renewed our conversation with the Bishop, and asked whether the accounts we had received of several Christians having adopted the Buddhist religion and become Talapoins, were correct. He assured us that the statement we had received was much exaggerated, and that he knew but of one example of a Christian becoming a Talapoin, which was that of a dissipated youth, who had fallen upon this easy means of evading the demands of his Christian creditors. The Bishop drew an animated picture of the Siamese character. He said that they were firmly of opinion that they were the first people on earth, and that they treated with ridicule the notion of having any equal, especially among European nations. This, however, he observed, did not prevent them from entertaining, in secret, very serious apprehensions of the power of the English. As to the French, he said, they were not known to the Siamese of the present day; and that the connexion which once subsisted, was now remembered only as a tale of other times.

May 25.—I had another long conference last night with the Prah-klang, the results of which, I am sorry to say, were far from satisfactory. When the English ship in the river had first arrived, an assurance was given that the import duty would be reduced from eight to six per cent. and that she should be allowed to dispose of her cargo freely, without any of the usual interference on the part of the officers of Government. This arrangement having been most completely evaded, and in a manner the most irksome and disingenuous, it became necessary to bring the matter to the notice of the Minister. In explanation, it was pretended that the reduction of duties should take place only when the English ships frequenting Siam should amount to five in number, as first stated. As to the unrestricted trade, it was constantly insisted upon that this was granted, but that the goods were so high in price that no one would buy. The fact was, as I had been well informed, that a secret order had been issued by the Prah-klang, forbidding all persons to hold any dealings with the English vessel, under pain of fine or corporal punishment. The determination, indeed, of the party who profited by it to maintain their monopoly was resolutely taken, and it seemed almost in vain to struggle against it. On this question they finally informed us, that the reply to the letter of the Governor-general would be ready for delivery on the 26th.

By far the greater part of the conference was taken up in discussing the affair of Quedah. The Prah-klang said that the Governor of Ligor had been ordered to Court to render an account of his proceedings in that country. He observed, however, that a dispatch had been received from him yesterday, and that all seemed to be well, as he represented the country in a state of perfect tranquillity, and a friendly intercourse going on with Prince of Wales's Island. He insisted, at the same time, that it was still necessary for the Rajah of Quedah to appear at the Court to vindicate himself. The words which he made use of, as translated to me, were nearly as follow. "The Governor of Ligor and the Rajah of Quedah are alike slaves of the King of Siam; and if a dispute arise between them, they must both repair to the Court to have the matter settled. The King of Quedah is not a child, he knows the customs of the kingdom, and if he wishes to be restored to his country, he must understand the necessity of appearing in the presence." Considering the threatening language which the Chief of Ligor had used towards the Governor of Prince of Wales's Island when he demanded the delivery of the King of Quedah's person, I thought it my duty to make a firm and distinct reply to this observation; and stated, that if the King of Quedah were of his own free will disposed to come to Siam, the British Government would put no obstacle in his way; but that if otherwise, no power should remove him, since he had thrown himself upon our hospitality. The Prah-klang asked whether if the King of Siam addressed a letter to the Governor-general, requesting him to seize the King of Quedah, and send him forcibly to Siam, such request would be complied with. I readily assured him that it would not; and farther explained that such request would not be considered friendly, as it would necessarily imply a belief that we were capable of violating the laws of hospitality, by delivering up an old friend who had sought an asylum amongst us.

The point of getting possession of the person of the Rajah of Quedah seemed one upon which the Siamese Court was fully bent, and in which they believed their honour or character implicated. The restoration of this prince being a point of considerable moment to us, I proposed, as an easy means of settling the quarrel between him and the Rajah of Ligor, the sending of a Siamese commissioner, superior in rank to both parties, to the spot, to inquire into and adjust the affair. This proposition, which the Siamese imagined would have brought their authority within the influence of our power, owing to the neighbourhood of the Quedah territories to ours, was without hesitation rejected. The

Prah-klang feigned to understand that the proposal amounted to sending a Siamese commissioner into the British territories there to make the inquiry; and he said, that he was convinced that if two tributaries of the British Government were to quarrel, and one of them were to fly to a foreign power for protection, we should never think of deputing a commissioner into the territory of such foreign power to investigate the quarrel; but on the contrary, that we should direct the parties to repair to the seat of Government, for the purpose of having the matter adjusted. I explained the real nature of the proposal which I had made, but the Prah-klang still insisted that it was contrary to the customs of the country, and that the King wished to look into all matters of this kind "with his own eyes," which was the expression he made use of.

The Prah-klang, after this, inquired whether the King of Quedah exercised sovereign authority over his own followers, who had fled along with him to Prince of Wales's Island. The reply to this was, that no foreigner whatever could exercise such an authority within a British settlement, as all were equally under the protection, and equally amenable to the local laws. The Siamese Minister observed, that such a state of things must be extremely inconvenient to the Rajah of Quedah, and that he wondered how he continued to reside at Prince of Wales's Island, instead of coming to seek redress from the King. In a letter which I had sent a few nights ago from the Rajah of Quedah, this prince had thrown himself upon the mercy of the King of Siam, and petitioned for his restoration to the throne as an act of grace. The Prah-klang, in reference to it, now observed: "The Rajah of Quedah himself has acknowledged his fault, and therefore why does he not repair at once to the Court and ask forgiveness?"

The language which I was compelled to use at this interview was such as a Siamese Minister could not have been much accustomed to listen to, and such, of course, as must have been offensive to his pride. The reception given by our Government to the King of Quedah, and our refusal to deliver him up, wounded the vanity of the Siamese; and there can be no doubt but that this had throughout a prejudicial influence upon the main objects of the Mission, although these, indeed, might not have been attainable without such obstacle.

May 27.—Ko-chai-sahak waited upon us yesterday, bringing with him, for our satisfaction, a copy of the dispatch from the Governor of Ligor, referred to in the conference of the 24th. The following is nearly a literal translation of this specimen of Siamese diplomacy, which appears to have been got up with considerable art.

"The army of Quedah is now at rest, and there is no misunderstanding with the people of Penang. The Governor of that place has given, according to former custom, two small vessels of war, to guard the coasts against pirates. The commander of one of these vessels came to me, and a friendly intercourse took place between us. The Governor of Penang and the English are satisfied that the Siamese army intend them no mischief, and the Governor allows the Siamese to frequent the island as heretofore. The commander of one of the vessels of war above alluded to, returned a second time with three English officers of consideration along with him. These stated, that two vessels, loaded with rice, had brought a letter from the Governor of Bengal to the Governor of Penang, directing him to consider Quedah as a tributary of Siam, and prohibiting him from interfering.

"The people of the island Langkawi having rebelled, the army went thither, beat them, and obtained possession. I sent news of this to Penang, accusing the King of Quedah of having stirred up the Malays of Langkawi to rebellion. The Governor of Penang replied, saying, that the English would not encourage the Rajah of Quedah, contrary to the interests of the Great King, and that they would by no means interfere in the affairs of Langkawi or the other dependencies of Quedah, nor permit the King of Quedah to send out stores or ammunition to assist the rebels of Langkawi.

"The different traders who come to Quedah represent the country now as in a state of greater prosperity than at any former period, and they describe the people of Penang as saying among themselves that small boats, with four or five men, can now go over to Quedah with safety, for there is no longer any fear of pirates. News from the same place also states, that the Tangku Abdullah, son of the Rajah of Quedah, took a Malay woman and offered her for sale as a slave. The woman made her complaint in the court of justice. The Governor of Penang replied, 'that if the Prince did so again, he should be considered an offender.' A great number of the slaves of the King of Quedah have become free since they came to Pulo Penang. The King had punished some slaves. This came to the knowledge of the Governor, who sent word to the King to say, 'That he had sought protection under the English flag, and that he must submit to the customs of the English, which did not admit of individuals taking the law into their own hands, and that if he had any grievance, he must seek redress in a court of justice."

The evident object of sending this letter to

us, was to convince us that every thing was right, and that perhaps we were no losers in having the Siamese for our neighbours instead of the Malays.

Last night, at the usual hour, I had another and my final public interview with the Prah-klang, which was as unsatisfactory as any of those which preceded it. One of the principal objects of it was, to read to me a draft of the reply intended to the letter of the Governor-general. With their wonted procrastination, however, the draft was not ready, but was promised to be produced during the course of the day. I took this last opportunity of recapitulating the arguments which I had already so often made use of in favour of an unshackled trade; but as I was by this time fully aware of the strong interest which militated against them, I was not surprised that they were repeated to little purpose. I dwelt particularly upon the favourable treatment which Siamese vessels had received in our ports. This was acknowledged, and nothing very reasonable could be said against what was urged, the constant answer being the difficulty of changing the long established usages of the country. The proposal of introducing us to a second audience of the King was now altogether abandoned, without any cause being assigned for it; but I have reason to believe that the Prah-klang and his party apprehended, that from the freedom of the communications which had already been made on the subject of the affair of Quedah, the interview might have been attended with disclosures unfavourable to their own peculiar views.

May 28.—At three o'clock yesterday afternoon, messengers came to inform us, that a draft of the letter to the Governor-general was now ready for our inspection. I proceeded accordingly to the house of the Prah-klang. The Chief was himself absent, under pretext of indisposition; but his deputy, Pia Pipat-kosa, the venerable old Chief who had come on board to receive the letter of the Governor-general, but who had not been present at any of the former conferences, received us in his stead. Along with him was Pia Raja Chula, the head of the Mohammedan settlers, who had also not been present at any of the former conferences. Two drafts of letters, in answer to that of the Governor-general, were exhibited. One of these was in the name of the Prah-klang, and addressed directly to the Governor-general; and the other was from his deputy, addressed to the Secretary to Government. The purport of both was the same, and the cause of preparing the two was to afford us an opportunity of selecting whichever we might prefer. A direct address from the King to the Governor-general had been declared contrary to the etiquette of the Court; and on the other hand, I had caused it to be made known, at an early period, that no direct address from a Minister to the Governor-general would be received. The great object which the Prah-klang, although but a Minister of inferior rank, had in view, was to place himself upon an equality of station with the Governor-general of India. This pretension was of course to be discouraged; and the draft which was in his name was at once rejected, and the other approved. The pretensions which were thus set up were indeed sufficiently absurd, and yet certainly less ridiculous than those made by the Burman Ministers, who, when preparing the draft of a letter to the Governor-general in 1810, wished to style the King of England a tributary of his Burman Majesty!

A third document was then exhibited, which was a letter from Pia Raja Chula, the Superintendent of the Customs, addressed to myself; and this contained such concessions to our trade as the Siamese Court had resolved to grant. It stipulated for an unlimited admission of British ships into the port of Bang-kok, and for the reduction of the present import duty of eight per cent. to six, as soon as the annual number of vessels arriving should amount to five. The document in its present form, I concluded, was an ultimatum, and I had no intention of offering any objection to it; but the Siamese officers having requested to know whether I had any alteration to propose, I requested that the stipulation for the reduction of duties might not be contingent upon the number of ships arriving, but unconditional. This proposition, very unexpectedly on my part, gave rise to a discussion of two hours' continuance. They earnestly requested that I would be satisfied with a verbal assurance to the effect which I required; but this, with the knowledge which I now had of Siamese assurances, as well as the character of the proposal itself, I necessarily declined.

The person who took the most active share in this day's conversation, was Pia Raja Chula, the chief of the Mohammedan settlers, from the west of India. This class of persons, possessing a large share of the characteristic disposition of the natives of Hindustan for intrigue, have considerable influence, and in our affair it was certainly exercised prejudicially. They subsist upon the perquisites and plunder of the foreign trade; and to have placed this upon a fair and equitable footing, would have deprived them of a considerable share of their emoluments. Their friendship, therefore, was not to be expected.

June 6.—The letter of the Governor-general was ready on the third instant, but I heard nothing of the commercial document until last night, when it was reported to me to be ready, and I had another interview with the Siamese chiefs for the purpose of hearing it read. It was translated passage by passage by our own interpreter, and I was surprised to find the whole document much altered. It now stipulated for no reduction of duties in any case, but instead of it there was an express stipulation for that free and unrestrained trade which I had all along struggled for. I of course accepted this document at once, without offering any comment upon it.

June 7.—In the course of this forenoon, our attention was attracted by a handsome and gay procession passing down the river towards one of the temples: it consisted of four magnificent gilded barges, each pulled by twenty-four rowers in scarlet dresses. The vessels were decked with royal umbrellas and banners, pointing out that they had come from the Palace; and from the gay appearance of the procession, we expected to hear of some Prince or Princess going upon an excursion of pleasure. We were therefore surprised to find, that the boats conveyed the *sordes* of the body of the Princess, who had died on the 15th of the epidemic *cholera*, and of which a party of her friends were proceeding in charge, for the purpose of having them consumed on a funeral pile at one of the temples.

June 9.—Ever since the arrival of the Cochin Chinese Ambassadors, I was anxious to form an acquaintance with them, believing that this might possibly be of use as an introduction when we should arrive in their country. Every thing that bears a political character, however, it must be again repeated, is received in Siam with so jealous a suspicion; that I was aware that to succeed in this was a matter of no small difficulty. Both the British and Cochin Chinese Missions were, in fact, strictly watched. Yesterday I sent one of our interpreters to make some preparatory inquiries at the residence of the Cochin Chinese Envoys. He found it surrounded by Siamese guards, and inaccessible. His inquiries were answered with rudeness or incivility, and he was in some danger of being taken into custody as a spy. It was necessary, therefore, at once to desist from all farther attempts. The Portuguese Consul informed me, that he had requested permission of the Prah-klang to pay a visit to the Cochin Chinese Ambassadors, and that he had received a pointed refusal.

June 12.—The Cochin Chinese Ambassadors left Bang-kok yesterday afternoon, on their return to their own country. We saw them drop down the river quietly in the small junks which had conveyed them to Siam, and no ceremony whatever attended their departure.

In the course of the evening, the reply to the Governor-general's letter, and the commercial document, were finally brought to us. In compliment to them, a ladder was put up against the end of the house, and in this manner they were conveyed to the apartment where we received them. The originals of both were in the Siamese language, but they were accompanied by Portuguese translations, which last only were open for inspection,—the former being inclosed in silk envelopes, duly sealed, and deposited in large red lacquered bowls, according to the custom of the country. A request to have copies of the originals in Siamese was refused, most probably under an apprehension that on examination this might give rise to some unpleasant discussion respecting the phraseology made use of. It was necessary to open the silk envelopes to ascertain the true contents of the original letters. This was accordingly done, and translations having been effected, I had the mortification to discover that the pledge of unrestrained trade, or, as it was expressed in the original draft, "free permission to British merchants to buy and sell with the merchants of Siam," was entirely omitted, and an ominous one of assistance from the Superintendent of Customs substituted for it. After the struggles I had already made, I felt that farther remonstrance would be useless, and might even, in the present state of things, be productive of such additional irritation, as might prejudice our future prospects. Under this impression, I forbore from noticing the deception which had been practised in the terms which it well merited.

The answer to the letter of the Governor-general, as translated through the medium of the Malay, was as follows :—

"The letter of Paya Pipat-Racha Balat Kosa, second Prah-klang at the Court of Prah Maha Nakon Si-Ayuthia, to the Secretary of the Government of Bengal, makes known to him that the Governor of Bengal sent a letter by Mr. Crawfurd, the subject of which was to explain that England has been at peace with all the nations of Europe for a long time, and that the Governor of Bengal * is anxious to be in friendship with the kingdom of Siam, and to increase it beyond the friendship of other times; and farther, that he wishes that the merchants of Siam should trade to English ports, whether in Europe or in other parts of the world; and that the English should have the same liberty to frequent this kingdom; and moreover, that as the imposts on trade in Siam are high, he requests the King of Siam would make them lighter, to the end that by this means English merchants might be encouraged to extend their trade in Siam. Mr. Crawfurd having come as the Envoy from the Governor of Bengal to offer presents to his Majesty, and representing the person of the Governor of Bengal, &c. the

* In the original, the Governor-general is styled Chao Muang Bangkala, which may be translated Lord of the kingdom or principality of Bengal. This title, Chao Muang, is applied by the Siamese to the governors of great provinces, as well as to the dependent princes of Lao.

Chao Pia Prah-klang, first Minister in this department, gave him all assistance, and introduced him to his Majesty's presence, with the letter and offerings of the Governor of Bengal, and explained the contents of the said letter fully to his Majesty. His Majesty on this caused it to be distinctly made known to his grandees of every rank, that the Governor of Bengal, with good-will, had chosen Mr. Crawfurd to convey *offerings* to his Majesty, having a desire to strengthen the existing friendship, and farther to increase it; and, in consequence of that, that merchants might be encouraged to resort with their ships to the kingdom. His Majesty was much gratified at all this; and, in regard to the imposts upon trade, Mr. Crawfurd was directed by his Majesty to confer with the principal officers connected with this department, according to custom. His Majesty has ordered the officers in charge of the royal magazines to return presents to the Governor of Bengal as follows:—Ten elephants' teeth, weighing two piculs; eagle-wood, two piculs; benzoin, two piculs; cardamums, of one sort, one picul; of another, three piculs; tin, fifteen piculs; pepper, one hundred and fifty piculs; sugar, one hundred piculs; and gamboge, five piculs. These presents have been delivered to Mr. Crawfurd.

Written on Tuesday, in the seventh month, on the eight day of the bright half of the Moon, in the year of the Horse. (26th May, 1822.)

The commercial document was as follows:—

"The Governor of Bengal commanded Mr. Crawfurd to come to Siam, to open a way to friendship and commerce, and to request permission for English ships to trade to this capital, buying and selling with the merchants of Siam, and paying duties as heretofore. The Pia Prahklang, by authority of his Majesty, directs me, in consequence, to express his satisfaction at the contents of the letter of the Governor of Bengal, and to address a letter to Mr. Crawfurd in the form of an agreement, to say, that if English merchant-ships come to the port of the capital, upon their arrival at the mouth of the river, they shall be searched by the Governor of Pak-nam, and their small arms and cannon landed according to former custom, and then that the ships shall be conducted to the capital. As soon as they are anchored, the Superintendent of Customs shall afford all assistance in buying and selling with the merchants of Siam, and the duties and charges shall not be more than heretofore, nor afterwards be raised. Let the English merchants come to Siam to sell and buy in comformity to this agreement."

This letter of agreement is written on Thursday, in the seventh month, the second day of the dark half of the Moon, in the year of the Horse. (10th June, 1822.)

CHAPTER VII.

Obstacles to European Trade in Siam.—Not applicable to that of the Chinese.—Ordination of Siamese Priests.—The wild race denominated Ka.—A Servant belonging to the Mission drowned.—Consecration of an image of Gautama. —Son of the Minister initiated into the Priesthood.—Visit from a Portuguese Christian.—Visit to the Prah-klang.—Visit from a French Priest.—Anecdote of a late King of Siam.— Visit to the Prince Krom-chiat.—Departure from Bang-kok. —Land in dropping down the River.—Colony of Peguans. —Mouth of the River and its neighbourhood infested by Musquitos.—Ship crosses the Bar of the River.—Description of it.—Arrival at the Sichang Islands.—Incidents there.

June 21.—OUR business in Siam having now been brought to a conclusion, we should have been happy to have embraced the earliest opportunity of quitting the country,—as well to avoid the risk of any collision with the Siamese, as to avail ourselves of the most favourable season for the prosecution of the remainder of our undertaking,—but unfortunately the result of another examination of the bar of the River was unfavourable, and it was declared that there was not yet water enough to enable the ship to pass out.

The American ship sailed about this time, after being detained near six weeks; and the commander, although he required but a small quantity of sugar to make up his cargo, and had paid for it in ready money, was subjected to much vexation and imposition. The English vessel from Calcutta was treated in the same manner. The Chinese, in fact, are the only foreigners whose trade is upon a fair footing: they are allowed to buy and sell without any inconvenient restriction; and fourteen or fifteen of their junks, which had arrived from Penang and Singapore long after the English and American vessels, had already disposed of their cargoes, although these included at least a hundred thousand Spanish dollars' worth of opium, *an article which is contraband.*

We had last night a violent thunder-storm, with a heavy fall of rain. A celebrated gang-robber, whose apprehension had cost the Siamese Government a great deal of trouble, and who was placed in charge of the Prah-klang, took this opportunity to effect his escape. The mode in which he accomplished this, afforded some insight into the character of the servants of the Siamese Government. The robber seduced the whole guard, and walked off with them,—thus not only effecting his own escape, but taking with him an armed and organized body of depredators.

June 26.—It was now the eighth month of the Siamese year, which is that set aside for the ceremony of the ordination of the Talapoins. The Siamese were seen everywhere busily engaged in this important concern,—for such it is, whether viewed as a civil or religious institution. To defray the expense of ordaining a priest, is considered on the part of the wealthy as an act of piety; and every person who is able, is at the expense of ordaining one or more, according to his means. The Prah-klang on the present occasion ordained seven; which afforded us an opportunity of seeing part of the ceremonies. The principal wife of the Minister, and her handmaids, had for many days before been busily employed in dyeing of a yellow colour, and making up, great quantities of dresses to be presented to the Talapoins. Yesterday afternoon a number of priests made their appearance, to whom these dresses were distributed. The seven *Nen*, or noviciates, presented themselves at the same time for ordination, with their heads newly shaved. White scarfs (upon this occasion, of Bengal silver-flowered muslin) were thrown over their shoulders, and prayers and hymns were chanted at great length. These last did not appear to us to differ from the usual ones, except in this particular, that their monotony was frequently interrupted by loud and most barbarous yells, which we did not hear upon other occasions. The principal portions of the ceremony were, however, performed at the Prah-klang's new temple, and these we did not witness because the whole females of the Chief's family were present; and we thought it on this account a matter of delicacy to absent ourselves, although indeed, in points of this nature, the Siamese are not over-scrupulous.

Among the young priests ordained by the Prah-klang on this occasion was a Javanese youth, one of the individuals who had been kidnapped, as I have already mentioned. I had met this person, a few nights before, near the temple of the Prah-klang, after he had made up his mind to change his religion. He was a native of the interior of Java, and had all the docility, simplicity, and carelessness which are so characteristic of the primitive inhabitants of that island. I inquired into the motives of his change of religion. Without adverting at all to the principles of the faith he had abandoned, or the new one he had adopted, and about which he neither knew nor cared any thing, he proceeded at once with considerable vivacity to a detail of the temporal immunities and advantages of the Siamese priesthood—such as respect from the people, fine clothes, abundance of food, and, above all, a total exemption from labour. One of my interpreters, a staunch Mohammedan, upbraided him for his apostasy; but he got nothing for his pains from the apostate but to be laughed at for his own scruples.

June 29.—I had brought to me to-day an individual of the wild race called Ka. This people inhabit the mountainous country lying between Lao and Kamboja, and still preserve their rude independence. The Siamese make no scruple in kidnapping them whenever they can find an opportunity. In consequence of this practice, a good number of them are to be found in a state of slavery at the capital. My present visitor had been taken about three years before. His features differed strikingly from those of a Siamese, and so did that of others of his nation who had been pointed out to me in my walks. In intelligence I found him greatly superior to what might reasonably have been expected.

July 3.—Notwithstanding the discouraging reports which had been made respecting the state of the bar of the River, we resolved to attempt to cross it with the next spring-tides, and were now busy in making preparations with this intention.

Our baker, a Chinese, with one of his countrymen, was drowned last night by the upsetting of a boat within a few yards of the bank of the River, and opposite to our dwelling. It was a bright moonlight night, and assistance was immediately rendered,—for both the Siamese and Chinese, unlike the natives of Hindustan, are very prompt upon such occasions,—but it was ineffectual. The bodies were picked up this afternoon, about five miles down the stream, and immediately burned by the Siamese, according to custom upon such occasions. It is, after all, surprising to find how few serious accidents take place on the Menam: the face of which is covered with boats night and day, some of them the veriest cockle-shells that can be imagined, and often managed by old men, women, and children. Numbers of them are upset, but commonly without any fatal consequences.

July 8.—The Prah-klang suddenly made his appearance yesterday morning, in a sort of workshop close under our windows, where the woodwork for his new temple was preparing. The carpenters, as it happened, were asleep, or smoking segars, when they should have been at work. Six of them received the punishment of the bamboo on the spot, under the personal direction of this minister of state. These symptoms of patriarchal government, however, are by no means so frequent in Siam as we afterwards found them in Cochin China.

In the evening, the Prah-klang was busy consecrating a new image of Gautama. The idol, which was of brass, and gilded, was placed in the centre of the saloon which I have so often mentioned, and had a silk cloth of gold tissue thrown over it. A band of Talapoins surrounded it, repeating their orisons. At certain passages of these, a crowd of boys and young men in the court-yard raised horrid shouts, seemingly, to all appearance, more suited to raise an evil spirit than to invoke a god, as was their ostensible object. To aid them in these yells, they forced their hands into their sides, making all the while hideous grimaces. Part of the ceremony consisted in the priests passing round from one to another a flaming torch, each waving it twice or thrice over his head before delivering it to his neighbour.

The eldest son of the Prah-klang, the youth whose tonsure I lately described, assumed, within the last few days, the yellow garment of the priesthood, in the character of a *Nen*, or noviciate, in conformity to the almost universal practice of the Siamese, of whatever rank. This morning, between six and seven o'clock, we saw him, for the first time, going forth to beg, in his new character. He had a large scrip upon his back; but as he was a delicate and weakly lad, a servant followed him, to carry it occasionally. Fifteen or twenty women, retainers of the Minister, threw themselves in his way as he was going out, and bestowed charity upon him, in the shape of boiled rice and fruit. His father and mother appeared at the same time, and now made him an obeisance, for which, in conformity with the sacred character, he made no acknowledgment.

July 10.—I had, in the course of this forenoon, a visit from a person of singular modesty and intelligence, Pascal Ribeiro de Alvergarias, the descendant of a Portuguese Christian of Kamboja. This gentleman holds a high Siamese title, and a post of considerable importance. Considering his means and situation, his acquirements were remarkable; for he not only spoke and wrote the Siamese, Kambojan, and Portuguese languages with facility, but also spoke and wrote Latin with considerable propriety. We found, indeed, a smattering of Latin very frequent among the Portuguese interpreters at Bang-kok, but Señor Ribeiro was the only individual who made any pretence to speak it with accuracy. He informed us, that he was the descendant of a person of the same name who settled in Kamboja in the year 1685. His lady's genealogy, however, interested us more than his own. She was the lineal descendant of an Englishman of the name of Charles Lister, a merchant, who settled in Kamboja in the year 1701, and who had acquired some reputation at the Court, by making pretence to a knowledge in medicine. Charles Lister had come immediately from Madras, and brought with him his sister. This lady espoused a Portuguese of Kamboja, by whom she had a son, who took her own name. Her grandson of this name also, in the revolutions of the kingdom of Kamboja, found his way to Siam; and here, like his great uncle, practising the healing art, rose to the station of Maha-pet, or first physician to the King. The son of this individual, Cajitanus Lister, is at present the physician, and at the same time the minister and confidential adviser of the present King of Kamboja.* His sister is the wife of the subject of this short notice. Señor Ribeiro favoured us with the most authentic and satisfactory account which we had yet obtained of the late revolution and present state of Kamboja.

July 12.—I addressed a letter to-day to the Minister, informing him of our approaching departure, and containing expressions of general good-will. I received a verbal message in return, with a request for an interview.

July 13.—I called at the house of the Minister this afternoon, and had a long conference with him. He said he had a message to deliver to me from the King, and pointed out to three chank shells which lay before him. These, as is well known, are sounded by the officiating Brahmins in performing the ritual of Hindu worship in the temples of Hindustan, and the

* As Resident of Singapore, I afterwards maintained a correspondence with this individual.

Buddhists also employ them for religious purposes. Ordinary ones are of little or no value; but when nature produces a *lusus*, by inverting the usual order of the spiral convolutions of the shell, they are in great request, being valued, according to their size or beauty, at from one to two hundred pounds sterling a-piece. One of the shells exhibited by the Minister was of this description, and had been presented to the King by the Rajah of Ligor. Over and above its own supposed value, it was richly set with pearls and rubies. In Siam no subject is allowed to be possessed of one of these shells. They are not employed in the common ceremonies of the Buddhist worship, but upon solemn occasions only, when they are filled with water, over which certain incantations being repeated, the element is considered holy, and thought to confer a blessing upon whomsoever it is sprinkled. The object of exhibiting the shells upon the present occasion, was, to point out the difference between them, and to beg that I would request one of the precious ones from the Governor-general for the King.

The subject of our commerce, and the dispute respecting Quedah, were introduced in the course of the visit. Respecting the former, the Prahklang plainly stated, that what the Court most required in an intercourse with the English were fire-arms; and on the latter subject he said, that the Governor of Ligor would soon be at the capital, and that all matters should be amicably arranged. At parting, the Minister wished us a safe journey, and with the characteristic aversion of a Siamese for the sea, asked if we were not afraid of so long a voyage. I replied, that such of us as were sickly, hoped to gain benefit by the change of climate, and by the sea air. He smiled at this remark, and appeared quite incredulous,—observing, that the Siamese and English must differ widely in this respect, for that even a few days of a sea voyage made a Siamese miserable, altering his appearance to such a degree that his acquaintances could scarcely recognize him!

In the evening, the Christian bishop sent one of the priests of the establishment to pay us a visit. This was a French gentleman who had recently arrived at Bang-kok, from Prince of Wales's Island, by a journey across the peninsula. He made the bishop's apologies for not visiting us in person,—taking pains to explain, on his behalf, the extreme circumspection which the character of the Siamese Government rendered indispensable in his situation. We had indeed ourselves seen quite enough, to render these explanations on the part of the bishop superfluous. Our visitor enforced his explanations, by recounting to us the story of the punishment inflicted upon the Christian priests in Siam, about forty years before, and which, as I have heard it told more at length from others, is as follows. Pia Metak, the adventurer of Chinese parentage, who mounted the throne of Siam upon the expulsion of the Burman invaders, was partially deranged for some years before he lost his throne and life. He had become fanatical, and entirely devoted to the priests of Gautama, to whom his charities were unbounded. In one of his religious frenzies, he took it into his head, that by still more intense devotion than he had hitherto practised, he might attain the supernatural gift of flying, and by this means be enabled to ascend direct to Heaven, as if it were by a sort of short cut, or, as it was explained to me, in the easy and rapid manner in which a bird soars to the sky. He sent for the priests of Gautama, who declared the project to be quite feasible. The bishop and other Christian clergy were then sent for and asked their opinions. They had the temerity to attempt to reason his Majesty out of the delusion with which he was possessed, by explaining that flying was incompatible with the physical form of the human body. For this small piece of philosophy, and also for certain opinions offered about the same time, concerning the unlawfulness of polygamy, deemed heretical in Siam, the bishop and his clergy received each a hundred blows of the bamboo, and were banished from the kingdom.

July 15.—Every thing being prepared for our departure, we embarked at five o'clock last evening. Just as we were going on board, we received a message from the Prince Krom-chiat, expressing an earnest desire for a farewell interview. Although such a visit was rather inconvenient, I resolved to comply, and accordingly waited upon him in the course of the night, accompanied by Mr. Rutherford. He received us very courteously, and seemed anxious to make a favourable impression upon us at parting. He began by informing us that he had a message to deliver to us from the King. The purport of the message in question was, that his Majesty expressed his regret that he was not able to give us an audience of leave, owing to the great distress he was in, occasioned by the deaths which had recently taken place in his family,—thus alluding to the loss of his sister, his brother-in-law and favourite, and the high-priest; but the Prince added, that the friendly sentiments which his Majesty entertained towards the English, would hereafter be proved by the protection he should afford to all the merchants of our nation who should visit his country. The Prince then proceeded to offer assurances of his own friendly sentiments, and condescended to say that he would direct prayers to be offered for our safe voyage. He dwelt at length upon his anxiety to prosecute a trade with the British possessions, and referred to the circumstance of his having twice sent the King's ship to Calcutta with this view. These voyages however, he said, were unsuccessful, owing to the great distance of Bengal and the unskilfulness of the Siamese mariners. After an audience of about an hour and a half, we took leave.

July 16.—Yesterday forenoon the ship was unmoored, and we dropped down a few hundred yards only. In the evening an officer came on board from the Prah-klang, with a message and a present of fruits and vegetables. The officers of police or customs also visited us, in order to take a census of the ship's crew and followers of the Mission, with the view of ascertaining that we carried away none of the inhabitants of the country—a matter respecting which the Siamese Government, viewing as it does the population of the country as its own private property, is especially jealous and tenacious. It ought here to be mentioned, that no description of charge whatsoever was made against the ship—her bearing a foreign embassy being considered to exempt her from all the numerous charges incident to a merchant-vessel.

As soon as it was daylight this morning, and we could steer clear of the Chinese junks and other craft in the River, we again dropped down, and, passing along many fine and highly cultivated reaches of the Menam, anchored at noon at the village of Klong-toe, the same spot where we had anchored on our voyage up. Here the banks of the river, to the depth of several hundred yards, were occupied by villages, and by a belt of orchards and gardens. The lower ground behind these again presented a wide extent of rice-lands. Shortly after anchoring, we landed on a shooting excursion, but were not successful. The country indeed now was nearly inundated and impassable. The peasantry, often up to their middle in water, were engaged in preparing the ground for the ensuing crop. The Chief of the village informed us, that he expected a return of forty-fold for the seed which he sowed, and that he would consider thirty but an indifferent crop.

In the course of our visit to the shore, we came accidentally upon a village temple, near to which there were about half-a-dozen priests. This was an oblong building of brick and mortar, composed of a double colonnade all round, supporting an ordinary tiled roof. At one end of it there was an altar crowded with gilded image of Gautama and his disciples. It may be presumed that either these were of little or no value, or that the crime of sacrilege is not common in Siam, for the temple was open all round, and there was no one watching or in attendance. In the course of the present excursion, as well indeed as upon all other occasions when we went amongst the peasantry, we met with nothing but good-nature, and, as far as regarded our persons and property, felt the same confidence and security, in rambling through the villages, that we should have done in the most civilized country in Europe.

July 17.—We weighed again this morning, and at nine o'clock arrived off the Pegue forts. As the ship dropped slowly down, a party went on shore and examined the fort which is on the right bank of the River. This was a square building of masonry, slightly constructed without a ditch, bastion, or any other defence, save the bare rampart or wall. I felt surprised, in going up, to hear that this and the opposite fort, which had the appearance of places of some consequence, should be intrusted to refugees from Pegue; but a nearer acquaintance explained the matter. Both forts are completely dismantled, their cannon had some years before been carried off to the capital, and even the gates had been removed. In the one which we examined, the peasantry of the neighbourhood were employed in converting its area into a rice-field. This particular part of the Menam, if adequately fortified, might, no doubt, be made sufficiently strong, for it does not seem above 250 yards broad. This is, however, what cannot happen in the hands of the Siamese, either here or at any other part of the river; and their capital, as now situated, must always be exposed to destruction by the sudden invasion of any active enemy.* Refugees from Pegue seeking protection, under the Siamese Government, from the excesses of the Burmans, are the only inhabitants of the immediate neighbourhood of these forts, where they have been planted by the Government in the manner of a colony. We could easily distinguish this race from the Siamese, by the long hair of the women, and the painted, or rather tatooed, limbs of the men. This latter practice is sometimes carried to a great degree of extravagance. One person of some consideration whom we met, had, for example, not only his legs and thighs tattooed, but an inscription tatooed, across his breast, in the Pegue or Mon character, every letter of which was at least an inch long. In the little intercourse we had with these people, we found them cheerful and communicative, and seemingly anxious to be upon good terms with us.

July 18.—After dropping down the river slowly all night, we found ourselves, at about six o'clock in the morning, opposite the village of Pak-nam, and at noon anchored beyond the mouth of the Menam. The view of the sea, which now presented itself, and of the high mountains to the eastern side of the Bay, formed a cheering and enlivening prospect, after our four months' confinement to the Siamese capital, with all the

* These forts were repaired, and cannon mounted on them, after the commencement of our contest with the Burmese.

irksome restraints incident to the relation in which we stood with the despotic and suspicious Government of Siam.

The village of Pak-nam, which I have just mentioned, is about two miles from the mouth of the River, on its left bank—a long, straggling, and poor place. It is not, I am told, unhealthy, which is surprising, for the situation is low, swampy, and comfortless. The swarms of musquitoes which infest it are prodigious, and render it intolerable to strangers. This plague must even render it miserable to the inhabitants themselves; the very lowest orders of whom are compelled to use musquito curtains, and cannot get a moment's rest without them. Our own experience of them, in the course of last night, more than realized the accounts which we had read of them in the travels of voyagers to Siam, and which we before considered as exaggerated. In going up the River, a fresh north-east monsoon had blown, and we then felt no inconvenience whatever from these insects, but the opposite monsoon now prevailed; and when it fell calm, about six o'clock yesterday evening, they came on board in such swarms, that we were compelled to betake ourselves to the protection of boots, gloves, fans, and finally our musquito curtains. They appeared to be not only more numerous, but more venomous than the oldest of us had experienced in any other part of India.

July 19.—The Christian interpreter, Bastian, came on board this morning with a message from the Chief of Pak-nam, expressing his regret that we had not stopped at his residence and afforded him an opportunity of paying us attention. It is but justice to this person to observe, that he had been constantly polite to every individual of our party with whom he had any intercourse, since our first arrival in the country.

July 25.—About nine o'clock last night, we crossed the bar of the River, having taken no less than seven days in warping the ship over a mud flat, ten miles in extent. The outer edge of this flat is sandy and of harder materials than the inner part, being little more than two hundred yards broad. The rest of the flat is so soft, that when the ship grounded during the ebb, she often sunk five feet in the mud and clay which supported her upright, so that we were subjected neither to risk nor inconvenience. The highest water on the bar of the Menam in the hot months, from February to September, is about thirteen and a half feet; and in the remaining four months, somewhat more than fourteen feet—a difference probably produced by the accumulation of water at the head of the bay, after the south-west monsoon, and by the heavy floods of the rainy season. The extensive mud flat and bar of the Menam are serious obstacles to its navigation, and, on this account, foreign trade ought perhaps to be confined to vessels not exceeding two hundred or two hundred and fifty tons burthen. In all other respects, the River is extremely safe and commodious. Its mouth is no sooner approached, than it deepens gradually; and at Pak-nam, two miles up, there are six and seven fathoms water. This depth even increases as you ascend, and at Bang-kok is not less than nine fathoms. The only danger is, or rather was, a sand-bank off Pak-nam, bare at low water. On this a fort or battery has been erected since we left the country, which affords at all times a distinct beacon. The channel of the River is at the same time so equal, that a ship may range from one side to another—approaching the banks so closely, that her yards may literally overhang them. The navigation is said to be equally safe all the way to the old capital.

July 26.—Two of the Christian interpreters came on board this morning, with an answer to a letter which I had brought to the Prah-klang from the Resident of Singapore. The reply to that from the Governor of Prince of Wales's Island had only arrived three days before. All this was perfectly agreeable to the spirit of procrastination which characterises every measure of the Siamese Government that came under our knowledge.

August 4.—From the 26th of July till the 2nd

of this month, we were occupied in putting the ship in a condition to enable her to sail with safety to a group of islands close at hand, called by our old navigators the Dutch Islands, and by the natives Ko Si-chang; for, in order to enable her to pass the bar, she had been dismantled, and her draft of water reduced from fifteen to twelve feet. During all this time, and indeed from the moment we quitted Bang-kok, we had a constant succession of fine and serene weather. We reached the group of islands in question yesterday afternoon, and had here the satisfaction to find a safe and beautiful harbour, formed between Si-chang, the principal island, and Koh-kam, the next in magnitude. A party landed in the evening. On the large island we discovered nothing but an uninhabited hut, close to which it was evident there had been a considerable extent of culture not many years back; for a number of hardy plants, such as capsicums, yams, and the indigo plant, were still propagating themselves over a tract of two or three acres of ground close by. At this visit we could discover no other signs of occupation or habitation than what is now mentioned. We afterwards visited Koh-kam, forming the eastern side of the harbour. This island, composed of one hill of moderate elevation, about a mile long, is generally cleared of forest, cultivated with maize, cucumbers, gourds, and bananas; and on the shore of the harbour is a village of ten or twelve fishermen's huts. The inhabitants showed no marks of timidity; but on the contrary received us with much kindness,—readily offering to share with us their yams, bananas, and fish, without bargaining for any remuneration.

Early this morning we paid a second visit to Si-chang, and landed on a sandy beach farther up the harbour than the spot which we had reached last night. Here we perceived a shed covered in with a tiled roof. Near to the shed a good pathway led into the forest, and conducted us, after a walk of a quarter of a mile, to a fountain of clear and fine water. The same path, after a distance of a quarter of a mile more, ascending the hills of which the bulk of the island is composed, led to a second fountain of water, near to which we unexpectedly perceived a Prachidi, or "holy spire," of solid masonry, and about thirty feet high. Still there was no sign of inhabitants. This edifice was, in fact, a place for the traders between Bang-kok and the east side of the Gulf to pay their devotions at. We also paid a second visit to Koh-kam, the inhabitants of which received us with the same familiarity and attention as before. Several of them accompanied us to the summit of the hill, from which we had an extensive view of the neighbouring continent, not above ten or twelve miles distant, as well as of the innumerable islands scattered over the eastern shore of the Gulf.

August 5.—We had this forenoon a visit from the commander of two small Chinese junks, with their followers, which had come in, in the morning, bound from Tung-yai to Bang-kok, with cargoes of pepper. Our visitors were of various races—some being Chinese, others Cochin Chinese, and others Siamese and Kambojans; for the provinces on the eastern shore of the bay are inhabited by a mixture of all these different nations, as well as by other tribes still ruder. The Chinese commanders informed us, that the country of Tung-yai and Chan-ti-bun produce pepper, cardamums, and eagle-wood; the first, however, only in large quantity, and which, at Tung-yai alone, might amount to 15,000 piculs yearly. They stated that the coasting trade of Tung-yai and Chan-ti-bun was greatly harassed by the depredations of pirates from Tringanu, and other parts of the Malayan peninsula.

Among our visitors, I found an individual of the wild race of the Chong, who appear, as far as I could learn, to be the aboriginal inhabitants of the territory of Chan-ti-bun and Tung-yai. In features and complexion, the individual whom I now saw appeared to differ essentially from the Siamese: the hair was softer, the beard more copious, the features more prominent, and the complexion much darker. This might however have been all peculiar to the individual. He gave me a short vocabulary of his dialect,—

judging by which, it seems to be essentially an original language, although borrowing a considerable number of extrinsic terms from the Kambojan.

August 9.—We buried two of our people this morning, a sepoy and a washerman: the first, a weakly young man, died of a chronic diarrhœa; and the second, an old man, of a hemorrhage from the lungs. These, with the exception of a Lascar, who died of pulmonary consumption, were the only deaths from sickness during a voyage of thirteen months' continuance, and the only casualties in our party, with the exception of the Chinese who was drowned in the Menam. When it is considered that we amounted in all to one hundred and thirty persons, including the ship's company, and that we lay in the Menam for four months, during the most unfavourable season of the year, and not very comfortably situated, this statement may be adduced as strong evidence in favour of the salubrity of the climate of Bang-kok.

August 14.—We had now been nine days at the Si-chang Islands, without suspecting that there was a single inhabitant on the larger one. Yesterday morning, however, directly abreast of the place where the ship lay at anchor, we discovered a foot-path, which conducted us through the forest, until it brought us to a plot of cultivated ground, ten or twelve acres in extent, surrounded in every direction by the deep forest. In the centre of it was a single hut, the inhabitants of which were an old man and woman, each seemingly above seventy years of age, and very frail. The man was a Chinese, and his companion a native of Lao. Although we came suddenly upon them, and were probably the first Europeans they had ever met with, they received us familiarly, and without apprehension invited us immediately into their cabin, and cheerfully offered us plantains and Indian corn. The old woman was particularly earnest and kind in her attention. They stated to us, that their business, in that sequestered spot, was to cultivate vegetables for the supply of the trading boats and vessels which passed and re-passed between Bang-kok and Chan-ti-bun; and that one of the party, the husband of the old woman, was absent at the time at Bang-kok. The ground was neatly laid out in the Chinese style of husbandry, and planted with maize, yams, battatas, capsicums, and cucumbers. This part of the island presented a greater extent of level and good ground, than might have been looked for from its rugged aspect from the harbour.

This morning the old man, conformably to a promise which he had made, paid us a visit on board, and returned very well satisfied with the presents which we made him for himself and his companion.

CHAPTER VIII.

Departure from the Si-chang Islands.—Description of them.—Crossing the Gulf of Siam.—Sam-roi-yot, or the "Three Hundred Peaks."—Group of Islands called Pulo-panjang.—Mission visits Pulo Condore.—Ruins of an English factory.—Description of Pulo Condore.—Cape St. James.—Arrival in the River of Saigun.—Intercourse with the Chief of Kandyu, and description of the place.—Visit to Saigun.—Audience of the Governor.—Elephant and Tiger fights.—Description of Saigun and its River.—Departure from Saigun for the Capital.

April 5.—Having completed our wooding and watering, and otherwise prepared the ship for sea, we weighed anchor at ten o'clock this forenoon, in prosecution of our voyage to Cochin China, and stood across the Bay, making for the projecting land on the western coast, called in European charts the Point of Cin.

The following is a brief description of the Si-chang Islands. They are eight in number, and the largest five miles in length, and about a mile and a quarter in its broadest part. Their coasts are in general bold and rocky, with here and there a sandy cove intervening. With the exception of a few spots, where the rocks are so steep and abrupt, as to preclude any soil resting upon them, their surface is covered every where with forest-trees. The rock formation is primitive, consisting of granite, occurring so low in position, as generally to be visible only during the ebb of the sea. There then occurs quartz rock, and finally blue granular limestone, on which repose the soil and vegetable mould. The occasional minerals found were white quartz, in veins intersecting the limestone, quartz, and granite—veins of dolomite occurring in the limestone only; and on one of the smaller islands, veins of jaspery iron-ore in the quartz rock. On the bolder parts of the coast of the larger island, there were several caverns to which we had access from our boats, and which, from the fantastic forms of the stalactites and stalagmites with which they were commonly lined, presented a very singular and picturesque appearance.

Mr. Finlayson described the botany of the island as highly interesting, and as having afforded him a number of new species. Among the plants, no palm is to be found,—a novelty in countries so close to the Equator. Tuberous rooted plants abounded; amongst which, one was of so singular a description, that it deserves particular mention. This, according to Mr. Finlayson and

Dr. Wallich's opinion, was a new species of menispernum. What was chiefly remarkable in it, was the enormous size of the tuberous roots. One of these, which we brought on board, weighed 150 lbs.; another, 350 lbs.; and a third, 474 lbs. The last measured nine and a half feet in circumference. These, with several smaller ones in a living state, were conveyed to the botanical garden of Calcutta. Not above one-fourth part of the enormous mass of these roots was buried in the soil, the rest being entirely exposed. The small size of the stem, which was scandent, formed a singular contrast with the bulk of the root: it was scarce half an inch in diameter in its thickest part. We found this extraordinary plant growing on two or three of the smaller islands, generally in a scanty and rocky soil, not far from the shore, and always under the shade of trees. Its substance was white, dense, farinaceous, and somewhat bitter to the taste. The natives, with some propriety, called it Pai-pun-chang, or the "elephant yam;" and informed us that it was capable of affording an esculent farina, which they sometimes had recourse to in times of scarcity, but they evidently put little value upon it.

The only quadrupeds which we observed on these islands, were a large species of rat, and a small squirrel about a foot long. This last was numerous in the forest, and we obtained several specimens. It was of a milk-white colour, the paws excepted, which were black.*

Among the birds, the most frequent was the white pigeon, already mentioned. On one of the small islands, we saw and succeeded in obtaining specimens of what we considered a new species of pigeon. This was somewhat larger in size than an ordinary domestic pigeon, of a reddish brown colour, with a metallic gloss over the neck and back, having the wings and tail black, and the head ash-coloured. It was a very shy bird. A small species of green pigeon, or dove, with a yellow breast, was also procured. Fishing eagles, of a large size, were seen in considerable number, and specimens obtained.

The harbour of Si-chang and the neighbouring seas appeared to abound in fish; but the natives were indolent and unenterprizing, and seemed satisfied with taking what was sufficient for their own immediate wants, and no more.

Hamilton† is the only writer whom I have met with that takes notice of this group of islands. He calls the whole, the Dutch Islands, and the principal one, or Si-chang, "Amsterdam." They appear to have received these names on account of the ships of the Dutch East India Com-

* This appears to be a new species, and Dr. Horsefield has appropriately named it after the late Mr. Finlayson.

† Hamilton's new account of the East Indies, from 1688 to 1723, vol. ii.

pany which frequented Siam in the seventeenth century, being in the habit of taking shelter at them in the south-west monsoon. English ships, it would appear, had been occasionally in the habit of doing the same thing.

August 15.—A fine steady breeze brought us yesterday quite across the gulf, which, at its head, does not appear to be above fifty miles broad. In the passage, the high land was generally visible on both sides. At noon, to-day, we were in the latitude of 13° 2′, close to the western shore, and in five fathoms water. A few miles to the north of us was seen the entrance of a river, upon which is situated the town of Kwi. The view to the west of us was novel and imposing. The shore was a sandy beach, and behind it was a narrow strip of land, beyond which nothing was to be seen but a succession of peaked mountains to the verge of the horizon. Some of the peaks appeared to be not less than 3000 feet high. Several were insulated, and, rising abruptly from the plain to the height of many hundred feet, presented the appearance of artificial cones. The Siamese give to these mountains, with some propriety, the name of Sam-roi-yot, which means, in their language, "the 300 peaks."

August 17.—We continued all yesterday and last night to work along the western shore of the gulf; and when we had made the headland, which is called in the charts the Point of

Cin, but correctly written Kwi, we stood across the bay with a six-knot breeze for Pulo Ubi.

August 20.—On the 17th and 18th we continued our course across the bay with a favourable wind, and yesterday afternoon, at three o'clock, anchored off the group of islands called Pulo Panjang, to the north side of the largest island, in eighteen fathoms water. A party landed immediately. The island, which is about three miles long and two broad, is composed of a mass of sand-stone, in which we found some common jasper, of a reddish brown colour, and some veins of jaspery iron-ore. The coast, wherever it was visible to us, consisted of huge fragments of this rock, piled one upon the other, and rendering the landing difficult and precarious, even with the fine weather which we enjoyed at the time. The island, elevated every where, but exhibiting no peak or hill distinct from the general aspect, was as usual covered with thick wood, into which we found it difficult to penetrate even for a few yards, on account of the prevalence of climbing plants. The only quadruped we saw was a handsome greyish brown squirrel, which was new to us.

This group of islands consists of seven. The name Pulo Panjang, or "long island," is Malayan, and has probably been imposed by the Malay pirates, who occasionally visit it in their passage across the gulf when engaged in their predatory expeditions against the Siamese and Kambojan establishments on the eastern coast. In the course of our excursion we came accidentally upon a copious fall of fresh water, and leading to it saw a pathway, which, however, had not lately been trodden. This spot was most likely the usual place of resort of the rovers in question.

At daylight this morning we set sail, passing close to the two islands which lie immediately south of the principal one. These exhibited several sandy bays, upon which a landing might be effected without inconvenience.

August 21.—Last night we passed the false Pulo Ubi, and, at four this morning, the true Pulo Ubi, at the distance of two miles, and between it and the main of Kamboja. We had now fairly entered the Chinese Sea, and pursued our course towards Pulo Condore.

August 22.—Yesterday afternoon, we passed the little islands, or rather rocks, called The Brothers. The largest is not above a mile in circumference; a steep and almost inaccessible rock, with a few stunted shrubs growing on the summit. We passed within half a mile of it. It was covered with innumerable sea-fowl, chiefly black and white mews. We came within a few miles of Pulo Condore in the course of the evening, and lay to all night, that we might have daylight to enter the harbour. We accordingly sailed into the bay this morning, which presented a very noble prospect. An amphitheatre of steep mountains terminating in a bold and rocky coast, forms the harbour to the southern and western sides. The northern and eastern are formed by six islets of various sizes, which afford a much less effectual protection. We had scarcely come to an anchor, when a native boat came alongside;—thus affording an example of early confidence on the part of the Cochin Chinese, which pleased us when we compared it with the distrust and timidity always evinced by the Siamese throughout their intercourse with us.

After breakfast, a large party landed, and passed several hours in visiting the village, or rambling over the shores and woods. Opposite to the place where we anchored was a sandy beach about two miles in extent, with a tract of low land behind it, extending to about a mile and a half to the foot of the hills. This plain is sandy, and covered with a tall forest, which, being free from underwood, admitted our walking through it without difficulty. Towards one extremity of it there was a brook of fresh water, in following which, and about half a mile from the shore, we came suddenly upon the ruins of the English factory which had once existed at Pulo Condore. These consisted of the foundations of the fort; scattered bricks and stones; fragments of coarse earthenware, and porcelain.

in very considerable quantity, and broken pieces of tobacco-pipes of European manufacture. The forest about the ruins, was as tall and luxuriant as any where else. The establishment had been destroyed one hundred and eighteen years before, having been formed in the year 1702, and treacherously cut off by its own native garrison in 1704. The English who had formed the settlement at Pulo Condore, were the same who had been forced to abandon the factory of Chusan in China; and the remnant of whom having afterwards formed the settlement of Banjarmassin, in Borneo, were driven from this place also through their great imprudence. The Governor, Mr. Ketchpoole, had, according to the practice of those times, engaged some natives of Celebes as soldiers, stipulating to discharge them in three years—an engagement which he failed to fulfil, and the breach of which provoked these sanguinary people to rise upon the English, and murder all who were within the fort, in the dead of the night, and as they lay in their beds. A few who lodged outside the fort, hearing the cries of their countrymen when attacked, took the alarm, and, gaining the beach, embarked in a boat that happened to be ready; and after a perilous voyage reached the territories of the King of Jehor, who received them with humanity and kindness. I found, on inquiry, that the natives were not unaware that Europeans had once been settled amongst them; but it was an affair of mere vague tradition, and they could give no precise information on the subject.

At the only village in the plain before-mentioned, the natives welcomed us with great frankness, and with a confidence which was extraordinary, considering that they have little or no intercourse with Europeans. As we approached the village, we found the young men playing at foot-ball on the sand. They interrupted their sport to accompany us to an interview with the Chief. This person, a respectable-looking man, of about forty-five years of age, received us at first under a shed, but, as our acquaintance and familiarity grew, conducted us to his own house, and communicated without reserve on every topic of our inquiries. We were, in every respect, highly gratified by our intercourse with these poor people. After returning on board, the Chief and a large party of natives paid us a visit. Almost every one had a small present to offer. The Chief, on his part, presented us with some fresh fish and a turtle; and from the rest we received fowls, eggs, cucumbers, melons, and other vegetables. They were reluctant to take payment in money for any thing they offered, but gladly accepted cloth, cutlery, and other articles of European manufacture. In the conduct of this little traffic between us, there was a degree of delicacy shown on their part, favourably opposed to the rapacity which pervaded every class of the Siamese, with which we held any intercourse. One of our gentlemen presented an old man with a piece of white cloth, while we were on shore. He immediately produced a hen, in return. This the gentleman at first declined accepting, but was compelled to do so when the old man threatened to return the cloth. The gentleman, upon this, made him an additional present; upon which, the old man produced two additional fowls, resolving not to be outdone. We parted very good friends in the evening, after a pressing invitation, on their part, to prolong our stay. The chief, on going away, begged us to furnish him with a writing, stating that the Mission had called at Pulo Condore, which he might show to any English ships that might hereafter frequent the place. This I gladly complied with, and, I think, I may safely recommend future navigators, visiting the islands, to the hospitality of Cham-Kwan-Luang, which was the name of this worthy person.

The islands known by the name of Pulo Condore are twelve in number, of various sizes. The largest is twelve miles in length, and about four in its greatest breadth, but not above half this in some places. Others of the group are little better than rocks. Pulo Condore is the farthest limit of the Malayan navigation to the eastward. For what purpose, or under what circumstances, these people were in the habit of frequenting the island, I am unable to tell; but I think it not improbable that it was a station from which, in the days of their power, and probably before the arrival of Europeans, they conducted their piratical depredations against the peaceable coasts of Kamboja and Cochin China. The two words Pulo Condore mean, in the Malay language, the *Island of Gourds*--a name not known to the Anam language, in which it is called Kohnaong. The centre of the large island lies in latitude 8° 40′ North, and in longitude 106° 42″ East, about forty-five miles distant from the mouth of the western branch of the Kamboja river. The general aspect of this group of islands, compared to all that we had hitherto seen, was bleak and rugged. The land is mountainous and precipitate, commonly ascending at an angle of even beyond 45° from the very sea. The great island especially is one mountainous chain of this description, the highest part of which is, to all appearance, little less than 1800 feet above the level of the sea. Wherever the hills are exposed to the direct influence either of the south-west or north-east monsoons, they are either altogether bare, or covered only with coarse grasses or herbaceous plants; but, on the contrary, where there is shelter, the forest is as luxuriant as in the countries upon the Equator itself. The geological structure of the island is primitive, consisting, wherever we examined it, of sienite or sienitic granite, and common grey granite; the latter, however, only in small quantity. The rock was so hard, especially where the sienite prevailed, that it destroyed our hammers, and we found great difficulty in obtaining even a few hand specimens. Nothing can be more unfavourable to the accumulation of soil than such a structure as that of Pulo Condore, — where the rock is so hard, as to be little liable to decomposition—where the hills are precipitate, —and where heavy rains prevail, which must wash down the little soil that might otherwise be disposed to rest upon a surface so unfavourable.

Mr. Finlayson found the botany of the island exceedingly interesting by its novelty and variety; more especially, as many of the plants were at the time in flower or fruit. The common mango *(Mangifera Indica)* was discovered in the forest, where we also found an esculent grape. Dampier, whose account of Pulo Condore is marked by his wonted fidelity, says, that both these, as forest fruits, were ripe when he visited the island in the months of March and April. He states that the last of these was agreeable to the palate, and the first equal to any cultivated variety of the same fruit which he had ever eaten. In respect to the mango, we had no opportunity of bearing testimony to his accuracy.

Of quadrupeds we saw only monkeys and squirrels. The most frequent of the last was a small animal of a jet black colour all over. Of this we obtained a living specimen. It had been reported that wild oxen were to be found in the forests of Pulo Condore, the descendants of those introduced by the English settlers; but the natives stated that this was not the case. The white pigeon was again seen with a very large green pigeon, common in the Malayan peninsula and the adjacent islands, and which I believe to be no other than the copper-coloured nutmeg-eater of the Moluccas.

The village on the large bay consists of three hundred inhabitants. There are two other establishments upon the island, and the whole population, according to the information supplied to us by the Chief, amounts to eight hundred persons. These are all natives of Cochin China; and there are neither Chinese amongst them nor Kambojans, as has been asserted. Among those whom we saw, there was certainly no appearance of want of comfort. The houses were all built upon a level with the ground, the dry and sandy nature of the soil precluding the necessity of raising them upon posts. Persons of all ages had a healthy look, and many of them, being well clothed, had even a decent and respectable appearance. Numbers were marked with the small-pox—showing that this disease had been committing its ravages among them. There was nothing seen to warrant a belief of what has been reported of the unhealthiness of the climate. The inhabitants of Pulo Condore cultivate a small quantity of rice, of which we saw some patches in the forest; but their principal supply is obtained from Saigun. Besides rice, they plant a little maize and some cocoa-nuts, and raise a few cucumbers and other common esculent vegetables. Their principal occupation, however, is catching turtle, fishing, and extracting dammer, a kind of pitch, and wood oil, from the large forest-trees. It is these last objects, with live turtles, oil made from turtle fat, and dry fish, which they exchange for clothing and food at Saigun. In live turtle also they pay their tribute to the King of Cochin China, to whom the islands belong.

Of late years, Pulo Condore has rarely been visited by European voyagers. Lord Macartney, in his way to China, in 1792, touched at it with the expectation of receiving refreshments for his sick, but was disappointed, and went on to Turan. The Chief of the island informed us, that although he had seen many ships pass close by the island, none had ever come into the bay in his recollection. Five years ago, one European vessel sent her boat in, and received a few refreshments.

The Hai-nan junks carrying on the trade between that island and Siam, and now the Cochin Chinese junks trading with Singapore, make a practice of touching at Pulo Condore for wood and water, and these are the only description of vessels which frequent it. Its convenient and favourable position, as a commercial emporium, are sufficiently obvious, and did not escape the sagacity of Dampier.

We heard at Pulo Condore, that the King of Cochin China was at present residing at his capital, the city of Huè; and that Chao-Kun, the Governor of Lower Cochin China, the person of greatest influence in the kingdom, was at Saigun. We were particularly desirous of having an interview with this last individual, as well as of visiting the city of Saigun, which, with the exception of Kachao in Tonquin, was reported to be the richest and most commercial part of the kingdom. Accordingly, with this object in view, we sailed from the bay of Pulo Condore at five in the evening, directing our course for Cape St. James.

August 24.—Early yesterday morning, Cape St. James was visible at the distance of about twenty-five miles, having then the appearance of three small islands. It falling calm, however, and the tide being against us, we anchored until the afternoon, when we again made sail, and early this morning reached the Cape, and anchored off the bay of Cocoa-nuts. Cape St. James's, a promontory of from three to four hundred feet high, forms the eastern entrance of the river of Saigun, and occurring, after passing a low coast of two hundred miles extent, where not a hill or elevated spot is seen, forms an excellent land-mark for the entrance of the river, which cannot well be mistaken. Being within little more than a mile of the shore we landed, while the ship was waiting for the flood-tide. The prevailing rock which forms the hilly range of Cape St. James, is a tough, hard granite, intermixed occasionally with sienite. The mountains are wholly uncultivated, being covered with a scanty forest, of which the bamboo forms a considerable part. We heard the crowing of the wild cocks in the woods, and saw some fishing-eagles and ring-doves, but no quadrupeds.

In the afternoon, when the flood-tide made, we sailed for the anchorage of Kandyu, which we reached before dusk. As we passed the village of Pungtăo, which lies in the angle of the bay, where the ridge of hills forming Cape St. James's ends, the Mandarin, or petty officer of the place, came on board with a large party of followers. He was a little, lively old man, whose age was little short of sixty. We were forcibly struck with the contrast which he and his followers formed with the first Siamese with whom we became acquainted at the entrance of the Menam. The Cochin Chinese were more decently clad, and instead of being sluggish and sullen in their manners, were lively and civil. This officer recommended to us to write a letter to the Governor of Saigun, to be forwarded through the Chief of Kandyu, who was his superior officer. We accordingly wrote an English letter to His Excellency, with a French translation, understanding at the time that several French gentlemen were at Saigun, and that it was possible there might be no person there who could understand the original. This letter we transmitted to the Mandarin of Kandyu. He sent a polite message, in answer, to say that a list of the persons attached to the Mission, of the ship's company, and of the guns, arms, and ammunition, in the Chinese character, would be necessary to send to the Governor of Saigun, with our letter. This requisition was complied with.

The point of Kandyu may be looked upon as the actual mouth of the river on its right or western bank. From Cape St. James to this place, a distance of nine nautical miles, may be viewed rather as a bay of the sea than a portion of the river. On the western side, opposite the high lands of Cape St. James, an extensive mud-bank, proceeding from a flat shore, narrows the channel for ships entering to about two and a half nautical miles. From the edge of this bank to the shore on the eastern side, this spacious bay is not less than four and a-half miles broad. In mid-channel there is every where from six to nine fathoms; and after you have fairly entered the river, rarely less than ten; so that this fine stream is navigable for ships of almost any burthen, and it scarcely requires a pilot throughout. Relying upon our bearings and soundings, and on our charts, we stood boldly on at night, as if we had been entering a harbour well known to us. The actual breadth of the true mouth of the river is about one and a half English mile.

We were now anchored immediately behind the Point of Kandyu, secure from every wind. To the eastward, the hills of Cape St. James, and more to the north an elevated range of mountains, seemingly about twenty-five miles distant, were visible. Every where else nothing was to be seen but the low and wooded shore, with fishing villages here and there thinly scattered over it. The extraordinary clearness of the water, for so large a river, coming through an extensive alluvial tract, forms a striking contrast with the disturbed and muddy streams of the Ganges and Menam.

August 25.—The Mandarin of Kandyu, whose authority seems to extend over all the inhabitants about this part, amounting, as we were told, to about two thousand in number, had promised last night to pay us a visit in the course of to-day, and accordingly he came on board as early as seven o'clock in the morning, with a great number of followers. He was superior in appearance to any of those who came on board yesterday. He seemed near seventy years of age, but full of vivacity. Neither he nor those who accompanied him were, in any respect, less civil or obliging than our visitor of yesterday. We soon found our new acquaintances to be great and vehement talkers, and their conversation was accompanied by a more than moderate portion of gesticulation. It readily occurred to us, that there was in exterior, although it unquestionably amounted to nothing more, some foundation for the Cochin Chinese being called the French of India. The old chief brought us a supply of fresh fish, and we presented him, in return, with some cloth, cutlery, and, what seemed to be no less welcome, some brandy. He promised to forward, with all speed, our letter to the Governor of Saigun, and said, that in a day, or a day and a half, we should have a reply; and that he rested assured the Governor would be gratified with the visit which we proposed paying him.

August 26.—Mr. Finlayson, Mr. Rutherford, and myself, visited the old chief last night, and were received with great cordiality. Tea and tobacco were served to us. Kandyu is but a poor place, and the chief's residence a very paltry one; but the hospitality of our reception made some amends for the homeliness of our entertainment. At an early hour this morning he visited us again. A number of fishermen had come on board in the course of yesterday, and furnished us with an ample supply of fine fish at very low prices. Encouraged by our prompt payment, they had repaired to us again this morning, and the old chief found two of them on board. It appears they had come *without orders*, and the followers of the man in office began, in a manner quite unexpected to us, to punish them summarily on the spot for this alleged breach of duty. Our attention was called to this practical illustration of Oriental government, by seeing one of the fishermen taken into custody; the officer, as he carried him off, cuffing him over the face, and kicking him with such ludicrous address, that his foot, at every effort, reached sometimes the loins and sometimes the shoulders of the alleged offender. The fisherman's defence consisted in throwing himself on his face, on the deck, making three prostrations, acknowledging his offence, and crying for mercy. I complained to the chief of this piece of violence; but he treated the matter very lightly, and seemed to regard the fisherman's offence rather as a breach of etiquette, or neglect of customary forms, than as any thing more serious; and assured us that it should be attended with no inconvenience to us, or farther injury to the fisherman, who was immediately released. The old man, after partaking of tea and liqueurs, left us.

In the forenoon, Mr. Rutherford and myself went on shore, and were received by the old

Mandarin with the same cordiality as upon the first occasion. Requesting us to leave our Indian attendants behind, he conducted my companion and myself into his private apartments. Here we found a respectable-looking middle-aged woman, the chief's wife, and three young and comely girls, his daughters. The ladies did not appear by any means abashed or discomposed by the appearance of strangers. Seeing that we were disposed to take the diversion of shooting, the old man sent two of his principal people to accompany us, and we wandered over the fields near the village, passing through the principal part of the latter on our return. The village of Kandyu is built upon a creek, connected with the river. The inhabitants consist of about three hundred families, or between one and two thousand inhabitants. The men were, I believe, chiefly out fishing; but the women and children were very numerous. Although the land lies here so low, the houses are all upon a level with the ground, and not raised on posts as amongst the Siamese. Our appearance excited a good deal of curiosity, and the inhabitants flocked round us in numbers, observing a very civil and respectful demeanour. The village appeared well stocked with hogs and poultry, and there were at least no outward marks of want or misery.

During our excursion, we visited two temples about a mile distant from the village. They were built of brick and lime, and roofed with red tile, having the ridges and eaves ornamented with figures of animals carved in wood and painted. Each consisted of two chambers, in the first of which was an altar of brick and lime, having upon it two figures of storks opposite to each other. The inner chamber contained a number of elevated masses of brick and mortar, resembling tombs. The walls were painted with figures of tigers and fish, and with dragons and other monstrous animals. There seemed no distinct object of worship, either statue or picture. We were told, however, that the temples were dedicated to certain great fishes, which were represented as the tutelary deities of the place, and the protectors of the fishermen of Kandyu and its neighbourhood. The mounds of brick and mortar, resembling tombs, of which I have spoken, were alleged to contain the remains of some of the fishes in question, which had been stranded on the shore of the bay of St. James.

Connected with each of the temples, was a poor mean-looking house, where justice, we were told, was administered. Near at hand was an extensive burying-ground, the tombs commonly consisting of rude mounds of earth, the outer sides now and then cased with rough stones.

August 28.—This morning early, the Mandarin of Kandyu came on board to inform us, that a reply to our letter had arrived late last night, and that a deputation had reached the place from the Governor of Saigun, to invite and escort us up to his residence. We were informed that the persons who composed the deputation, waited only for our sanction to come on board. Upon receiving this, they accordingly came off without delay. The deputation consisted of seven Mandarins in four boats, the two largest of which, meant for our accommodation, were manned each with forty oars. The rowers were dressed in scarlet, and had on a kind of helmet, with a plume of cock's feathers. They rowed the boats standing upright, and facing the prow.

The members of the deputation were well dressed in silks, and had in all respects an air of much respectability. Their manners were brisk and lively; they spoke and laughed a great deal, and seemed under no constraint. Our conversation only touched upon our visit to Saigun. We endeavoured to provide as well as we could against detention, and were assured by them that we should not be delayed there beyond three days. We had at first intended to have gone up in the ship, but finding that our passage up and down in this manner would be tedious, we abandoned the project, and resolved to proceed in the barges now sent down to receive us. In the discussion which took place, perfect urbanity and good humour were observed on the part of all the members of the deputation. Few questions were put by them, and these few were not ill-bred or importunate, as in our first intercourse with the Siamese. The most material one had for its object to ascertain whether the Mission came from the King of England, or from the Governor-general of India. To this we generally answered that His Majesty the King of England sent no embassies to any of the princes of the East, and that when they were necessary, he usually deputed his authority to the Governor-general of India. After partaking of tea and liqueurs, the deputation took their leave, and were saluted.

August 29.—At six o'clock yesterday evening, Mr. Finlayson and I embarked for Saigun. The whole of our party consisted of thirty-three persons. One of the boats afforded very comfortable accommodation for Mr. Finlayson and myself, but the rain poured down in torrents during the night, and we could not avail ourselves of the moonlight to observe the appearance of the country as we ascended. As soon as day broke we observed, on each side of the river, a wide extent of champaign country, cultivated every where with rice, and over which villages were thickly scattered. At eight o'clock the city of Saigun was visible on the right or western bank of the river. Before coming to it we saw for several miles, on each side of the stream, a fine avenue of trees, and a public road, which we were told led to the city. At nine o'clock we reached the usual landing-place, where we had to wait for a considerable time before the house destined for our accommodation was determined on. The apology offered for this detention was, that the day was a great festival, and that the Governor and other Chiefs were engaged at the temples in their devotions.

We were, at length, conducted through a large creek, or canal, which falls into the western side of the river, and which communicates with the fortress, to the place destined for our reception. This was a large public edifice, a kind of town-hall, exactly in the form of an Indian bungalow, with a porch and arcade in front. A number of persons were employed in preparing it for our reception, and there was a great bustle. An officer and twenty soldiers were ordered as a guard for us, and double sentinels were placed at the gate to keep off the crowd, that from curiosity was pressing in to see us. A number of servants were also appointed to wait upon us. About one o'clock a deputation of two Mandarins of rank came to compliment us upon our arrival, and, losing no time, also to discuss public matters with us. These two persons, we were given to understand, were judges of the principal tribunal of the city. Their manners were very good, but had more of Chinese gravity in them than those of the persons who had come to meet us at Kandyu. They were far superior in rank to even the senior of the latter, who, I observed, stood up in their presence; for this is the attitude of respect towards superiors among the Cochin Chinese. They began by requesting that we would recommend to our followers and people a guarded conduct in their intercourse with the inhabitants of the country; for that, if any disputes arose, it would be an unpleasant matter to us, and an affair of great scandal to the Cochin Chinese Government. We assured them that the strictest injunctions had been given to our people upon the subject. After this we were asked whether the Mission was deputed by the King of England, or by the Governor-general. We replied, by the Governor-general, by whom the diplomatic intercourse with the princes of India was commonly conducted, since his Majesty the King of England was too far away to conduct such matters directly with convenience. We were then asked how long we had been from Bengal, what countries we had visited, how long we had remained in them, &c. &c. When Siam was mentioned, we were asked if we had had an audience of the King, and whether there were now any English ships there; to which questions we answered in the affirmative. The evident object of such interrogatories was to ascertain the nature of our reception, and the result of our mission. We were now asked, if we had been directed by the Governor-general of India to visit the Governor of Lower Cochin China. We said, that we had the Governor-general's sanction to do so, if we thought it necessary. The deputies answered, that if this was the case we had a letter for the Governor of Lower Cochin China, as a matter of course. We said we had no letter, for it was not the custom of our Government to address a subject, however high his rank, without the authority and sanction of his own sovereign. The deputies then demanded to know for what purpose we had visited Saigun. To this question a full, and to all appearance a satisfactory explanation was given. It was then asked, if there were any presents for the King of Cochin China. In reply to this, a few of the principal articles were enumerated. This was deemed quite enough, and no farther questions were put respecting this matter.

A more difficult topic, however, was now started. The deputies had informed us, that the Governor of Lower Cochin China wished to see the letter of the Governor-general to the King, that he might have an opportunity of making a report upon it to the Capital.—We mentioned, in a few words the purport and contents of the letter, and gave the deputies to understand, that we had offered to show it to the deputation that came to wait upon us at Kandyu, and that we had also tendered a copy and translation of it to be presented to the Governor of Lower Cochin China, but that both proposals were declined as unnecessary. We dwelt on the inconvenience and delay, at such an advanced and precarious state of the monsoon, that would attend our sending for the letter to the ship, as even a day or two was now of consequence to us. In their reply to this, they took no notice of the circumstance of the Mandarins who went to Kandyu, declining the proposal of seeing the letter there, or bringing copies of it to Saigun, but asked us how the Governor, in writing to Hué, could reasonably describe a letter, the contents of which he had no opportunity of verifying by his own inspection. We now offered to exhibit the letter to any officer who might be sent down to the ship to inspect it, and in the meantime to bring up copies and translations. This, however, was not deemed sufficient. Several messages passed and repassed between the deputies and the Governor during the conference, the purport of which we could not learn. This business ended by the Mandarins informing us that the matter would be taken into farther consideration to-morrow morning, when we should have a final answer. During this long conversation, in accordance with their mixed character of lawyers and diplomatists, no inconsiderable share of skill and dexterity in questioning and cross-questioning was displayed by the Cochin Chinese deputies. The interview lasted between five and six hours, so that, with our journey, it left us thoroughly fatigued. At parting, the Mandarins presented us, on the part of the Governor, with a quantity of rice, fruit, sugar, fowls, poultry, and a hog. The last is a description of present peculiarly demanded by the customs of the country, and never omitted on an occasion of any importance. Mr. Finlayson, who understood the Portuguese language, acted upon this occasion as interpreter, and his words were rendered into Cochin Chinese by a very intelligent native Christian, whose name was Antonio, and who, during our stay at Saigun, proved very useful to us.

Monsieur Diard, the only French gentleman at present in the place, dined with us in the evening. This gentleman is a naturalist and physician, and travels under the latter name. He has been at Saigun only three months, having come from Hué. He had before visited Bengal, Sumatra, and Java, and is well known for his active pursuits in the department of natural history.

Aug. 30.—Immediately after breakfast this

morning, we had a visit from a Mandarin of the military order, called Ong-kwan-beng. This person, a man of about fifty, of very respectable appearance, with a flowing white beard reaching nearly to his girdle, was of higher rank than our visitors of yesterday. His object was to urge the request already made for the Governor-general's letter to the King. Finding this could not be evaded, we yielded with as good grace as possible, after receiving a pledge that we should not be detained beyond three days, and that the letter should not go out of our own hands. The Mandarin was quite satisfied with this; and, in concluding the conversation, assured us that the Governor's request was strictly conformable to the laws and usages of the country, and hoped we should put no unfavourable construction upon his conduct.

While Ong-kwan-beng was with us, the two Mandarins who had visited us yesterday made their appearance. They bowed to him respectfully, but not servilely, as they came in, and seated themselves on the same bench with, but behind him. During the conversation, both to-day and yesterday, I was a little surprised to find that instead of avoiding to explain themselves through our interpreters, as was always the case in Siam, the Chiefs frequently volunteered this, and seemed indeed to give them a preference to their own.

A message came to us in the course of the day from the Governor, to say that we were at liberty to go abroad, and visit any part of the city we might think proper, and that either elephants, horses, or boats, would be supplied to us as we might prefer.

The letter of the Governor-general arrived to-day about half-past ten o'clock; the boat sent to the ship having proceeded with such despatch as to have taken in all no more than twenty-two hours in going and coming. Notice of this was, without delay, sent to the Mandarins charged with our business, and the three persons, who had visited us before, presented themselves in less than half-an-hour.

We had by this time found that our Cochin Chinese friends were extremely ceremonious, and partial to display and parade in little matters to the extent of ostentation. This humour was complied with, in exhibiting the letter of the Governor-general. As soon as it was opened, the Mandarins proceeded to inspect it minutely, examining by turns the writing, the illuminated paper, and above all the seal of the Governor-general. This being done, we proceeded jointly, through the medium of a Portuguese translation which accompanied it, to render it sentence by sentence into Cochin Chinese. After this process had gone on a little time, the deputation considered it unsatisfactory, and begged that a written translation in the Chinese character might be effected. This was done accordingly. They now examined my credentials, and begged a Chinese translation of those also, and they farther required English and Portuguese copies of all the documents. This too was acceded to. On perusing the translation in the Chinese character, the Mandarins expressed entire satisfaction at the general purport of the letter; but advanced many objections to particular expressions, which they declared it was impossible to submit to his Majesty the King of Cochin China; the use of them, they said, however respectfully meant, being against the laws of the country. For example, towards the conclusion of the letter of the Governor-general, "His Excellency sends certain presents in token of his profound respect and esteem for His Majesty the Emperor of Cochin China." This was not to be endured, because, as the matter was explained to us, profound respect and esteem must be considered as matters of course from any one that addressed His Majesty of Cochin China. At the suggestion of the Mandarins, the passage was rendered as follows: "I send your Majesty certain presents, because you are a great King." Strong objection was made to the expression in which His Excellency had disclaimed any wish for lands or fortresses; because it was not to be imagined for a moment that any one could desire lands or fortresses belonging to the King of Cochin China, and the disclaiming the wish to obtain commercial factories alone was inserted. In the letter of the Governor-general, His Majesty was styled Emperor of Anam, a common term for Tonquin and Cochin China; and as it was well known that he had conquered a great part of Kamboja, and, as was asserted of Lao, Sovereign of these countries, also was added to his titles. This was much objected to, and the Mandarins informed me that it was no honour to the King of Cochin China to be styled "a king of slaves," for ás such, it seems, the inhabitants of the conquered provinces are deemed by the governing race, that is, by the Anam nation, which includes both Cochin Chinese and Tonquinese. After the conference was over, I asked the Christian interpreter, in consequence of hearing this last observation, what opinion the Cochin Chinese entertained of the people of Kamboja. He had visited Bengal, and said without hesitation, "pretty much the same opinion that the English entertain of the black inhabitants of Hindoostan!!" The whole of this tedious conference lasted eight hours. The luckless interpreter, Antonio, was so overcome with the intricacy, not to say the danger of his part of the task, and the difficulty of pleasing every body, that he declared, that to have done it justice, would have required the head of an elephant!

Sept. 1.—Not satisfied with the tedious details of yesterday, and the pains taken to satisfy his Majesty's, the King of Cochin China's, feelings in the Chinese translation, one of the Mandarins returned this morning to inform us, that, on mature consideration, it was decided that there were still two improper words in the Chinese translation. These were accordingly rectified. He then informed us, that duplicate copies of the Governor-general's letter in English, in Portuguese, and in Chinese; of my credentials in the same languages, and duplicates of my letter to the Governor of Saigun in English and French, with a Chinese translation, also in duplicate, were farther wanted. The object of these voluminous documents was, that one copy of them might be sent to Court, and another kept at Saigun. They were so particular, in regard to these papers, that each required my personal seal and signature.

All this was completed by twelve o'clock, at which hour we set off to pay a visit to the town of Saigun, accompanied by Monsieur Diard. The town properly called Saigun, is about three miles distant from the residence of the Governor of the province. It is situated upon a small river, navigable for good-sized boats all the way to Kamboja, with which it is the principal medium of communication. Straggling houses nearly join the fort and residence of the Governor with Saigun. The banks of the stream are well cultivated on both sides, and extensive plantations of areca palm form the principal object of culture. At the town of Saigun the river forms many branches and canals. Over these are bad bridges, consisting of one or two planks. The river, however, is usually ferried over in boats. The regulation of these ferries is a little singular. The women alone pay, and all the men, under pretext of being the King's servants, that is, public officers, pass freight-free. A similar regulation exists in the Menam. The principal bazar is a wide and spacious street. The numerous shops were not rich, but sufficiently neat. The principal articles exposed for sale were Chinese earthenware, manufactured silks, chiefly of Tonquin, and of the place itself, and commonly made up into dresses, paper, and great quantities of amazingly coarse tea from the northern provinces, which had more the appearance of broken tobacco-leaves than real tea. There was abundance of poultry, including the common fowl, ducks, and geese, which last are not reared in Siam, and rarely in any Malay country, except where Europeans reside. Here were also plenty of hogs, of an excellent breed. The want of intercourse, direct or indirect, with European nations, was sufficiently evinced by the general absence of European manufactures. A few common glass-bottles, and some broad cloth, were all that was to be seen.

Women alone attended in the shops. The sex was to be seen going broad every where, without any reserve. Judging from the specimen we saw to-day, the Cochin Chinese women appear to be well and becomingly attired. Many of them were much fairer in complexion than we could have expected, and some were handsome, making due allowance for the peculiarity of their features, or what, at least, is considered such, according to our notions of beauty. The appearance of Saigun is respectable for an Indian town. A large proportion of the houses are covered with tiles instead of thatch. The houses of the Chinese are all good, and such as we visited during the day, spacious, comfortable, and, after their fashion, well furnished.

Our appearance excited a good deal of curiosity, unaccompanied however by the slightest appearance of rudeness. The reception we met with from the Chinese merchants was most hospitable and flattering. Three of the principal families, without giving us any previous notice, presented themselves at the doors of their respective houses, and invited us separately to come in. In each house we found a handsome entertainment ready prepared for us, served up with much neatness and propriety. Not satisfied with providing for ourselves, a board was also spread for all who accompanied us, including our Indian servants and Cochin Chinese escort. The persons whose hospitality and urbanity we now experienced, were all descendants of Chinese long settled in the country, and in point both of manners and intelligence were of a very superior order. The Chinese of Saigun amount in all to between three and four thousand in number. They have several temples, and that which belongs to the Chinese of Canton is the handsomest building of the sort that I have any where seen. We returned about five o'clock in the evening, well satisfied with our visit.

Sept. 2.—Every thing was arranged last night for our audience, and, at the desire of the Mandarins, a Chinese list of the presents, written according to the custom of the country upon a scrap of pink-coloured paper, was transmitted. Little previous arrangement was made for our reception, or for the ceremonies we were to perform on our introduction; indeed, no stress appeared to be laid upon matters of this last description. Every thing being ready, about half-past seven o'clock I made a demand for the palanquins or elephants that were to convey us. There were none ready, and I was given to understand indirectly, that it was expected we should go on foot. I gave those that communicated with us to understand, that we would not move a step without a suitable conveyance, and in less than ten minutes five elephants were produced to accommodate us. This was evidently an attempt of some of the lower Mandarins to impose upon us, and I make no question was wholly unknown to the Governor. About eight o'clock we quitted our house for the palace, accompanied by thirteen of our attendants, but leaving the guard of sepoys behind us. Mr. Finlayson carried the letter of the Governor-general. A number of spearmen on foot, and some horsemen mounted on small spirited ponies, similar to those of the Indian islands, accompanied the procession. In about twenty minutes we reached the fort, to which the canal, on the banks of which our house was situated, leads by a straight course, having a good road on each side of it. A great number of spearmen were drawn out to receive us along every avenue of the fort through which we passed, and especially in front of the hall of audience. We did not dismount from our elephants until we came within a hundred yards of the latter. This building was quite open in front, very long but narrow, and entirely constructed of wood, no where either varnished or painted. It was altogether a poor place; and the houses of the Chinese, which we visited yesterday at Saigun, were real palaces compared to it. It is the custom of the Cochin Chinese to sit either upon broad tables, elevated about a foot and a half from the ground, or upon platforms raised about eight or nine inches from it; those of highest rank, in either case, sitting in front, and those of inferior rank behind. These benches, or platforms, are always covered with handsome mats. In the middle of the hall was one of the platforms in question, somewhat higher than usual, on which the Governor was seen sitting. We advanced in front and made him a bow, which was not returned. Chairs were pointed out to us to the Governor's right-hand, of which we took possession. On his left was seated by himself the second in authority, a venerable and fine-looking old man about seventy. The rest of the Governor's Court were seated on the same side with us, but behind us, upon another platform. The first in place among these was Ong-kwan-beng, the military Mandarin who had transacted business with us. The old Governor is by repute an eunuch, but without having been told so, we probably should not have discovered it. He was, indeed, totally destitute of beard; but the beards of the Cochin Chinese in general, although they are fond of wearing them, are usually very scanty. His voice also was feeble and feminine, but not to so remarkable a degree as to excite suspicion.

This individual, who acted a distinguished part in the late wars and revolution of Cochin China, was, at the period of our visit, fifty-eight years of age. His countenance was animated and intelligent, his person rather short and slender, but he appeared active and subject to no bodily infirmity but the tooth-ache, which had deprived him of a great part of his teeth. The other Mandarins were richly dressed in figured silk. The Governor, on the contrary, seemed to be careless and indifferent about his dress, which consisted of a plain black silk gown and a crape turban of the same colour.

He began his conversation with us, by asking how long we had been on our voyage; after getting a reply to which, he proceeded at once to the main subject, and said that the English were welcome to trade in Cochin China, complying with the laws of the country; that the imports were not heavy, and that they were the same to all nations. We answered, that this was exactly what the Governor-general of India desired, and no more. The Governor added, that if the Cochin Chinese, for the purposes of trade, visited the British dominions, they must submit to our laws; and if we came to Cochin China, we must do the same thing. It was replied, that friendship and good understanding could not exist among nations on any other terms. The Governor then observed, that he would forward a particular account of our Mission to the capital, and recommend us to the Mandarin of Elephants, the chief of the foreign department. He now observed, that kings only wrote to kings, and that his Majesty the King of England should have written to the King of Cochin China, and that the Governor-general should have addressed himself to the Mandarin of Elephants. We explained, as we had done on similar occasions before, that the King of England was at too great a distance to be able conveniently to maintain a direct correspondence with the princes of the East, which, therefore, was principally conducted by the Governor-general of India. He answered, that this practice was totally contrary to the customs of Cochin China, but that the informality, on the commencement of a friendly intercourse, should prove no obstruction to the Embassy. We now offered to present his Excellency with a few presents from the Governor-general of India, and the Chinese list of them was read by a secretary. His Excellency, after the list was read, said that he felt obliged to the Governor-general of India for his politeness in sending presents to him; but that the negociation being in a state of abeyance, he could not now with propriety accept of them; but as he hoped many English vessels would visit Saigun hereafter, there would be time enough for presents. We made no objection whatever to this, which struck us at the time as forming so remarkable a contrast with the rapacity of the Siamese officers on similar occasions.

We were now asked when we wished to leave Saigun. The time was mentioned. The Governor answered that every thing would be in readiness for our accommodation. We fully expected that the Governor-general's letter would have been opened, if only out of curiosity; but the Chief simply looked at it, without even taking it from its silk envelope, and politely returned it immediately, requesting, that as we were about to amuse ourselves, it might be sent back to our residence; and he ordered, as a mark of respect, three caparisoned elephants to accompany it. In the course of conversation, the Governor asked my companions' age, and my own. Our Indian servants and their dresses excited his notice, as they did that of every body else during our visit. The Cochin Chinese are total strangers to the inhabitants of Hindustan, of whom not an individual is found residing at Saigun. Their persons, features, manners, and costume, therefore, excited a far greater degree of curiosity than any thing respecting ourselves.

After tea was served to us, we were invited to be present at an elephant and tiger fight; and for this purpose mounted our elephants, and repaired to the glacis of the fort, where the combat was to take place. The Governor went out at another gate, and arrived at the place before us in his palanquin. When the hall broke up, a herald or crier announced the event. With the exception of this ceremony, great propriety and decorum were observed throughout the audience. The exhibition made by the herald, however, was truly barbarous. He threw himself backward, projecting his abdomen, and putting his hands to his sides, and in this absurd attitude uttered several loud and long yells. The tiger had been exhibited in front of the hall, and was driven to the spot on a hurdle. A great concourse of people had assembled to witness the exhibition. The tiger was secured to a stake by a rope tied round his loins, about thirty yards long. The mouth of the unfortunate animal was sewn up, and his nails pulled out. He was of large size, and extremely active. No less than forty-six elephants, all males of great size, were seen drawn out in line. One at a time was brought to attack the tiger. The first elephant advanced, to all appearance with a great show of courage, and we thought from his determined look that he would certainly have dispatched his antagonist in an instant. At the first effort he raised the tiger upon his tusks to a considerable height, and threw him to the distance of at least twenty feet. Notwithstanding this, the tiger rallied, and sprang upon the elephant's trunk and head up to the very keeper, who was upon his neck. The elephant took alarm, wheeled about and ran off, pursued by the tiger as far as the rope would allow him. The fugitive, although not hurt, roared most piteously, and no effort could bring him back to the charge. A little after this, we saw a man brought up to the Governor, bound with cords, and dragged into his presence by two officers. This was the conductor of the recreant elephant. A hundred strokes of the bamboo were ordered to be inflicted upon him on the spot. For this purpose he was thrown on his face upon the ground, and secured by one man sitting astride upon his neck and shoulders, and by another sitting upon his feet, a succession of executioners inflicting the punishment. When it was over, two men carried off the sufferer by the head and heels, apparently quite insensible. While this outrage was perpetrating, the Governor coolly viewed the combat of the tiger and elephant, as if nothing else particular had been going forward. Ten or twelve elephants were brought up in succession to attack the tiger, which was killed at last merely by the astonishing falls he received when tossed off the tusks of the elephants. The prodigious strength of these animals was far beyond any thing which I could have supposed. Some of them tossed the tiger to a distance of at least thirty feet, after he was nearly lifeless, and could offer no resistance. We could not reflect without horror, that these very individual animals were the same that have for years executed the sentence of the law upon the many malefactors condemned to death. Upon these occasions a single toss, such as I have described, is always, I am told, sufficient to destroy life.

After the tiger-fight we had a mock battle, the intention of which was to represent elephants charging an intrenchment. A sort of *chevaux de frise* was erected to the extent of forty or fifty yards, made of very frail materials. Upon this was placed a quantity of dry grass, whilst a show was made of defending it, by a number of spearmen placed behind. As soon as the grass was set on fire, a number of squibs and crackers were let off; flags were waved in great numbers; drums beat, and a single piece of artillery began to play. The elephants were now encouraged to charge; but they displayed their usual timidity, and it was not until the fire was nearly extinguished, and the materials of the *chevaux de frise* almost consumed, that a few of the boldest could be forced to pass through.

After these amusements were over, the Governor begged us to come near and converse with him. He wished to know the precise time we wanted to depart, and hearing that we had fixed on to-morrow morning, was extremely anxious that we should put off our journey for a couple of days, that we might see more of the town, and above all, that he might exhibit to us a dramatic entertainment. We urged the precarious state of the monsoon, and our great anxiety to secure our passage to Hué. Seeing that we were intent on proceeding on our voyage without delay, he said that every thing should be ready for us at as early an hour as we might think proper to name. The orders respecting our departure were accordingly given on the spot, and we had thus an opportunity of seeing how such matters are conducted in Cochin China. The Governor delivered his commands personally, in a high tone of official authority, and twelve or fourteen inferior Mandarins received them standing before him. As soon as he had done speaking they made the accustomed obeisance, which consisted in prostrating themselves four successive times upon the ground, their faces being prevented from touching the earth only by their joined hands, which were placed before them. His Excellency asked what provisions we required for ourselves and the ship's crew, and requested us to specify them, that our wants might be fully supplied. We answered, that we stood in need of nothing, but made suitable acknowledgments for this liberal offer. Having made our bow we took leave, after thanking him for the polite and handsome reception he had given us, and we returned to our residence. In our progress to the Governor's palace and back, a great crowd of the populace followed us. Their conduct was lively and playful, but by no means disrespectful. The soldiers who accompanied us never interfered with them, as long as they took care not to mix with the procession; but whenever they did, the rattan was liberally applied, and the offenders retreated, generally with a hearty laugh.

We had scarcely reached home, when one of the principal Mandarins came with the compliments of the Governor, and a present of provisions. These consisted of a live buffalo, a hog, a quantity of poultry, rice, and fruit. This Mandarin informed us, that the Governor, though he could not publicly accept of any present, would be happy to accept privately of the pistols and telescope which we had offered. I returned my respects to say, that I should be happy to send them. They were not however taken; the Governor, in lieu of them, requesting we would send him some fine gunpowder, on our return to the ship, which was done. A little time after this, arrived, with great ceremony, a hog roasted whole, with a large quantity of dressed rice, another present from the Governor. This, according to the customs of the country, is considered a token of proffered friendship.

In the afternoon we took an early dinner with M. Diard, and viewed his collection of animals. From this gentleman we received many marks of civility and attention, during our short residence at Saigun. In the evening we went through the markets and town of Pingeh, for this is the proper name of the Governor's residence. The streets for an Indian town are wide and regular, and the bazars well supplied with every thing necessary to the comfort of the people according to their notions. We visited a pretty, gaudy, little Cochin Chinese temple, dedicated to the Chinese form of worship. We expected to have found many temples of Buddha, in a place so near to those countries where his religion is universal, but hitherto we had met none. As we passed along one of the streets in this excursion, our curiosity was excited by observing two persons in violent altercation. They were sitting upon the ground, and one had a hold of the waistband of the other from behind. This last was a woman, who charged her prisoner, an eunuch, as we were informed, with defrauding her of some property. This was according to a custom of the country. When one person charges another with an offence, he has only to lay hold of him or her by the waistband, and the law expects that the accused shall forthwith submit to this species of arrest without offering any resistance.

Sept. 3.—At six this morning, the hour appointed for our departure, every thing was ready for our accommodation, with a punctuality any thing but Oriental, and we left Saigun with the same number of boats and attendants with which we had come to it. The river of Saigun, which is called by the natives the Saong, does not appear to me to be quite so broad as the Menam, but it is broad enough for all useful purposes, and so deep and free from dangers every where, that the largest ships may go with perfect security up to the city, and much farther if it were necessary. Its banks, for twenty-five miles below the city, are one extensive sheet of rice cultivation, but from thence to the sea the water is salt, and unfit for irrigation or culture, and the country is extremely low, and covered by a forest of undersized trees, fit for no purpose but fire-wood. At eight o'clock we came to the mouth of the river which leads to Dong-nai, a considerable town about two days' journey from Saigun, which gives name to the whole province. The river of Dong-nai is navigable for vessels of considerable burden. About fifteen miles before coming to Kandyu, there is the mouth of another considerable river, to the same side which leads to a place called Bariya, towards the hills which are visible to the east. Here there are said to be manufactories of silk. We reached the ship between four and five o'clock, the whole voyage having taken up little more than ten hours, and having proved a very agreeable one. Neither in ascending nor descending the river did we observe any defences whatever. The smallest vessel of war might, therefore, go up to the city without a pilot, and destroy it without risk or opposition.

The city of Saigun is, as I think I have already mentioned, about fifty miles from the sea. The place consists of two distinct towns, at the distance of three miles from each other. Pingeh, the seat of the Governor and of the citadel, lies on the western bank of the great river, and Saigun, properly so called, is situated upon a small river, which communicates directly with Pingeh. Saigun is the principal seat of commerce, and the residence of the Chinese and other merchants, though the river on which it lies is navigable only for small craft, and the larger junks all lie before Pingeh. This seems to be a matter of very little inconvenience, where the navigation is always so sure and easy for cargo-boats. These two towns are nearly about the same size, but I could not gain any specific information respecting the amount of their population. During the period we were at Saigun, the whole of the junks for the northward and eastward were absent, having sailed on their respective voyages, and there remained only six junks for the Straits of Malacca and Siam. As we saw Bang-kok, it certainly presented a far busier scene of commerce than Saigun, and its actual commerce is indeed much superior. By the accounts we obtained at the latter place, the actual foreign commerce of the place amounts to no more than between 7 and 8000 tons.

The citadel of Saigun, or rather of Pingeh, is, in form, a parallelogram, distant from half a mile to three-quarters of a mile from the western bank of the river, the principal part of the town intervening. I conjecture, from appearance, that the longest side of the square may be about three-quarters of a mile in length. The original plan appears to have been European, but left incomplete. It has a regular glacis, an esplanade, a dry ditch of considerable breadth, and regular ramparts and bastions. With the exception of the four principal gateways, the whole of the fortress is constructed of earth, now covered every where with a green sward. There are no guns mounted any where, though there be several hundred lying in the arsenal. The gates consist of four large and as many small ones. The large gateways are built of stone and lime, and are very substantially constructed, although a Chinese tower, with a double-canopied roof gives them a grotesque and unmilitary appearance. The approach to them is by a zig-zag in the glacis, and they are connected with the counterscarp by a mound, without any drawbridge. The two angles of the fort which came within our view were protected by horn-works. The fortress, as it now stands, is not capable of regular defence. One angle of it approaches so near to the river, that a ship of war might breach it in a few hours. The interior is neatly laid out and clean, and presents an appearance of European order and arrangement. The principal buildings consist of the officers' quarters, barracks, arsenals, and the residence of the Governor. There is a good parade, and the place is not incumbered, as usually happens in Indian fortifications, with a motley assemblage of huts, sheds, and petty buildings. The late King made this place the seat of his Government during the rebellion, but on recovering the northern provinces he removed to the old capital.

Saigun proved to us a far more agreeable residence than Bang-kok, and I have no doubt that the character of the people, and the nature of the country itself, would always render it so to any European visitor. The average of the thermometer at noon, during our six days' stay, was 81°. Venomous and troublesome insects, the plague of all hot and low countries, are fewer at Saigun than it is easy to imagine in such a situation. We saw few ants or flies while we were there, and mosquitoes were so little troublesome that we might have slept with little inconvenience without gauze curtains. This could not be ascribed to the season, for it was the very height of the rains, when insects are always most abundant; nor to our situation, for we were upon the very banks of a canal which was always dry at low-water. The markets afford the necessaries and even comforts of life in great plenty and cheapness. For hogs and for poultry, the latter consisting of geese, ducks, and common fowls, the soil and climate appear to be peculiarly favourable. A hog weighing 200lb. may be had for seven Spanish dollars, which is less than twopence a pound; ducks and common fowls are found in greater perfection here than in any other part of India, being remarkable both for size and flavour. The first, which are in great demand among the Cochin Chinese themselves, may be had eight for a Spanish dollar; and of fowls, which are hardly ever eaten by the natives, twenty-four or twenty-five may be had for the same money. The latter are all of the game breed. The Cochin Chinese are great cock-fighters; his Excellency, the present Governor, fights cocks regularly twice a month, and invites the chiefs to be present. Goats are in considerable numbers, and the sheep, an animal which seldom thrives in the damp climates near the Equator, thrives tolerably at Saigun. The race is a small hardy breed, similar to that of Lower Bengal. They are much more cheap and abundant, however, I am given to understand, at Kang-kao in Kamboja than at Saigun. The buffalo and the ox are both of them very good and very cheap, and may be had in any quantity. The variety and the excellence of the fish can scarcely be equalled. Besides river-fish, great quantities of sea-fish are brought up fresh for the market of Saigun; the largest kind being conveyed by dragging them after the boats, and the smaller in wells in their bottoms. During our short stay, we were daily supplied from the ordinary markets, with the three best fish which the Indian seas afford, the cockup, the pomfret, and the mango fish, all exquisite in their kind. There are however, besides the articles now enumerated, others exhibited for sale in the market of Saigun, not so well suited to the European taste, such as the flesh of dogs and alligators. These, indeed, are in little esteem, and not eaten by persons of any consideration. The first day we arrived, we saw two whole alligators carried upon men's shoulders to the market, and afterwards frequently saw the flesh of this animal cut up in large junks, and exposed for sale in the stalls and booths. The price of rice, when we were at Saigun, was a dollar a picul. This was considered extravagantly high. For fruit, the season of our visit was the most unfavourable in all tropical countries to the north of the Equator. We found, however, abundance of oranges, and plenty of ordinary fruits, such as pumplenoses, bananas, and custard-apples. In their proper seasons, I am told, that the mango, the lichi, and orange, are in great perfection; but, upon the whole, Saigun, for variety of fruits, is far inferior to Bang-kok. Neither the mangostin nor the durian, so abundant in the Malay countries to the south of Saigun, and in Siam to the north of it, are found here. Whether this has arisen from carelessness, or real unsuitableness of soil and climate, we could not learn; but, in all probability, to the former.*

Sept. 4.—Early this morning, Antonio, the Portuguese interpreter, who had come down with us from Saigun, came on board, bringing us a small present of fruit from the Chief of Kandyu. He received a sum of money and a piece of cloth for his services. The amount of the donation, although far from extravagant, surprised him exceedingly; for persons in his situation are miserably rewarded in Cochin China. He begged for a certificate of his skill and good conduct, which he might present to English merchants frequenting the place; for on the visits of strangers, he said, his fortune depended. This favour was readily granted. He took this opportunity of informing us, that his pursuit was a very difficult and critical one, and that even since our arrival he had been in constant terror of the bamboo, which he complimented us by saying he had escaped through our discretion. When the two American ships visited Saigun about a year be-

* At Singapore we afterwards received occasional supplies from Saigun of the largest and finest oranges I ever saw.

fore, he told us he had received fifty strokes for an error in judgment respecting the delivery of a certain supply of rice to one of the ships in question.

At eight o'clock in the morning we set sail, and at ten passed Cape St. James with a strong and favourable breeze. When about two and a half miles to the east of it, and pursuing the course laid down in the common nautical directions, we came suddenly upon the edge of a sandbank and struck soundings in two and a half fathoms water, nearly the ship's draft. We immediately hauled up, and, steering a westerly course, were soon out of danger. This shoal is not laid down either in the charts of M. Dayot or Captain Ross. At night we had heavy squalls and much rain, and were, notwithstanding, compelled to pass through the channel between Cow Island and the De Brito Shoal. This last has its name from a Portuguese navigator, who suffered shipwreck upon it.

Cochin Chinese State Boat.

CHAPTER IX.

Voyage along the Coast of Cochin China.—Account of its Harbours.—Arrival in Touran Harbour.—Visit from the civil Mandarin of the place.—Description of the Town of Touran.—The Mission receives a Letter and Presents from the Governor of Fai-fo.—Visits made to the Villages in the neighbourhood of Touran.—Invitation to the Court.—Voyage to Hué, the Cochin Chinese Capital, and arrival there.

Sept. 5.—To-day, at noon, we were in latitude 11° 26′, after passing Cape Pandaran, considered the Cape of Good Hope of Cochin Chinese navigation, on account of the difficulty of weathering it, and the heavy sea which rolls in upon it, owing to its exposed situation, the coast immediately changing its direction after passing it, and trending suddenly to the north. All the way from Cape St. James, there was nothing but high coast, and many chains of mountains running in a north-east and south-west direction. The shores, in many situations, consist of sand-hills — the mountains are covered with a scanty forest, and the whole aspect of the coast is that of great sterility. Thus far the south-west monsoon blew strong and steady, and we sailed, with little exception, between eight and nine knots an hour, during the last twenty-four.

Sept. 6.—Yesterday afternoon we lost the monsoon, were becalmed at night—had a regular land-wind, and to-day a sea-breeze. The coast was here extremely bold, and the country as far as we could see very mountainous; the peaks of some hills appearing to be not short of three thousand feet high. The coast of Cochin China, after passing Cape Pandaran, becomes a great deal more broken and indented,—has small islands scattered along it, and abounds with ports and harbours, perhaps beyond any other country in the world. To-day, at noon, we were in latitude 12° 6′, having the bay of Ya-trang within a few miles of us. This, which is protected by the large island Tre, forms a good harbour. A river which falls into it, and is navigable for vessels drawing seven and eight feet water, conducts to the town of Ya-trang, which gives name to the bay. At this place the late King caused a fortification to be constructed, after the European manner, under the direction of M. Olivier, a French engineer. The place was besieged in the years 1794 and 1795, by the rebel brothers, the Tysuns, and relieved by the King's fleet, after a siege of six months. It is well situated, and commands the province of Ya-trang and the neighbouring ones. This place is the entrepôt of the commerce of all this part of the country, and the seat of considerable manufactories of silk. It is four days' long journeys by land from Saigun, and five from the capital.

Sept. 7.—Yesterday evening we passed the harbour of Kon-köe, represented by M. Dayot as a very fine one; but at which a few fishermen only reside. Early this morning, we were off Cape Varela, the most remarkable point of Cochin Chinese navigation. The mountain forming the Cape, seems to be between fifteen hundred and two thousand feet high. On one of the peaks is a remarkable rock, representing the appearance of a huge broken and falling column; which is seen from fifteen to eighteen leagues distant, either from the north or south. This mountain has the reputation of containing veins of silver, and is known to contain, at about half its height, a hot-spring of remarkably high temperature. Immediately after passing Cape Varela, the land recedes, and the coast is much less elevated. This recess forms the great bay of Fu-yin. In this bay is situated the finest port in all Cochin China, and which consists of three distinct harbours, all represented as excellent. The province of Fu-yin which gives name to the bay and port, is the finest in Cochin China. In entering the harbour, according to M. Dayot, the prospect is highly pleasing. The land is cultivated from the sea-side all the way to the tops of the hills, and the country every where interspersed with houses and cottages, giving to the whole the appearance of one extensive garden. From the rugged mountains with which the coast is bound, so rich a country could scarcely be looked for. Rice is the great object of culture in the province of Fu-yin, as, indeed, in every tropical country of the East distinguished for fertility. The town of Fu-yin is about four short days' journey by land from Hué. Our Chinese interpreter, who had travelled from Saigun to the capital, stated that the road from Fu-yin as far as Hué was excellent; but that that from Fu-yin to Saigun was mountainous and difficult.

We had now regular land and sea-breezes. Our latitude at noon was 13°. In the morning early, we could count, coasting close to the shore, thirteen small junks, of from five to seven hundred piculs burthen, returning, as we were informed, from the Capital to Saigun, after discharging their cargoes of rice, and other articles of revenue and contribution.

Sept. 8.—In the course of the night, we passed the harbour of Kwinnyon (Quin-hone,) about the latitude 13° 41′. This place is accessible only to vessels drawing no more than three or three and a-half fathoms water. Its principal protection is formed by a narrow tongue of land, about four miles in extent, which is fortified. Within fifteen miles of the port is a city of the same name, before the late rebellion a place of great trade. A river nearly connects it with the port, and a number of other small rivers fall into the latter, which give great facilities to the communication between the harbour and the country. Lying nearly in the centre of the kingdom, Kwin-nyon is looked upon as of much importance by the Cochin Chinese, but does not appear at present to be a place of any considerable trade. The vicinity is a country of extensive rice culture. M. Dayot informs us, that it was here, in the year 1792, that the late King obtained a signal and decisive victory over the rebel brothers, capturing six ships of war, ninety large galleys, and upwards of a hundred of inferior size, and three hundred and thirty-seven pieces of artillery, of which forty-six were good brass cannon. Kwin-nyon is three long days' journey by land from the Capital. The coast still preserved the same appearance of low hills after passing Varella Point, but appeared less rude and rugged than that to the south. Our latitude at noon was 14° 30′, nearly in the parallel of Tang-kwan, in the river of which the late King, in 1793, obtained another and final naval victory over the rebel brothers, capturing sixty galleys. Land and sea-breezes continued regularly.

Sept. 10.—We had nothing on the 8th and 9th but calms and light airs. We were to-day, at 12 o'clock, in the latitude of 15° 14′, in the channel between the main and Pulo Canton, called Callao Rai by the Cochin Chinese. This island appears to be about four miles in length, and consists of a tract of low land, with three distinct hills running through its length. It is, although apparently not rich, well cultivated, and well peopled. The appearance of the main-land is here much changed. There is an extensive tract of low land, interspersed with rising grounds between the sea and the high-land, and this last appears to be cultivated and inhabited. Nearer the shore there are extensive downs, with only a tuft of trees here and there. We counted off the coast, this morning, about ninety fishing-boats, all of good size, and under sail. This seemed to show that we were in the vicinity of a populous country.

Sept. 12.—Calms and light winds still continued to prevail. Last evening we passed through the cluster of islands called Cham Calao, which lie within a few miles of the point which forms the northern entrance of Touran harbour. This group consists of eight islands, of which one only is of considerable size, probably four miles in length. Their aspect is bold and barren, covered with a low wood, and exhibiting, both on the shore and throughout their surfaces, the huge bare masses of rock. All these islands are uncultivated, but in a bay lying on the south-west side of the great island, there is a small village of fishermen. A strong current running through the channel, between the Cham Islands and the main, and which was adverse to us, compelled us early at night to come to an anchor. At daylight this morning we weighed, and stood on our course. We counted forty fishing-boats which had come out of the river of Fai-fo as we ran close along the coast. These were of a different construction and equipment from the neater vessels which we had seen near Saigun. The latter had two masts, which raked much aft, and lug-sails; the former had three masts, with a small sail on each, and a fourth between the main and foremast.

Sept. 15.—Light airs and calms, and an adverse current running at the rate of three miles an hour, baffled all our efforts to gain the entrance of the harbour of Touran until yesterday afternoon, when a favourable sea-breeze of a few hours' continuance enabled us to accomplish our object. In the evening we anchored off the great cape which forms the southern entrance of the harbour. This morning being calm, a party landed to examine the coast, which was within a mile and a half of us. The ridge of mountains of which it is composed is not less than 1400 feet high, and its acclivity very steep. The shore itself is so bold, and the swell of the sea was so considerable, although a calm, that landing was a matter of some difficulty and even peril. No rock was to be seen but granite of a grey colour and small grained, exhibiting frequent embedded masses of mica and quartz. The forest which covers the mountains is very stunted, and fit for no purpose but fire-wood. A number of wood-cutters were close at hand, employed in felling it for this purpose, and several boats were loading with it on the coast. In a very short search we obtained a number of interesting and beautiful plants, differing entirely from what our travels had yet afforded us, and indicating plainly that we had arrived in a new vegetable zone. The sea-breeze sprung up about ten o'clock in the morning, and we got, with great facility, into the harbour, where we anchored between twelve and one o'clock. The harbour of Touran is spacious, secure, and easily defended. It is completely land-locked. Two-thirds of the circumference of the bay is formed by an amphitheatre of mountains, the feet of which are washed by the sea, and some of the peaks appear to be not less than 2000 feet high. To the south-east side alone the mountains are wanting, and here is the seat of culture and population, and where lies the arm of the sea or gullet which conducts to Fai-fo.

We saluted the fort, after anchoring, with

twenty-one guns, which was returned with three. At half-past two o'clock, a Mandarin came on board. This was the Civil Chief of the place. His appearance was respectable, and his manner unassuming. He informed us that he and the Military Mandarin were only deputies of the Governor of Fai-fo or rather Fuchim, for this last is the name of the chief town and province, and that it was necessary for him to make a report of our arrival to this officer; for which purpose he requested a list of the persons composing the Mission,—of the ships, crew, &c. The list had been prepared beforehand in Chinese, and was immediately put into his hands. The questions put by this visitor were neither numerous nor importunate. He wished to know, as others did, whether the Mission was from the King of England, or the Governor-general of India. We satisfied him upon this subject, and gave him a similar explanation to that which I had occasion to give at Saigun. He said, that in three days there would be an answer from the Governor of Fai-fo, and that he hoped in ten days more we should be invited to the Court. This person, who had visited China, spoke the Chinese dialect of the province of Canton fluently; and as our Chinese interpreter was a native of that part of China, we had an easy means of communicating with him.

Sept. 16.—M. Borel, a French gentleman, who

had a commercial establishment at Touran, and who, with his brother, were the only Europeans at the place, paid us a visit this forenoon. M. Borel informed us, that our visit to Saigun had been known for the last six days at Court, and that, of course, our arrival was every hour expected.

Sept. 19.—Yesterday forenoon we had a visit from the Civil Mandarin of Touran, the same person who had come on board the first day of our arrival. We thought he had brought some decisive answer from the Governor of Fai-fo; but the visit, ostensibly at least, was one of mere ceremony. He entered into very familiar converse with us, asking many questions respecting the ship, her cannon, equipment, &c. At his particular desire, he was shown every part of the vessel.

In consequence of an invitation from our visitor, I went on shore to-day with Mr. Finlayson and Mr. Rutherford, to pay him a visit. The village of Touran is a little way up the creek which leads to Fai-fo, on the right-hand as you enter it. At the angle formed between the sea and the river, there is a neat earthen redoubt; and on the opposite side, but a good way back, are two more. The ramparts of all these redoubts were manned with armed men—a spearman and a musqueteer being alternately posted. This was done in compliment to us. After being presented with a dessert of sweetmeats and tea, at the public hall where the Mandarin met us, we were sent with proper guides to see the village and its market. It is superior to what I expected, and is probably greatly improved since the time of Lord Macartney's visit, in 1793. The creek, on which it is situated, is about two hundred yards broad at its entrance, and probably half as much at the village. Within there is every where a sufficient depth of water; but it is obstructed at its mouth by a bar of sand, on which there is no more than six feet at the highest spring-tides, and it is often bare at low water. The whole of this part of the country, including the site of the village, is nothing but a plain of sand, over which there is here and there a little scanty soil. The place is dry, and, I should suppose, generally healthy; for there are no noisome mud flats, or other obvious sources of insalubrity, near it—the shore and even banks of the river consisting every where of nothing but hard, clean sand. The market appeared to be well supplied with every thing necessary to the comfort of the people. Fish, poultry, rice, pulses, and coarse tea, were in abundance. All the venders and the greater proportion of the buyers were women. Europeans are by no means such strangers here as at Saigun, and therefore our appearance excited no particular curiosity. The inhabitants were every where, however, remarkable for their civility and good humour. The distance from the village to the anchorage cannot be less than three miles; which is an inconvenience to trade. We now met no obstruction or inconvenience in our intercourse with the people, which was as unconstrained as we could desire. Fishing-boats were constantly alongside of the ship.

Sept. 20.—We received a message this morning from the Mandarin of Touran, informing us that a messenger had arrived from his principal, the Governor of Fai-fo, bearing a letter and present, and that he would come on board himself at noon to deliver both. He came accordingly at the hour promised, accompanied by three boats carrying the presents, which consisted of an ox, two hogs, a quantity of poultry, and an ample supply of fruit and vegetables. The letter was received with a salute of eleven guns. This compliment was due to the rank of the writer, who was Governor of an extensive province, and bore a high title. The Mandarin of Touran, after coming on deck, put on his gown of ceremony at the gangway, before he would advance to deliver the letter. After this preparation, he strutted forward with it with much formality. The letter simply announced the presents, and felicitated us upon our safe arrival. A verbal message from the Governor of Faifo, was now communicated. We were requested by it to communicate in writing our desire to visit the Court, and to state in a few words the nature of our business. This was done immediately in a letter, in the Chinese and English languages, addressed to the Governor of Faifo, and the Mandarin of Touran, at his own request, stayed to receive it. We were asked, during this visit, whether our Embassy was undertaken with the knowledge of the King of England, or otherwise. I explained again, in answer to this, that every act of our Government was with the virtual knowledge of His Majesty the King, and had the sanction of our laws. The Mandarin left us at three o'clock, after passing several hours in the same social and easy manner as at his former visits.

Sept. 22.—We were now daily in the habit of making excursions on shore, and, wherever we met the natives, were invariably treated with kindness and attention by them. We seldom passed through a village without being invited into some house or another, and requested to partake of tobacco and betel. This morning we visited some of the villages situated on the narrow isthmus which divides the bay of Touran from that of Fai-fo. The soil is scarcely any thing but sand, and yet the cultivation exhibits considerable appearance of industry. The villages have a remarkably neat and clean appearance, to which, I have no doubt, the nature of the soil contributes perhaps still more than the habits of the people. There is, however, an appearance of real comfort and plenty,—at least we no where observed any traces of abject poverty or want. The culture of silk has extended even to this arid spot. In one house which we visited to-day, we observed several baskets full of cocoons, and others in which the worms were feeding upon the leaf of the mulberry, of which there were several fields in the vicinity. Returning home, we passed through an extensive burying-ground, among the sand hills, close to the shore. The tombs consisted of mere tumuli of loose sand surrounded by a circular trench. A great number of the graves were open, for, it seems, it is the custom of the Cochin Chinese, after the body has been three years interred, to disinhume the bones, and remove them to another situation, close to their dwellings, the ground in which they are then deposited being in a great measure viewed as a place of worship.

Sept. 23.—I made an excursion this morning to a village, which is the first stage from Touran to the capital, and distant from the common anchorage about six miles. It is situated in a beautiful little cove, on the west side of the bay. This place is of considerable extent, very neat, clean, and supplied with a good market.

For the accommodation of travellers of rank, that is, of public officers, but particularly of the Sovereign himself, there is here a spacious and handsome house, after the Cochin Chinese fashion, capable of affording room to several hundred persons. It is in the centre of a square fort, of from one hundred and forty to one hundred and fifty paces to a side, having a glacis, a ditch, and a rampart, but no bastions. This little fortification is very neatly constructed, every part of it being cased or paved with round stones. The gates were open, and we entered without any obstruction. We at first saw nobody, and thought the place uninhabited, until we stumbled by accident upon two persons wrapped up in mats, and fast asleep. These were the sentinels, or watchmen, who had charge of the place! Going into the environs of the village, we there found the whole male population of the place occupied in hunting the wild hog. They were all armed with spears, and accompanied by dogs, these being common curs, such as are found in numbers in every part of the East. Their object was to insulate a woody promontory, which composes one side of the little bay; and for this purpose they were affixing nets, consisting of thongs of buffalo-hide, to stakes driven in the ground. In the mean time, a great number of persons were engaged in beating up the wood and alarming the game with dogs, horns, and incessant shouting. They received us with their usual good humour.

In the evening, as we were sitting down at dinner, our former visitor, the Civil Chief of Touran, came on board, without having previously given any notice of his visit. He came, he said, to inform us, that a Mandarin had arrived at Touran, with an invitation to us from the King to go up, and with two galleys, of forty oars each, for our accommodation. He explained, that he was charged to inform us, that the number of persons of our party who could be conducted to the Court, could not in all exceed twelve individuals. We informed him, that our party consisted of more than four times this number; and that leaving our servants and escorts behind, would be extremely inconvenient as well as contrary to usage. He answered, that the orders from Court were peremptory, and that he was convinced the deputy dared not depart from them; and he insisted that neither the Embassy from Siam, nor the French Mission, had been so well accommodated. I had nothing to offer in reply to this last circumstance, because I was possessed of no information on the subject. In the evening we sent our interpreter on shore, to remonstrate on this topic with the Mandarin, who had arrived from Hué.

Sept. 24.—Our interpreter returned this morning, with a message from the deputy from Hué, to say that he regretted he could not depart from the orders he had received with respect to the numbers of our party who were to proceed to Court. It was useless to offer any resistance; and, making therefore a merit of complying promptly, we sent word that we should be ready to start on our journey at two o'clock. The two galleys were alongside precisely at that hour—the Cochin Chinese exhibiting in this, as on many other occasions, a degree of promptitude and punctuality rarely, if ever, shown among an Eastern people, and which, I think, must always be looked on, where it is found, as indicating a certain advance in civilization. The Deputy was a military Mandarin, and of the rank of "Commander of 2000." A number of inferior Mandarins accompanied him. He was received with a salute of thirteen guns. Our visitor was a man of sixty-five years of age, a hale and active person, above the usual stature of the Cochin Chinese, and of a manly and striking deportment. His manner was very frank and cheerful. He ran over every part of the ship with the activity and curiosity of a young man, and nothing escaped his notice. A little after him, the civil Mandarin of Touran came on board. After a great deal of discussion, they agreed to augment our party to fifteen, including the crew of the ship's launch, which was allowed to accompany us to convey our baggage. During this conversation, I happened to say, that I did not suppose that two or three individuals, more or less, would be considered of any moment by the Court. The Mandarins answered, that they did not know how it might be in our country, but that the slightest deviation from the express order of the Sovereign was looked upon in Cochin China as a crime deserving the severest punishment; and they gave us plainly to understand, that if they complied with our wishes, the least risk they ran would be to receive the bastinado.

At six o'clock we left the ship; Mr. Finlayson alone accompanied me, it being impracticable, from the restricted numbers, that Captain Dangerfield or Mr. Rutherford should proceed. During our voyage, we had an opportunity of examining our conveyances, and observing the discipline of the crews. These galleys are the regular war-boats of the King; they were each not less than ninety feet long, but very narrow in proportion; they were strongly built, and their rigging consisted of two lug-sails; they had each five large swivels, as handsomely cast and modelled as any European cannon, but they were intended to carry many more. Their crew consisted of forty rowers, besides the commander and officers, all well and uniformly clothed. The discipline preserved on board was more strict and regular than I could have imagined: the rowers plied incessantly and in perfect unison—an officer beating time by striking against each other two cylindrical sticks of sonorous wood, and cheering them with a song.

All communication between one galley and another was made by sound of trumpet; and while lying at anchor, a regular watch was kept, and the sentries challenged at intervals. Every soldier is supplied with a pair of the sonorous sticks which I have just mentioned, and with these the challenge is given and answered by the sentinels.

The low coast as we went along appeared to be nothing but a series of sand-hills, and the mountains to be of the same granite as we noticed along the rest of the coast. The weather we experienced was remarkably fine.

Sept. 25.—About two o'clock we arrived at the mouth of the river of Hué. Pilot-boats were in readiness to conduct us in, and the commander of the fort came out to compliment us upon our arrival. The breadth of the river at its mouth is no more than four hundred yards. On the right-hand going up, is a strong fort which completely commands the entrance of the river. It is of a quadrangular form, with a regular glacis and ditch. The rampart is neatly constructed of stone and lime, and the cannon mounted upon it in barbette, or without embrasures or parapet. In compliment to us, the walls as we passed along were manned with troops in regular scarlet uniforms, and amounting, as we were told, in number to three hundred. This, with the look of the little fortress itself, rising green amongst the sand-hills, made a very pretty appearance. At half-past two, we anchored a little beyond the fort. At this place, the river, receiving a great number of tributary streams at its western bank, is greatly increased in breadth, and forms an extensive basin and good harbour, nearly landlocked by the narrowness of the mouth and the bend which the river immediately makes. The river of Hué is fitted only for ships of a small draft of water. At high-water spring-tides, there are no more than nine Cochin Chinese cubits on the bar, which make exactly twelve feet six and three-quarter inches. The breadth of the bar, which is hard sand, is ten fathoms and the channel through it is no more than thirty fathoms broad. There seems, however, for vessels of small burden, no great difficulty. Three years ago, the *Henri*, a French ship drawing twelve feet, came over the bar without inconvenience. Out and inside of the bar there are four fathoms and a half water, sufficient for ships of almost any burden. A heavy surf rolls in, on both sides of the river, even in the most moderate weather, such as we now experienced; and at the height of the N.E. monsoon, the roadstead being totally exposed, there must always be a heavy and dangerous sea on the bar.

The spot we were now at, was the scene of the misfortunes of our predecessor, Mr. Chapman, the agent of Mr. Hastings, who was deputed for a similar object with our own. From real or imaginary fears of treachery on the part of the Government, then in the hands of the Tonquinese, he suddenly fled from Hué, and escaped on board his little bark, which lay where our galleys were now anchored. Hostilities commenced between him and some batteries upon the shore; and after more than twenty days of a perilous and unequal contest, at the height of the N.E. monsoon, when it was most difficult to get out of the river, he at last succeeded, by a fortunate slant of fair wind, in crossing the bar and effecting his escape. Besides his own interesting narrative of this event, I have had an account of the transaction from an eye-witness, one of his companions, the Chinese Lao Ami, a respectable and well-known inhabitant of Prince of Wales's Island, whom I have mentioned in another place.

In consequence of our launch not having arrived, our conductor dare not go up the river without first obtaining leave. This detained us until nine o'clock at night, when a despatch-boat sent up returned with orders for our galley to proceed, but for the Mandarin to wait the arrival of the launch. We reached the city about twelve o'clock at night. The river continues of a considerable size throughout, being little inferior in breadth to that of Saigun, or to the Menam at Bang-kok, but it is very shallow.

CHAPTER X.

Visit from the Intendant of the Port.—The Mission lands, and is placed in a state of surveillance.—Discussion respecting the letter from the Governor-general to the King.—Mission jealously watched by the officers of Government.—Visit to the Mandarin of Elephants, or Foreign Minister, and account of the discussion which took place with him.—Mission refused an audience of the King.—Visit to the fortifications of Hué, and description of them.—Visits to the two French Mandarins.—Posthumous honours paid to civil and military officers of distinction.—Negociations continued.—Excursions in the environs of Hué.—Royal Mausoleum.—Temples of Gautama.—Collation sent by the King to the Mission.—Negociations.—Cochin Chinese cookery.— Opinion of Chinese residents respecting Cochin Chinese Government.—French Mission to Cochin China.—Another visit to the Foreign Minister, and discussions which ensued.—Commencement of the monsoon with a gale of wind and heavy fall of rain, which inundates the town of Hué.—Visit from the two principal assistants of the Foreign Minister, and discussion with them.—Final visit to the Foreign Minister, and termination of the negociation. Striking circumstance, in illustration of Cochin Chinese manners.

Sept. 26.—AT six in the morning, one of the royal galleys came alongside, with the Intendant of the Port and other Mandarins on board, to invite us on shore. A house was prepared for us quite close to the place where we anchored, and we landed immediately. Our accommodation was very good, according to the habits of the people. The house was tiled, and consisted of ten apartments, constructed of substantial wood upon a well-raised terrace, with abundance of office-houses. There was a court-yard in front. One side of the house looked towards the river, and the other towards one of the principal streets of the town. At both these quarters, from which alone ingress or egress was practicable, there was raised for the occasion a stockade of bamboos, and a strong party of not less than an hundred men was directed to guard, or rather to watch us;—in a word, we were, for the time at least, state prisoners. The Intendant of the Port waited upon us immediately, and told us he was requested by the Mandarin of Strangers to receive the letter of the Governor-general and the translations. I made no hesitation in complying with this demand, and immediately produced the letter itself,—a correct Portuguese translation made at Calcutta, and a translation in the Chinese language made by Mr. Marshman, the learned missionary of Serampore. The only questions now asked respecting the letter or Mission were—whether the Governor of Lower Cochin China had actually seen the Governor-general's letter to the

King; and whether the letter itself was written with the knowledge of the King of England. The Intendant of the Port required of us, in civil terms, not to go beyond our house, or pass the sentinels of our guard, until the letter of the Governor-general was approved of by the King — this being the invariable usage of the Court, with regard to all missions from foreign countries.

About noon an officer came with a letter from the Mandarin of Elephants. He brought a quantity of provisions and thirty quans* in money. This last we were compelled to accept to avoid giving umbrage, which a refusal would unquestionably have done. The intention of the money, it was said, was to obviate the necessity of our servants going to market where there might be a risk of disputes with the inhabitants.

The Mandarin of Touran, who left that place the same night we did, and made his journey by land, arrived at the capital this morning, and paid us a visit. He had been directed to repair here on our account.

Sept. 27.—Shortly after breakfast, the Intendant of the Port and other Mandarins called with the Chinese translation of the Governor-general's letter. They informed us, that the translation which we had furnished to the Governor

* About fifteen Spanish dollars, in a miserable coin composed of zinc.

of Saigun was correct in its style, but that the present one was very objectionable; as, besides other errors, the Governor-general there claimed an equality of rank with the King of Cochin China. They admitted that the letter was good Chinese, but that the etiquette of the Court was greatly violated in it. It was stated in reply, that in the English letter the style was unequivocally respectful, and such as the Governor-general would have used in addressing his own Sovereign; beyond which, nothing farther could reasonably be expected from him. The alterations now required in the Chinese translation, however, were not material, and therefore submitted to without difficulty. The same objections were made here, as at Saigun, to our disclaiming any wish to possess forts or territory; and the expression in the Governor-general's letter, mentioning the death of the late King, was considered improper. His Majesty, it was observed, ought to have been represented as not dead, but merely gone to Heaven! The Mandarins, who had the conduct of this business, were not less fastidious, or less troublesome, in matters of minute detail, than their brethren at Saigun. They insisted that our interpreter should transcribe every word of the copies taken *in his own handwriting*, and that the documents should be signed by him as well as both signed and sealed by myself. This tedious matter occupied from ten in the morning to five in the evening, when the Mandarins left us apparently satisfied.

Sept. 28.—In our new residence we found ourselves treated with perfect respect, but we were close prisoners. Interpreters and Cochin Chinese servants were always at hand to do every office for us, but our Indian servants were not allowed to move beyond the doors without two or three persons to watch them, and this only once or twice in the course of the day. A singular exception was made in favour of our Chinese attendants. These were permitted to go abroad with entire freedom, and no suspicions entertained of them, any more than if they had been natural-born subjects of Cochin China itself. It is obvious from this, that all intercourse between European nations ought to be conducted through the instrumentality of the Chinese, and that the greater number of these people there are attached to an European mission, the fewer obstacles it will be likely to encounter.

A singular mixture of jealousy and respect was observed to us in this early stage of our intercourse with the Cochin Chinese Court. While we were not permitted to go beyond the threshold of our doors, an order was given, that all persons on horseback should dismount as they passed our dwelling, out of compliment to us, or rather, in all probability, in consequence of our being supposed to be under the immediate protection of the King; and it was expressly forbidden to any one to stand and gaze at us from the street. The bastinado was liberally applied to the passengers, in execution of these orders; and, for neglect of duly enforcing them, seven soldiers of the guard received fifteen strokes apiece this morning. The punishment, in such cases, follows the sentence and offence, with a rapidity truly summary. A sentinel, for example, neglects to strike his rattle when challenged with military promptitude; the officer comes out, throws him down upon his face, and forthwith gives him ten or more strokes of the bastinado! The former, by a prostration, acknowledges his obligations for the parental correction, and the business is ended. The military men are so regularly broken in to the bastinado, that they receive it without a murmur. When the seven soldiers, already alluded to, for example, were flogged, they threw themselves down upon their faces, and received the strokes of the bamboo as a mere matter of course,—duly making a low obeisance to the officer who directed the punishment, when it was over. The civil classes do not seem to be just so well trained, and, as we had ourselves an opportunity of observing, never failed to make some resistance, and occasionally an effectual one. Slight corporal punishments appeared to be carried inexorably into effect. One of the interpreters, detected in imposing upon our servants in the purchase of some trifling articles, was sentenced to receive ten strokes of the bamboo. We were informed of this, and requested, for our satisfaction, to send a person to see the sentence put into effect. We begged that no such chastisement should be inflicted upon our account, stating that the matter in question was not of the slightest moment; but our remonstrances were of no avail, and the punishment was duly inflicted; while the culprit was admonished, that the next offence would be punished by the infliction of the *cangue*, or, "wooden ruff."

It may indeed be said, that the Cochin Chinese are a well-flogged nation; and one might expect that the universality of this brutal system would render them not only servile, obsequious and cowardly, but also timid, gloomy and suspicious: but, in the latter respect at least, the case is quite the contrary; and the lower orders of the Cochin Chinese, as far as we could judge from outward appearance, seemed to be vain, cheerful, good-humoured, obliging and civil, beyond all Asiatic people whom we had seen.

Sept. 29.—The Intendant of the Port, and other Mandarins, called yesterday, requesting two additional copies of the Chinese translation of the Governor-general's letter, which were accordingly given, and they presented to us the compliments of the Mandarin of Elephants, saying that he would be prepared to receive us about ten o'clock, if we would favour him with a visit. We agreed to do so; and an accommodation galley being sent for us, Mr. Finlayson and I left our dwelling about half-past twelve. The Mandarin's residence is situated above the new fortress, or rather fortified city, on the banks of a highly picturesque and beautiful reach of the river; and our journey occupied near an hour and a half, being principally along two faces of the fortress. M. Chaigneau and M. Vanier, two French gentlemen who had the rank of Mandarins at the Court, met us as we landed, and accompanied us to the dwelling of the Minister. We found this personage seated in an open hall of great size. A crowd of people surrounded the place, but there were no persons of any distinction within, and the upper end of the hall was occupied by the preparations for a Chinese drama. It was hung with some Chinese pictures, and there were a few English prints representing naval actions. The place, although spacious, had but a mean, unfinished look, and, in point of neatness and comfort, was very inferior, indeed, to the habitations of those chiefs whom we visited at Siam. Its only handsome ornament was a large board of ebony, on which were written some Chinese characters, every one of which was not less than eight or nine inches in length. These were raised upon the wood, and formed of mother-of-pearl, constituting a brilliant and beautiful piece of mosaic. This was suspended over the place where the Minister usually sat.

The Minister, a little, lively old man, dressed in a rich habit of orange-coloured silk, covered with flowers and devices, received us with great politeness. We made a bow to him, and were requested to occupy a bench prepared for our accommodation beforehand. The French Mandarins sat on chairs on each side of us. The Cochin Chinese Minister began the conversation by apologizing for the trouble he had given in requiring so many copies of the Chinese translation of the Governor-general's letter, and then desired to know if we had any request to make verbally beyond what was contained in that document. We said, that we had no request whatever to make, except what was connected with the subject of the Governor-general's letter; and added, that since arriving in Cochin China, we were given to understand, that new and liberal regulations upon the subject of foreign commerce had been promulgated, which appeared to be entirely satisfactory; and that we wished to be furnished with official copies of the regulations in question. The Minister answered, that he was authorized by the King to communicate to us, that the request made by the Governor-general of India was acceded to; and that English ships would be admitted freely to trade in the King's dominions. He added, that a copy of the new regulation for foreign trade was already prepared for us, and would be sent without delay. On this subject he observed, that he farther pledged himself personally to use every means in his own power to insure despatch in the transaction of the business of such British merchant-ships as might visit Cochin China. He also said, that an answer to the letter of the Governor-general would be given before our departure, and indeed as soon as required. In alluding to the imports upon foreign trade, he observed, "In England, imposts are no doubt levied upon foreign commerce, as here; every nation has a right to do this, for its own benefit."

The Minister now stated, that in the letter of the Governor-general mention was made of certain presents for the King, and that they were specified in a communication from the Governor of Saigun. He wished to be more particularly informed on this subject. The necessary information was given, and the presents mentioned. He requested to be furnished with a written list of them, that he might lay it before His Majesty. This was supplied on our return home in the evening. The Minister, as if he wished to consider every thing as now settled, requested to know if we wished to gratify our curiosity by seeing the city and its environs,—observing, that when we desired to go abroad, he should be ready to supply us with barges or palanquins, as might be most suitable to the places we intended to visit. No notice having been taken of introducing us into the presence of the King, and it being evident that this was intentional, I now pointedly brought the subject forward, and desired to know whether a day had been appointed for granting us an audience. The Minister answered, that the subject of our Mission being a commercial one, it was not customary for the King, on such occasions, to grant an audience. It was stated, in answer, that it was true that one great purpose of the Mission was commercial, but that it had also for its object to congratulate the King upon his accession to the throne. The Chief shifted his ground, and said, that, according to the custom of the country, audiences were only granted by His Majesty to the bearers of letters from Kings; and that if the letter had been from the King of England, there could have been no question about an audience. The Governor-general, he was aware, he said, was the viceroy of a great country, but he was not a sovereign prince. I observed, in answer, that the Governor-general of India was in habits of direct correspondence with the first princes of the East, into whose presence his representatives were always received. It was also stated, that the present Mission had had an audience of the King of Siam a few months ago. To this he replied promptly, "What is done in Siam is no rule for this country." I added, on this subject, that it was so far from contrary, even to the customs of Cochin China itself, that His Majesty's father had granted two audiences to the representative of the Governor-general of India, no longer ago than eighteen years, and at a time when our Indian empire was neither so great nor powerful as at present. Upon this, I brought to his notice the circumstances connected with the Mission of Mr. Roberts, deputed by the Marquis of Wellesley, in 1804. The old Chief stated, that he remembered the circumstance well, and he intrepidly asserted that Mr. Roberts was never admitted to an audience. I was aware that M. Vanier, who sat at my right hand, had received Mr. Roberts at Touran, and that he must, therefore, have been present either at the audience or at the capital, at the moment of Mr. Robert's visit; and therefore I referred to him. M. Vanier stated, that he was sick at the time, and not actually present at the audience, but that there was no question of Mr. Roberts having had an audience of the King. This was explained to the Mandarin, who was once more compelled to change his ground; and now stated, what was perhaps nearer the truth, that the customs of the country, in this respect, had been changed by his present Majesty, whose policy, in all such matters, differed widely from that of his father. We afterwards indeed learned, that, since his accession the Court etiquette had, in every way, become more ceremonious and uncomplying, and that it was the great ambition of the King to mimic the ceremonial of the Court of Pekin. I finally requested the Minister to represent to His Majesty our desire to have the honour of an audience. He endeavoured, for some time, to evade this demand; but at last assented to convey our request, promising that we should have an answer on the following day.

In the course of this last part of the conversation, the national vanity of the Cochin Chinese, and the exalted opinion they entertain of themselves and their Sovereign, were sufficiently conspicuous. "It is natural enough," said the Mandarin, with a smile, "that you should employ every expedient in your power to attain the honour of being presented to so great a King."

During our visit, a handsome entertainment of meat, fruits, and wine, was served to us; and while the Chinese drama was acting, the Chief affably explained the most striking parts of it. This audience lasted from two to near six o'clock, and we returned home by the opposite walls of the new city from those by which we had proceeded, so that in going and coming we made the whole circuit of it. This was no doubt done to give us an opportunity of admiring this splendid and extraordinary work, to which I do not imagine there is any thing parallel in the East.

Sept. 30.—Notice was sent to us yesterday forenoon, that an accommodation-barge would be sent, to take us to whatever part of the city we wished to visit, and that the French Mandarins would accompany us. At three o'clock MM. Chaigneau and Vanier accordingly waited upon us, and said that they had orders from the King to conduct us into the new city, and to show us the works. We ascended the river, and landed on the west side of the new fortification, or walled city, where we found a Cochin Chinese Mandarin waiting to receive us.

The new city, which is of a quadrangular form, is completely insulated, having the river on two sides of it, and a spacious canal of from thirty to forty yards broad on the other two. The circumference of the walls, or of the city, which is the same thing, is upwards of five miles. The form of the fortification is nearly an equilateral quadrangle, each face measuring 1180 toises. The late King himself was the engineer who formed the plan, under the instructions and advice, however, of the French officers in his service, but whose personal assistance he had lost, before he commenced the undertaking, in the year 1805. This singular man proves to have been no mean proficient in this branch of European military science; for the works, as far as we could judge, are planned and constructed on technical rules, and the materials and workmanship are not inferior to the design. The fortress has a regular and beautiful glacis, extending from the river or canal to the ditch; a covert way all round; and a ditch which is thirty yards broad, with from four to five feet water in it, all through. The rampart is built of hard earth, cased on the outside with bricks. Each angle is flanked by four bastions, intended to mount thirty-six guns a-piece, some in embrasures, and some in *barbette*. To each face there are also four arched gateways of solid masonry, to which the approach across the ditch is by handsome arched stone-bridges. The area inside is laid out into regular and spacious streets, at right angles to each other. A handsome and broad canal forms a communication between the river and the fortress, and within is distributed by various branches, so as to communicate with the palace, the arsenal, the granaries, and other public edifices. By this channel the taxes and tributes are brought from the provinces, and conducted at once to the very doors of the palace or magazines. The palace is situated within a strong citadel, consisting of two distinct walls, or ramparts.

Within this we were not invited; but the roof of the palace itself was distinguishable by its yellow colour; and one handsome temple, consecrated to the royal ancestors of the King, was also noticed. This last, which has no priests attached to it, was the only place of worship within the new city.

In the whole of this extensive fortification, there is scarcely any thing slovenly, barbarous, or incomplete in design. Perhaps the only exceptions are the Chinese umbrella-shaped towers over the gates, and the embrasures of one or two of the bastions finished by his present Majesty, and in which he has taken it into his head to invert the rule of science and common sense, by making the embrasures to slope inwards instead of outwards. The banks of the river and canal forming the base of the glacis, are not only regularly sloped down every where, but wherever the work is completed, for it is still unfinished in a few situations, they are cased from the foundation with a face of solid masonry. The canal within the walls is executed in the same perfect and workmanlike manner; and the bridges which are thrown over it, have not only neat stone balustrades, but are paved all over with marble brought from Tonquin.

The first object in the interior to which our curiosity was particularly pointed, was the public granaries. These form ranges of enormous length in regular order, and are full of corn, being said to contain many years' consumption for the city. It has been the practice of the late and present King, to add two or three ranges of granaries every year to the number. The pernicious custom of hoarding grain against years of scarcity, and the unavoidable effect of which is to aggravate, or even to create, the evil it is intended to obviate, seems to be a received and popular maxim of Cochin Chinese government. It has its use in maintaining the tyranny of a despotic government.

The barracks were the next object pointed out to us, and here we found the troops drawn out. These buildings are excellent, and, in point of arrangement and cleanliness would do no discredit to the best organized army in Europe. They are extensive, and surround the whole of the outer part of the citadel. We were informed that from twelve to thirteen thousand troops were constantly stationed at the capital.

The most extraordinary spectacle was still to be exhibited—the arsenal. A violent fall of rain, and night coming on, prevented us from inspecting the whole of this; but what we did see, was more than sufficient to excite our surprise and gratify our curiosity. The iron cannon were first pointed out to us, consisting of an extraordinary assemblage of old ship-guns of various European nations—French, English, Dutch, and Portuguese. These were objects of little curiosity compared with the brass ordnance, the balls, and shells, all manufactured in Cochin China, by native workmen, from materials supplied by Tonquin, and after French models. The ordnance consisted of cannon, howitzers and mortars. The carriages were all constructed, finished, and painted, as substantially and neatly as if they had been manufactured at Woolwich or Fort William, and the field-carriages especially were singularly neat and handsome. The cannon are of various calibres, from four to sixty-eight pounders, with a large proportion of eighteen pounders. Among them were nine remarkable guns cast by the late King; these carry each a ball weighing seventy Chinese catties, or, in other words, are ninety-three pounders; they are as handsomely modelled and as well founded as any of the rest, and placed upon highly ornamented carriages. On these remarkable pieces of ordnance is inscribed the name of the late King, Ja-lung, and the day and year in which they were cast. The King used to say that these would prove the most durable monuments of his reign—no great compliment to his administration.

The art of casting good brass cannon, under the direction of Europeans, appears to have been long known in this part of the world, for among the cannon in the arsenal were a good number of very well founded ordnance, apparently of the size of ong nine-pounders, as old as the years 1664 and 1665. These had an inscription in the Portuguese language, importing that they were cast in Cochin China, or Kamboja, and bearing the dates in question, with the name of the artist. Although very inferior indeed to those recently cast under the direction of the French, still they were very good specimens of workmanship. The balls and shells in the arsenal throughout were neatly piled up, and arranged in the European method: the gun-carriages were all painted, and in short the arsenal was in the most perfect and complete order in all its organization.

The chief of the artillery had been directed to exhibit the whole of it to us, and we found him waiting for us on our arrival. This was one of the old warriors of the late King, a venerable and fine-looking old man, habited in a rich suit of velvet. Besides being chief of the arsenal and artillery, this Master General of the ordnance, was also intendant of the household, and in this last situation, according to all accounts, was charged with certain details scarcely compatible with his military character. It was his business, for example, to superintend the royal kitchen, and to make a registry of all the pregnancies and births within the seraglio, that all possible care might be taken to exclude illegitimacy from its sacred enclosures.

The whole of the cannon within the fortified city are not only raised on platforms to protect the carriages from damp, but placed for security against the weather in the arsenal; and there is not one mounted upon the works, with the exception of a few upon the walls of the citadel. The cannon, it is said, which are required for the sixteen bastions, amount to five hundred and seventy-six, and for the whole of the works the requisite number is about eight hundred. I do not know what the exact number in the arsenal is, but it probably far exceeds this amount.

The powder magazine is constructed with the same intelligence as the rest of the works: it is fenced by a strong wall, and has a broad and deep ditch completely surrounding it. Close to it is an extensive parade, for the exercise of the troops.

It is hardly necessary to say, that against an Asiatic enemy this fortification is impregnable: its great fault is its immense extent. I presume, it would require an army of 50,000 men at least, to defend it;—a force which would be far more effectually employed in harassing an European enemy, (the only enemy to be apprehended,) by those common desultory modes of warfare, which it is alone safe for an Asiatic enemy to oppose to a disciplined army. An European force, either by making regular approaches, or by a bombardment, could not fail to render itself soon master of the place; and this occurrence, by putting it in possession of the treasure, the granaries, and principal arsenal of the kingdom,—by destroying the principal army, and thus cutting off all the resources of the Government,—would be virtually equivalent to conquering the kingdom at a single blow. We did not reach our residence till eight o'clock at night,—well drenched and fatigued, but highly gratified at the novel and striking scene which we had witnessed.

M. Vanier called upon us to-day, and we accompanied him on a visit to his house. M. Vanier is the senior French Mandarin,—a gentleman of pleasing manners, and of much practical information respecting Cochin China, in which he had now resided thirty-three years. He was an officer in the King's marine;—served in the whole of his wars, and now held a high rank and title. In his youth, he served in the French navy, and was present with the combined French and American army, to which Lord Cornwallis surrendered at Little York, as well as in the action between the Comte de Grasse and Lord Rodney. He had prints of the battle of the 12th of April on the walls of his room, and dwelt upon its details,—pointing out how the French ought to have won it, and how they lost it through the errors of their commander, and the superior skill of the English admiral.

M. Vanier told us that he and M. Chaigneau

had been sent for in the morning by the King, for the express purpose of being asked what opinions we had given respecting the new fortifications and other public works; and that he was gratified when he understood that we had expressed great surprise and admiration at all we saw. In the course of conversation, he dwelt upon the jealousy and apprehension which the extensive conquests of the British in India had excited among the Cochin Chinese and other nations of the farther East. In reference to the Mission of Mr. Roberts, in 1805, he remarked upon the indiscretion of some of the presents offered by us, stating that one of them was a series of prints representing the capture of Seringapatam, and the death of Tippoo Sultaun!! When the late King saw these, he said, "The Governor-general of India wishes to intimidate me, by exhibiting to me the fate of this Indian prince."

Oct. 1.—We called this morning upon M. Chaigneau, the other French Mandarin. This gentleman had been twenty-eight or twenty-nine years in the country. He returned to France in 1819, and came back with the appointment of Consul-general for Cochin China, from the French Court We did not find M. Chaigneau at home; he had been summoned to a council by the King, but we were received by his son and nephew—the latter an intelligent young man, lately come from France. In company with these gentlemen, we visited the great market, which appeared to be well stocked with all the usual articles of native consumption.

Returning home, there was pointed out to us, but we were not allowed to visit them, some singular temples on the western side of the river. These, which I think were six in number, and constructed of stone and lime, with tiled roofs, were surrounded by an extensive wall of masonry and appeared altogether neat and spacious. They compose a sort of pantheon, built by the late Emperor, and consecrated to the manes of departed Mandarins of the military class. There is a similar group farther up the river, consecrated to the souls of worthies of the literary or civil order.

In these temples the bodies are not buried, and nothing more is done than dedicating a small pillar to each of the departed, on which his name is inscribed. These cenotaphs have no priests, and are kept constantly shut, except on the annual festival set aside for the performance of religious honours to the souls of deceased ancestors. Among the heroes whose names are honoured with a monument in the military cenotaph, are a Frenchman and an Irishman. The first was a corporal, of the name of Manuel, who blew himself up in a small vessel, when about to fall into the hands of the Tysons. Our countryman was an officer, —a person of great gallantry, and a favourite of the King, but I could not learn his name. The King was desirous of giving an eminent place in the literary cenotaph to the soul of the Bishop of Adran, and spoke to him on the subject;—but the catholic prejudices of the latter revolted against it; and it was one of his dying requests, that this pagan compliment might not be paid to his memory. The Bishop is buried within four miles of Saigun, at which place he died in 1799. A handsome monument was erected to him, at which, during the life-time of the late King, a guard of two hundred soldiers kept constant watch. We were not acquainted with this circumstance, when we were at Saigun, or we should certainly have paid our respects at the tomb of so remarkable a person.

Oct. 2.—Shortly after our return home from our excursion yesterday, the Intendant of the Port waited upon us with a communication from the Minister; and the two French Mandarins, by order of the King, shortly afterwards joined him, to assist in explaining the Minister's message. The Intendant of the Port began by informing us, that every thing being now settled, we were at perfect liberty to go abroad wherever we pleased; that we might again visit any part of the fortifications we wished, or go into the country, on shooting excursions, or, in short, take any other amusement we thought proper. This part of the communication was said to come directly from the King himself, who desired us not to take offence at the guards placed over our dwelling, which were intended only to protect us against the importunate curiosity of the lower classes of the people, and to prevent depredations upon our property, which, were they to take place, would be a matter of indelible disgrace to the Cochin Chinese Government.

The subject of the presents was then introduced. We were informed that the King could not accept of any part of them, because, as it was alleged, we had come here only to ask for trade, and had not yet gained any actual advantage from our intercourse. It was added, that as soon as we should have reaped any benefit from a connexion with Cochin China, the King would be happy to accept of any thing that should be presented to him. On this point we answered, that we had no observation whatever to make, and that His Majesty would accept or refuse the presents as he thought best. Great care was taken to show no disappointment at the refusal of the presents, and in consequence some uneasiness appeared to be felt by the Cochin Chinese at the indifference which we evinced on this subject. The Intendant of the Port intreated on behalf of his chief, that no unfriendly construction might be put upon the rejection of the presents by His Majesty, and a quiet assurance was given by us that no unfavourable impression whatever was produced by this circumstance.

The subject of trade was next introduced, and on this point entire satisfaction was given; more, in fact, being conceded, than was contemplated by the Indian Government, or than it was believed when the Mission was determined upon, that the supposed anti-commercial prejudices of the Cochin Chinese would have admitted. It was stated, that all the ports of the Cochin Chinese empire worth frequenting would be open to British commerce, upon the same terms as to the Chinese of Canton, and that official copies of the *tariff* and regulations of trade would be furnished. We desired to know whether the port of Kachao in Tonquin, and of Kangkao or Hattian in Kamboja, were included among those where British trade would be admissible. The Mandarin answered, that the ports contemplated by the Court were those of Saigun, Faifo, Touran, and Hué, but that Kachao and Hattian, at our desire, would be added to the number.

The French Mandarins, by authority of the King, introduced the subject of His Majesty's declining to grant us an audience, and stated expressly, that as this had been refused to others in our situation, it could not now be consistently granted. The circumstances connected with a recent Embassy from the Court of France, and which had scarcely been hinted at before, were now distinctly brought forward as a conclusive reason for His Majesty's declining to grant us an audience, and accepting the presents of the Governor-general. The French gentlemen stated that on the 25th of December, 1817, the French frigate Cybelle, of forty guns, arrived at Touran with a mission from the French Government. The Envoy was M. Achille de Kargariou, a captain of the first class in the French Navy. He was charged with a letter from the Minister of Marine to the first Minister of the Cochin Chinese Government, and with valuable presents from the King of France to His Majesty of Cochin China, but there was no letter from the one Sovereign to the other. The King of Cochin China consequently refused to grant the Envoy an audience, and even declined to receive any of the presents. This happened during the lifetime of his late Majesty; the same prince who lay under so many obligations, if not to the French nation, at least to many individuals of that country Whatever might have been the ostensible reasons for refusing to receive the French Envoy and the presents of the King of France, there is good ground for believing that the true cause was the nature of the demands which the Envoy was instructed to make. He is alleged to have required the fulfilment of the treaty of 1787, by which a considerable territorial cession, and many other political advantages, were yielded to France. But the situation of the Cochin Chinese monarch was now very different from what it had been when he signed that convention, the hard conditions of which were extorted from him by his necessities only, nor could he now, in his prosperity, be expected to receive with complacency a proposal for its renewal, especially since he had surmounted all his difficulties without its assistance. Upon this subject, of course, nothing was said by the French Mandarins, nor did it become us to put any questions.

Oct. 3.—In company with the French gentlemen, we made last evening an excursion into the environs of the town, taking with us our fowling-pieces. Our journey, which lasted several hours, took us over a good deal of the country on both banks of the river. Although the soil is light and sandy, it is every where in a high state of cultivation, and this consists of rice, mulberry-trees, cotton, and orchards of fruit-trees. It is thickly strewed with villages, universally surrounded by hedges of live bamboo; and I am told this last appearance is general throughout the inhabited country. The banks of the river are well raised, and in some places extremely picturesque and beautiful, more resembling the scenery of an European, than a tropical country.

Hué is, I dare say, the only Indian city in the East, the neighbourhood of which has good roads, good bridges and canals. Here are a number of highways, straight, broad, and well constructed, and besides the stone bridges connected with the fortifications, there are a number of wooden ones, extremely neat, and built on European rules. In the course of the excursion now described, we passed along the banks of a deep and regular canal, which extends, as we were told, for twelve or fourteen miles, and serves the double purpose of irrigation and navigation. Boats laden with rice, just as it had been reaped, were passing along it to the city. By means of many canals of the same description, and embankments towards the sea, extensive tracts of land have been rendered available to agriculture, which were before flooded by the tide, and therefore a waste.

All this was the work of the late King, whose active mind appears to have been devoted to projects sometimes of utility, but oftener of ostentation and ambition. It is probable, that his subjects lost at least as much by the last as they gained by the first. All public works are accomplished by corvées and forced contributions, which are an intolerable burthen to the people. The new fortress, scarcely yet completed, has been, for example, entirely constructed on this principle, and has been now seventeen years in executing. In such a state of society and government, there can be no security that the labour of the people shall not be wasted, even under the most respectable princes, in schemes of folly or ostentation, or in monuments of superstition. The late King, for example, constructed a splendid mausoleum and laid out extensive gardens, as a place of interment for himself and his favourite Queen, upon which thousands of his subjects were occupied for years. The following account of these gardens was given to us. They are situated in a romantic part of the mountains, and about ten leagues to the north of the capital. The tombs are the least splendid part of this undertaking, which consists besides, of spacious gardens and groves, laid out in walks and terraces, and, as it is said, with no mean taste. In the course of this splendid undertaking, hills were levelled,—mounds thrown across from one hill to another,—canals and tanks dug, and spacious roads constructed. The Queen, a woman of great beauty and merit, who had accompanied her husband in his exile in Siam,—in his retreat among the desert islands, in the Gulf of that name, and who was besides his constant companion in all his warlike expeditions by sea and land, was buried here about seven years before our visit. Four years afterwards, the King himself was placed by her side. The same spot, before being decorated in the present magnificent manner, was also the ancient burying-ground of the predecessors of the present race of kings. The place was represented to us as a delicious and a romantic spot, exceeding in beauty every other scene in the country. We wished for permission to pay it a visit, but were politely informed that the King was always reluctant to permit the visits of strangers, whose presence, he said, might "*trouble the repose of the spirits of his ancestors.*"

In the course of the day's excursion now described we visited two temples. One, a spacious and large building, was dedicated to the ordinary form of Chinese worship; but the other, a mean little building in one of the villages, afforded the first example which we had seen of the worship of Buddha or Gautama. There were two altars in this last, on the principal of which was an image of this Indian divinity sitting cross-legged. It was made of wood, but gilded, with the exception of the head, which was painted black. The features had a kind of negro cast, and, like the representations of the same object of worship in Siam, the hair of the head was curled. There were several paintings of Buddha also upon the wall. On the other altar was the figure of two storks in carved wood, such as we had seen at Kandyu. There was but one priest belonging to this temple, and he was sick, so that we could not see him. The priesthood, of whatever form of worship, is but in slender repute in Cochin China. Instead of stumbling on one at every step, as in our walks in Siam, here, from their small number, we scarcely ever met any.

In our excursion to-day, we were a good deal surprised at discovering, among the feathered tribe, an early and familiar acquaintance, which I had not seen before in any part of India; —this was the common European magpie *(Corvus Pica)*, which was in considerable numbers about all the villages. Its habits, manners, and appearance, seemed to differ in no respect from those of the European species.

Oct. 4.—Mr. Chaigneau entertained us yesterday, at his house on the banks of the river. The repast was entirely French. We had been entertained in a similar manner, the day before, at M. Vanier's. All the French at the place were on both occasions invited to meet us. These consisted of a gentleman of the medical profession, who was old enough to have been a surgeon of the first class in the fleet of M. Suffrein, of the nephew of M. Chaigneau, and of his two sons born in the country. The Missionaries are all in a place fifteen leagues distant, and we did not see any of them. The lady of M. Chaigneau is the daughter of a French gentleman, and accompanied her husband to France three years ago. Mad. Vanier is a Cochin Chinese, a fine-looking woman, tall, and as fair as a native of the South of Europe. Both the gentlemen and ladies dress in the Cochin Chinese fashion—a compliance with the customs of the country, indispensable to every stranger who takes up his permanent residence in it. Even the Chinese, who are not very tractable in matters of this nature, are obliged to submit to it; for such is the vanity of the people, that the dress of a stranger, of whatever country, is considered by them as nothing less than ridiculous, and is sure to attract so much curiosity as to prove very inconvenient.

Our hosts, the French Mandarins, were in politics decided Royalists; and it was their devotion to royalty that fixed them, and the greater number of their countrymen, in this remote quarter of the world. In short, it was the French Revolution which achieved the revolution in Cochin China, and established the existing order of things in that country. Whatever their political feelings, however, like all good Frenchmen, our friends were warm lovers of their country. In their conduct to ourselves, nothing could surpass their politeness, hospitality, and real kindness; and I trust we shall always have a grateful recollection of their attentions.*

While we were at M. Chaigneau's, a message

* These gentlemen have all quitted Cochin China since; and I had the pleasure of seeing the greater number of them at Singapore, on their way to France, in 1825.

was brought to us to say, that at 12 o'clock, a deputation of two Mandarins would wait upon us, at our residence, with a present of fruit and confectionary from his Majesty, and we were requested to return home without loss of time to receive it, that no mistakes or delay might take place on a subject of so much importance. We returned accordingly, and found the house already spread with mats, and all requisite preparation making, with great formality, for the reception of his Majesty's gift. This consisted of a ready-dressed entertainment, contained in four very handsome varnished and gilded cases, carried by porters, accompanied by a military guard, and preceded by a military and civil Mandarin of rank, with their secretary,—all in their dresses of ceremony. The Mandarins wore a cap of a peculiar form, and on a square piece of silk, on the breast of their gown, was embroidered the badge of their order. That of the military chief was a boar, and of the man of letters a stork. The utmost formality was observed throughout the whole of this affair, as if it had been a matter of the first consequence to both parties. We received the deputation at the bottom of the stairs. In the long portico of the house, Mr. Finlayson and myself, with our Indian servants, stood on one side, and the Mandarins, with their followers, on the other, forming a street for the presents which passed between us. A list of them

ANDARIN OF THE MILITARY ORDER, IN HIS DRESS OF CEREMO

Drawn by A. Ibrahim

Pub. by E. P. ... London 1822

MANDARIN OF THE CIVIL ORDER, IN HIS DRESS OF CEREMONY.

was then read by the secretary from a scroll of paper with much formality, and the honour conferred upon us duly notified. There is nothing of the slightest moment done here, in public matters, without writing—whereas at Siam, on the other hand, it was found impossible to get the officers of Government to commit a single sentence to paper upon almost any subject. After the list was read, we were politely requested to turn towards the presents, and make them an obeisance after our own manner, which Mr. Finlayson and myself complied with. After this ceremony the Mandarins were presented with tea, and took their departure with the same formalities as they had come. It was suggested to us through the Mandarin of Touran, that it would be a proper mark of respect to his Majesty's gift, to make an offer of a sum of money to the Mandarins who brought it, which, as a matter of course, would be declined, but that the offer alone would have the appearance of a handsome acknowledgment of his Majesty's condescension. This proposal I rejected, informing the Mandarins, that if the money were really to be accepted, it should be given, but that nothing would be tendered for the avowed purpose of being rejected, such not being our custom. This was acquiesced in, after some hesitation and a good deal of disappointment.

Oct. 5.—The Mandarin of Touran called upon

us this morning, and entered into familiar conversation. The points on which he was most anxious for information, were the reason of our long war with France, and the cause of our separation from the Americans, who, he observed, were, in look, manners, and language, the same as ourselves. These were intricate questions, to which it would have been extremely difficult to have given answers that would have been either satisfactory or intelligible to his mind, and no direct attempt at explanation was made on our part.

Oct. 6.—Yesterday forenoon, the old Intendant of the Port called with a message from the Minister, on the subject of our trade. It seemed that the question had been discussed yesterday morning in the council where the King in person was present. The question now put to us was, whether, in levying the duties upon our ships, we should prefer having a fixed sum for vessels of all dimensions, of 3000 quans, or a rated impost, as levied upon the Chinese junks, according to the breadth of the vessel's beam. The second proposal was of course preferred, not only as the most fair and advantageous, but as that least repugnant to custom and usage.

After this point had been disposed of, the Intendant of the Port requested to know what articles the English could import into Cochin China, cheap enough for the Cochin Chinese to purchase. Cotton fabrics, woollens, iron, fire-arms, lead, tin, and salt-petre, were mentioned as staple articles. He pointed out woollens as the most suitable of these, stating that the King's army was clothed in English woollens; and he suggested iron as a fit article of importation into Saigun. He strongly recommended that our ships, on their return from China, should touch at the ports of Cochin China for cargoes, bringing with them Chinese goods which were in universal demand in the country.

We had a message in the morning to say, that a deputation would wait upon us in the course of the day, with another present from his Majesty, consisting, as before, of an entertainment. About three o'clock it arrived, with the same forms and ceremonies as upon the first occasion; and one of the Mandarins, a matter which was pointed out as a mark of particular attention, was the fourth person in rank about the Court. After the entertainment was laid out upon six small tables in an adjoining apartment, the Mandarins requested that we would be pleased to go and "admire it," which was the expression made use of. In point of quantity it was certainly more than abundant for two gentlemen, one of them in delicate health, for it consisted of fifty-two covers. The cookery was by no means contemptible, and the feast was served up in a very neat and cleanly manner.

It principally consisted of pork, fish, and poultry, prepared in a great variety of forms, and of abundance of confectionary. One of the Cochin Chinese dainties served up on this occasion ought not to be omitted; it consisted of three bowls of hatched eggs. When we expressed some surprise at the appearance of this portion of the repast, one of our Cochin Chinese attendants observed, with much *naïveté*, that hatched eggs formed a delicacy beyond the reach of the poor, and only adapted for persons of distinction. On inquiry, we, in fact, found that they cost some thirty per cent. more in the market than fresh ones. It seems, they always form a distinguished part of every great entertainment; and it is the practice, when invitations are given out, to set the hens to hatch. The fête takes place about the tenth or twelfth day from this period,—the eggs being then considered as ripe, and exactly in the state most agreeable to the palate of a Cochin Chinese epicure. It is singular that the Cochin Chinese, who are in general indiscriminate, and even gross in their diet, have an antipathy to milk, amounting to loathing. They insist, that the practice of using it as food is little better than that of drinking raw blood. Our Indian servants, to the great scandal of the Cochin Chinese, not only declined partaking of the royal banquet, but felt their prejudices much shocked at some of the details of it. I proposed distributing the principal part of it among our Cochin Chinese guard, and for this purpose sent for the commander. He said, he dared not lay a finger upon what came from the King, without an express command; and it was found necessary to send a message to the Mandarins of the deputation, to obtain the necessary leave.

Oct. 8.—We made another short excursion into the country yesterday, accompanied by some of the French gentlemen, and in returning home passed through the principal part of the town. The appearance of the country was such as I have already described it,—thickly strewed with villages, all surrounded by bamboo hedges, and having good pathways communicating between them. The soil, as before experienced, was light and sandy. We entered several temples, none of them dedicated to the religion of Buddha. On the altar of one temple there was the figure of the cap or coronet of a female of rank, and under it an inscription. This temple, which was an extremely neat and pretty building, was, we were told, founded by a pious lady. We found all these temples carefully locked up; but, when requested, they were readily thrown open to gratify our curiosity. There was not a single priest, as far as we could discover, attached to any of them.

One of the most striking objects in Cochin

Chinese landscape is, the little religious groves which are here and there interspersed among the villages, and commonly near the burying-places. Of these we saw many in the course of this day's excursion. They are of a circular form, and consist of a variety of thick and umbrageous trees. A single entrance conducts by a winding passage to the centre of them, where there is an open space, and one or more little temples, or rather rude altars. These retreats are consecrated to the manes of the dead, and their gloom and solemnity render them well-suited to this purpose.

Oct. 10.—Having made application to the Minister to return to Touran by land, and afterwards to visit Faifo, we received a civil message from him yesterday, to say that we should be allowed to return in the manner most agreeable to ourselves, and that an order would be sent to Faifo to receive us with attention. A Chinese merchant of respectability called upon us in the course of this day, and furnished much information respecting the trade between Hué and China. The resident Chinese are the class of persons to be chiefly relied upon in these parts of the world for useful information, and I have seldom applied to them in vain. They possess a degree of practical good sense and intelligence scarcely ever to be found in the natives of the country. The individual in question spoke in discouraging terms of all commercial transactions with the

Court, and on this subject used the following strong expression: "Men of rank are full of caprice in this country, and there is nothing but vexation to be got by dealing with them. If, for example, you offer them for sale a set of tea-dishes, it may happen that they will fancy the cups and reject the saucers,—or the contrary. I never," he added, "have a transaction with them, that I do not feel my *neck the smaller* for it;"—meaning, of course, by this expression, that he never thought his life altogether safe upon such occasions. This person informed us, that a good deal of suspicion and jealousy regarding our views were entertained on our first arrival, which had now abated. I have reason, indeed, to confide in the fidelity of this report of the apprehensions of the Cochin Chinese, of which, in the course of our visit, we received many proofs. Among others, I may mention the following: A Chinese, on the day of our arrival, sent us word through our interpreter, an old acquaintance, that he did not believe the Court would allow the English to trade to the country, as they desired no intercourse whatever with them. The expression he used was, that "the Cochin Chinese looked upon the men with red hair and white teeth,—that is to say, Europeans,—to be as naturally prone to war and depredation as tigers."

In the evening we made another excursion into

the country. A little below the town we entered a considerable river, which is navigable almost all the way to Tonquin. Every spot of ground, as far as we could see, was well cultivated. This was the period of ploughing for the great rice harvest, and a number of ploughs were at work. The soil was so light, that a single buffalo was sufficient for a plough. In a few spots, favourably situated for irrigation, the grain was already in the ear. It appeared a very light crop, as might have been expected from the nature of the soil. In Java, or Bengal, or Siam, it would have been looked upon as a poor one. After proceeding some way on the river above named, we turned into a canal, or rather a branch of the main stream. This leads into a salt-water lake, about two miles distant, and also communicates with the great river of the capital. The salt-lake in question abounds in fish, and we met a number of boats on their way to it. The Cochin Chinese are great consumers of fish; and their seas, rivers, lakes, canals, and even brooks, afford a great supply. The fisheries indeed exhibit almost the only active display of industry which is to be seen among them.

At night we received accounts that our launch, which we had despatched some days ago with our heavy baggage, had fortunately succeeded in crossing the bar of the river, after having been detained by a heavy and dangerous surf, and which, now that the north-east monsoon had fairly set in, rendered the entrance generally impassable.

Oct. 12.—The French Mandarins called upon us yesterday, by order of the King, to inform us, that to-day the Foreign Minister would show us the answer to the letter of the Governor-general,—that to-morrow certain presents intended for the Governor-general would be presented to us in the hall of ceremonies in the palace; and that on the succeeding day, or as soon after as we should be inclined, every thing would be in readiness for our journey overland to Touran. At an early hour this morning, a barge was ready to convey us to the house of the Mandarin of Elephants, and we set out immediately after breakfast. The French Mandarins accompanied us. We found the Minister in the hall where he had formerly received us. Along with him were his two assistants, and two Mandarins deputed by his Majesty to present the letter to us. After some complimentary observations, we proceeded to business. The Minister began with some remarks touching our visit to Saigun, and asked whether it was the custom with us to send letters from one great personage to another open as our's was. I said, that it was not the custom in Europe; but that the princes of Western India simply inclosed their letters to one another in a silken envelope, and that in our correspondence with them we conformed to this practice. He said, "It is His Majesty's wish, when the Governor-general writes again, that the letter may be sealed, for this is the custom of Cochin China." We were now pointedly asked, whether we had voluntarily shown the Governor-general's letter to the Governor of Saigun, or whether it had been demanded of us? We stated the latter, explaining that we did not comply until assured that doing so was conformable to the customs of the country. The Mandarin replied: "It is not agreeable to the customs of the country, that any one should inspect letters addressed to His Majesty, before they reach his own presence. A copy, or a duplicate, would have been enough for the Governor of Saigun." These observations probably arose out of jealousy of the Court towards the latter personage. By the concurrent testimony of every person with whom I have spoken on the subject, this Chief is considered not only as the first subject in the kingdom in point of rank and power, but the most distinguished also for his firmness, his talents, and his integrity. His leaving the Court was regretted by the people as a misfortune; and I have been assured, that the corruption of the lower Mandarins has known no bounds since they have lost the restraint imposed upon them by his vigilance and severity. His Majesty is naturally jealous of his influence and popularity.

The Minister, after these observations, proceeded to inform us, that certain presents had been prepared, by order of his Majesty, for the Governor-general, and some for the Mission, and that they would be presented to us to-morrow morning at the palace, where we should be received in state by the Minister of Ceremonies, who would be in attendance for the purpose. I had full time to deliberate upon the subject of these intended presents; and had resolved to decline accepting those for the Governor-general, as a necessary consequence of his Excellency's presents having been declined on the part of the Cochin Chinese Court. It was at the same time necessary, in doing so, to avoid, as far as possible, giving offence to the pride and pretensions of the Cochin Chinese. With this view it was stated, that presents were now superfluous, as a friendly acquaintance had commenced; while to receive them would be contrary to custom and to our instructions, except in the event of those brought by us being accepted by the King. A direct refusal of them was as far as possible avoided, and the presents for the Mission were accepted with due acknowledgments. The Minister answered, that the presents tendered for the Governor-general of India were mere trifles, not given for their value, but as tokens of his Majesty's friendship. He showed great anxiety that the presents should be accepted; but, on our part, persevering in our first resolution, he at last waived the point; and it was agreed, that we should repair on the following morning to the hall of ceremonies to receive the presents for the Mission only. We hoped, that in this manner a question respecting which we had anticipated considerable difficulty, had been amicably and temperately disposed of.

Drafts of the different papers were now exhibited to us. The first of these was the letter for the Governor-general. It was explained by our own Chinese interpreter; and the language of it appeared, as far as we could judge through this medium, unexceptionable. It was not a letter direct from the King, but from the Minister, by command of his Majesty. It stated—that a letter in the English language, understood by nobody at Court, but translated by our interpreter, had been received from the Governor-general of British India—that this letter expressed a desire that a commercial intercourse should take place between the Cochin Chinese and the English; and that it disclaimed all desire for lands or establishments in Cochin China. His Majesty's answer to this was, that the wish expressed by the Governor-general had given him satisfaction, and that he had issued the necessary orders for the admission of English ships into the ports of his kingdom. The letter then proceeded to give the reasons for the King's declining to receive the presents of the Governor-general, being the same which I have already mentioned, and concluded with the list of the presents sent to his Excellency as tokens of his friendship. These last were as follow: three pairs of elephant's teeth; four rhinoceros' horns, set in gold feet; cinnamon of the first quality, three catties; of the second quality, five; and of a third quality, ten; agila wood, of the first quality, five catties; and of the second, ten catties; and three piculs of sugar-candy. These are the customary presents sent to foreign princes by the Court of Cochin China. The amount determines the rank of the person to whom they are sent, or at least that conceded to him by the etiquette or vanity of the Cochin Chinese. The cinnamon of the first quality here mentioned, I may observe, is reserved exclusively for His Majesty, and it is death to a subject to trade in it. An incredible value is put upon this commodity, viz. twenty dollars the tael, or three hundred and twenty dollars the catty, of one and one-third pound avoirdupois.

The subject of commerce was then introduced. The Minister observed, that His Majesty had granted permission to English ships to visit three ports of the kingdom only, viz. Saigun, Han or Touran, with Faifo, and the capital. With regard to Tonquin, he said, the river was too small for the navigation of English ships. We answered, that in former times the English, and other European nations, had conducted a considerable commerce with Tonquin, and that then the river had water enough for ships of large burden. The Minister replied, that the King was resolved not to permit foreign trade, at present, to Tonquin, as that country was a recent conquest, and for which reason it was not deemed convenient to encourage the resort of strangers to it. I was disappointed at this communication, after the assurance which had been made on the subject; but I saw, from the tone in which it was made, that it was conclusive, and that remonstrance would be useless, and might excite jealousy and suspicion. I therefore acquiesced at once in the decision; and only expressed a hope, that when we became better acquainted, the port of Tonquin would be thrown open to us with the same liberality as the rest.

Our Chinese interpreter, after this, translated the tariff and regulations at the three different ports at which we were to be licensed to trade. They were what had been promised, and without variation the same as those conceded to the Chinese.

After this conversation, the arrangements for our journey were made. We were allowed any number of porters and carriers that we thought proper to name, and the Minister offered us his own barge to convey us the first stage, which is by water. A very handsome entertainment in the Cochin Chinese manner concluded, as we hoped and believed, the whole affair, and we should have been glad to have taken leave. As soon as it was over, however, one of the Mandarins, the Chief of Touran, our earliest acquaintance, stood up and said, that it seemed extraordinary that because we had brought certain presents from the Governor-general of Bengal, and that these presents had been declined, we should dream, in return, of declining the gifts of so great a King as His Majesty of Cochin China. This was the very point the discussion of which we were so anxious to avoid. I felt much annoyed that the topic should now be renewed, after it had to all appearance been so well disposed of—even the Minister himself seeming to be entirely satisfied with the arrangement. We therefore requested, that as the matter had been finally settled, no farther discussion should take place concerning it. Several of the inferior Mandarins, however, agreed in the opinion expressed by the Chief of Touran; and the first determination of the Minister was evidently shaken; and he accordingly informed us, that the letters and papers which we saw sealed and placed in a casket upon the table before us, ready to be handed over, could not be delivered, as the presents were mentioned in the letter, and it would be necessary to take the farther orders of His Majesty on the subject. The Minister, and other Mandarins, with the two French gentlemen, repaired immediately to the palace, to report what had taken place to the King, and we returned to our own residence, which we reached about five in the evening. The Minister displayed great good-humour and affability during the whole conference. He spoke familiarly of his own private affairs. Four or five of his children stood beside him; and this led him to inform us, that he had in all fifty-four, thirty-six of whom were living in his house. During the entertainment he sat down to table with us, but did not eat. Not so the four inferior Mandarins, who did great justice to the feast. The Cochin Chinese, like the Chinese and Japanese, eat with chop-sticks, which, in point of delicacy, is not a whit better than the naked hand of other Asiatics. The bowl, in which the viands are contained, is applied to the very mouth, and the food dexterously tossed in, in immense quantities, and with a kind of beggarly scramble, as if the guest was fearful that any part of it should be snatched from him.

Oct. 14.—For the last three days it rained almost incessantly. I never knew rain more heavy or more continual. The river overflowed its banks and completely inundated the whole town. In the street before our door there were three and a half feet water, and boats were seen passing to and fro in it, as if it had been a regular canal. All the houses, with the exception of our own, which was raised upon a high terrace, were completely flooded; and the inhabitants were compelled, for the security of their property, to deposit it in boats at their doors. For ourselves, we were driven into the interior and higher parts of our dwelling for shelter, there being at least four feet water in the low court-yard in front, and even the verandahs of the house being overflown. At the same time there was a violent gale of wind from the N.E., so that our situation was extremely uncomfortable. For some days, indeed, we were completely insulated, and had no communication with the Government.

The Mandarin of Touran, Ong-hep, called upon us in the morning, paying his visit in his barge, and landing at the street-door. He spoke much on the subject of our rejection of the King's presents, and sought to excuse himself for the impediment thrown in the way of the negociation, by his unseasonable interference at the last conference. While he was with us, a message came from the Minister, to inquire how we were after the inundation, and to inform us, that as soon as the waters had subsided, our business should be proceeded in.

Oct. 15.—The two Mandarins, assistants of the Minister, called upon us this forenoon unexpectedly, and without giving us any notice of their visit. They came, they said, by order of the Minister, to inform us, that as we would not accept of the King's presents for the Governor-general, His Majesty had thought proper to decline sending any answer to His Excellency's letter, but that the commercial document was ready to be delivered. To this I answered, that this depended solely upon His Majesty's pleasure;—that if the letter was given, we would take charge of it; and that if it was not given, we should make a faithful report of this, as of every other circumstance connected with the Mission, to the Governor-general of India on our return. They were sensibly disappointed at this reply; and after consulting with each other for some time, they put the question pointedly, whether we would be glad to have the letter or not. We answered, that we should be happy to take charge of any letter from the King, as a matter of course. They then finally explained that if we would accept of His Majesty's presents for the Governor-general, the letter would be furnished; but if this form, which was according to the custom of the Court of Cochin China, was not complied with, no written answer could be given. In reply to this, we stated distinctly in a few words, that we had delivered our deliberate opinion upon this subject on Saturday to the Minister, and had nothing new to say now.

We explained, that our principal business in coming here was to settle a friendly commercial relation between the two countries, and that this being adjusted, we were perfectly satisfied. On hearing this, the Mandarins proceeded to deliver the commercial document. They finally asked when we wished to take our departure for Touran. We fixed on the 17th. They begged to know whether we would call to take leave of the Minister. We agreed to do so to-morrow, and they departed.

Oct. 16.—We called on the Minister to-day, according to promise. Neither the French gentlemen nor any Cochin Chinese of rank, were present. Although the visit purported to be one of mere ceremony and civility, yet the Minister immediately entered upon business. He stated, that in consequence of our declining to take the King's presents for the Governor-general of India, his Majesty could not answer the Governor's letter; as, according to immemorial usage, such presents as were named in it, must indispensably accompany it. He then proceeded to explain, that the King had declined receiving the Governor-general's presents only because the English had as yet gained no benefit by their intercourse; but that as soon as we had, he would accept of any presents which should be offered. We answered that we did not complain of the King's declining the Governor-general's presents, but that among us it was customary not to receive presents where those tendered by ourselves were declined. He said, if we would accept of the presents, they should be presented in the palace, with all due form; and he stated, as an inducement to comply, that His Majesty would be present on the occasion in person. To this it was replied, that if His Majesty desired to send the presents to the Governor-general, we would with pleasure convey them to Bengal, without, however, pledging ourselves to their being accepted. The Minister declined giving the presents on these terms.

He next adverted to our commerce; and said, that he hoped that every thing connected with this subject was settled to our satisfaction. He begged to assure us, that English ships visiting the ports of Cochin China would meet with every assistance that he could personally render them; and requested that his respects might be offered to the British Governor-general with this message. We now told him of our anxiety to leave Hué to-morrow. He answered, that the boat intended to convey us the first day's journey would be ready at an early hour, with four palanquins for the remainder of the journey.

During our interview, the permission to visit Faifo was confirmed; and we had also leave to visit the marble rocks or other curiosities in the vicinity of the Bay of Touran. The Minister paid us polite attention throughout, and entered into familiar conversation after our business was terminated. He told us with some exultation, that he had served three Kings of Cochin China. He was a great favourite of his late Majesty, whom he accompanied in his flight to Siam, throughout the desert islands on the eastern coast of the Gulf of that name, and, in short, through all his wars and peregrinations. With the present King, although permitted to retain office, he is not a favourite; and this accounts readily enough for the junior Mandarins having taken it upon themselves to oppose his opinion, even in our presence, in the conference which took place on the 12th. He took leave of us with great kindness, and wished us an agreeable and prosperous voyage.

During our visit, the females of the Minister's family, as they had also done upon the two former occasions, crowded to the skreen, which was in front of us and behind the Chief, to gratify their curiosity. Here they laughed, and nodded, and beckoned in such a manner, as to give us but a very indifferent opinion of Cochin Chinese female modesty in high life! All whom we saw were young, and two or three of them fair and pretty, after the manner of Cochin China beauties.

Another incident, of which we were eye-witnesses, deserves to be mentioned, as highly illustrative of Cochin Chinese manners and Cochin Chinese government. While we were entering the court-yard of the Minister's house, we saw a company of comedians, who had been exhibiting, as upon the first occasion. It seems that they were not perfect in their parts, or at least that their performance did not satisfy the taste of the great man. They were accordingly undergoing, the universal panacea for all breaches of moral, social, and political obligation,—for all errors of omission or commission; that is to say—the bamboo. The first object that caught our attention was the hero of the piece lying prone on the ground, and receiving punishment in his full dramatic costume. The inferior characters, in due course, received their share also, as we afterwards ascertained from hearing their cries, while we sat with the Minister. This conference virtually terminated the diplomatic intercourse of the Mission with the Cochin Chinese Court.

CHAPTER XI.

Departure from Hué.—Journey by land to Touran, and description of the Route.—Cochin Chinese Palanquin-bearers.—Arrival at Touran.—Presents for the Mission received.—Worship of Buddha.—Visit to the town of Faifo.—Marble rocks and grottos.—Account of the town of Faifo.—Temples of Buddha.—Account of the country between Touran and Faifo.—Typhoon.—Departure from Touran for Singapore.—Description of Touran.—Land-birds met at Sea.—Anambas Islands.—Arrival at Singapore.

Oct. 17. EVERY thing having been arranged for our journey, we left Hué this morning at eight o'clock. The first part of our route was performed by water, and the Mandarin who had conducted us from Touran accompanied us with an escort of soldiers. Our whole party occupied an accommodation-boat and two galleys. After ascending the river until we were opposite the citadel and palace, we sailed into a canal in a south-easterly direction. The appearance of the country here was strikingly beautiful and picturesque, and had more of the variety and interest of European landscape than of tropical scenery. After proceeding about a mile on this canal, we saw two or three excellent houses, surrounded by gardens and walls. The houses resembled large and spacious Indian bungalows. These habitations, were occupied by some of the princesses of the late King's family. Here the low hills, which approached close to the river, were naked of wood, with the exception of one, which exhibited the unusual spectacle, in a tropical country, of a plantation of timber-trees. A little beyond the residence of the princesses now mentioned, and on the opposite bank of the canal, was seen the manufactory of bricks, from which the fort and other public works were supplied. This extended, I believe, for not less than a mile and a half along the canal. We had the curiosity to count the number of kilns, and found them to amount to 255!

It took us four hours to pass through the canal, and, at the rate we were going, I suppose it to be about fourteen miles in extent. This was the work of the late King, now indeed highly useful to the agriculture and communication of the country; but effected, we were told, at a vast expense of labour and of life. During the first five miles, the canal is about twenty yards broad, and raised above the level of the surrounding country: it has a neat footpath on each side, and, at convenient intervals, flood-gates for inundating at pleasure the adjacent rice-lands. The rest of the work is wide, irregular, on a level with the marsh through which it passes, and destitute of foot-paths. The whole of the lands through which the canal passes, are rice-grounds. After the recent heavy falls of rain, these were so completely inundated, that they had more the appearance of a vast lake, than of a country under culture. Boats were passing and repassing over the fields, and some persons even engaged in fishing where crops of grain would be reaped in a few months.

The canal terminates by a narrow sluice, a great internal lake, or, more correctly, in a wide arm of the sea, with a very narrow neck. Either owing to the freshes, or the canal being elevated above the lake, there was a considerable fall and rush of water at the sluice, which made the passage a matter of some difficulty—and even danger, if a number of persons on each side, armed with long poles, had not directed the boats as they passed through. It took us two hours, with smooth water, to row across the arm of the sea just referred to, the breadth of which appeared to be about seven miles. The entrance into this spacious bay from the sea is to the north-east, and, as already said, very narrow. We had noticed it as we proceeded by sea to Hué, but had then no conception of the extent of the sheet of water into which it led. The depth of this bay is no more than two fathoms throughout, and therefore, as a place of shelter it is fitted only for small vessels. In the language of the country it is called the bay of Mukgot.

At four in the afternoon, we reached the end of the stage, the village of Kao-hai. This is a large hamlet, situated in a fertile valley, between the foot of a chain of hills and the bay, and to the southern side of the latter. The valley is well cultivated, and, we were told, contains a thousand families. A pretty rivulet winds through it, which was full of boats. From the favourableness of its situation, this valley gives two crops of rice a-year: one had just been reaped, and preparation was making for sowing the other. We had an excellent house to reside in, and every convenience that travellers in our situation had a right to expect. Our place of accommodation was a sort of caravansera resembling others of the same description, found regularly at intervals of eight or ten miles, all the way from Saigun to the extreme limit of Tonquin, where it borders on China. It was well raised upon a terrace, and was a hundred feet long, and half as broad. It consisted of one great hall, with a double row of pillars, having an elevated place at one end for the King's throne, and a large chamber at the other end for the security of property. It was substantially and excellently built.

Oct. 18.—We left Kao-hai at six o'clock this morning, and reached the foot of the first range of hills in about an hour. After crossing this, which is narrow, and not above three hundred feet high, we entered an extensive valley. Travelling through this, until half-past eight o'clock, we halted at Nuk-mang, "the place of sweet water," a remarkably pretty and neat village. We breakfasted here, and resumed our journey at half-past eleven. Still traversing low ground for three quarters of an hour, we reached a second range of hills, of nearly the same elevation as the first: this terminated the valley, which appears to be about nine miles broad. It is, generally speaking, sandy, sterile, and in a state of nature; but towards the hills, on both sides, the soil improves and is well cultivated. Here we saw reapers in the fields; among them were many women. They used a sickle, as in Europe; and their work was performed with something like the energy and vigour of European labour. As soon as we had reached the top of this second range of hills, a beautiful and unexpected view was presented to us. On one side was the valley which we had just quitted; on another, the open sea; on a third, high ranges of wooded mountains; and before us, what we took at the time for a great internal lake, surrounded every where by steep and wooded hills. This extensive piece of water proved, however, to be another arm of the sea. We skirted it along its eastern shore, passing a great deal of forest, but our journey being over a most excellent and well-finished road. In this part of our route in particular, and generally indeed throughout the whole of it, we observed along the road many monuments of Cochin Chinese superstition, in the form of little temples, at which votive offerings were presented as well as occasionally on the pinnacles of rocks. These offerings consisted usually of little bits of gilded paper and similar trifles, and were most usual in wild and solitary spots, considered by the Cochin Chinese to be the natural dwellings of evil spirits. At one spot which we passed, on the summit of a hill, and in the depth of the forest, there was erected a post, having on it a board, on which was represented a hideous human face with an inscription underneath. Our native companions informed us that the writing was a sacred text, and that it and the ugly face were intended to frighten away an evil spirit of peculiar malignity which haunted this particular spot. They said, that when people travelled in numbers, or in fine weather, the evil genius in question was not to be apprehended; but that he took advantage of solitary travellers, especially of women, and that he was most mischievous in storms and gloomy weather!

At two o'clock, we arrived at Hai-mung, the end of our stage. This was a considerable village on the sea-side, just at the entrance of the bay already mentioned, and which, in the native language, is called Vungdam, or the harbour of Dam. It appeared to be about five miles across, in its broadest part, and seven or eight long. The depth of water in the middle is ten Cochin Chinese cubits, or almost fourteen feet English. The entrance is extremely narrow, I should think not above one hundred and twenty yards, and here there is only a depth of from seven to eight and a half feet. For a mile inland, the bay consists of a narrow gut or channel, which expands all at once to the breadth which I have just stated. A tremendous surge rolls in upon the beach or rocks towards the entrance of the bay on both sides, the narrow channel alone being free from danger.

In the forests through which we passed in the course of this day's journey, we were informed that tigers and elephants were numerous. Of wild poultry *(Phasianus Gallus)* we saw several flocks. One of these, not far from a village, appeared so little shy that we at first imagined it consisted of domestic fowls, and hesitated to fire. In the winter, or cold season, innumerable flocks of ducks and other water-fowl are described as visiting Cochin China. These had not yet arrived, but we observed preparations making for insnaring them. These consisted of a number of artificial birds, intended for decoys. They were so well imitated, that one of our party fired twice among a flock of them, mistaking them for real birds.

This day's journey was performed in palanquins, of the fashion of the country. These vehicles consist of a net, hung from a single pole, and having a pent roof of very light materials. On each side, as well as behind and in front, there are curtains of wax cloth. The weight of a good one is about thirty catties, or forty pounds, and of a small one, not more than half that amount. Two men, and no more, carry these vehicles, and four is the greatest number of bearers employed for persons of any weight, including the relief. In this employment, the Cochin Chinese exhibit a degree of strength, dexterity, and activity, of which I had not believed them capable. They travel at a quick pace, and change the palanquin from shoulder to shoulder, or relieve each other without even halting. Each of our sets of bearers carried us at least nine or ten miles. In every respect, I conceive them superior to Indian palanquin-bearers. They perform the same work, at least equally well, with less than one half the numbers employed in Hindustan. This superiority is, in a good measure, owing to the greater lightness of the vehicle employed; but, I have no doubt, in some degree, also, to the superior physical strength of the Cochin Chinese over the natives of Western

ORDINARY MODE OF CONVEYANCE OF PERSONS OF RANK IN COCHIN CHINA.

India. We found the Cochin Chinese palanquin the most comfortable and least fatiguing vehicle in which we had ever travelled.

Oct. 19.—We commenced our journey this morning at half past five, by crossing the narrow channel which forms the entrance of the bay. Immediately before us was the high range of mountains, which divides the bay of Vung-dam from that of Han or Touran. We immediately began to ascend, and when we had got to the elevation of four or five hundred feet, had a beautiful and extensive prospect of the bay which we had just left—of the open sea, and even of a portion of the bay of Nuk-got, which we had crossed in the first day's journey. Here was a temple to the Spirit of the Mountain, and on the altar some incense still burning, left by travellers who had gone on before us. Our course was now along the sea, but at a considerable elevation over it, while it was generally concealed from view by the thickness of the forest. The scenery now, and for the rest of the day, was bold and romantic. The forest was as tall and luxuriant as close to the Equator itself, and the sound of brooks and waterfalls was perpetually murmuring in our ears. Two or three waterfalls were visible at a distance, one of which appeared to have a fall of about two hundred feet. Its white foam made a fine contrast with the uniform verdure of the surrounding forest. The road was frequently very steep. All that labour could do to make it good, had indeed been tried, but this was not much among the vast masses of granite of which the mountain consisted, and where there was scarcely an inch of soil, with which to form an even surface. Every step we took was from one block of granite to another, both in ascending and descending. The dearth of human inhabitants was ill made up by numerous herds of monkeys. We saw no less than five herds of these animals while we were passing the mountain. These were all of the same species which we had seen at the bay of Touran, the Douc *(or Simia nemoris)*, in colour one of the handsomest of the Ape tribe. At the elevation, as we conjectured, of six or seven hundred feet, we observed for the first time the tea plant cultivated. The trees seemed to be little attended to,—were at least twelve feet high, and the leaves appeared large and coarse. At half past eight o'clock, we reached the highest part of the mountain. The thermometer, which on the plain was the day before, at the same hour 83°, here sunk to 76°, and the barometer showed that our elevation above the level of the sea, was about 1600 feet. The high road, however, lay over a comparatively low part of the range, some peaks of which appeared to be at least 4000 feet high. Near the highest spot to which we ascended, was a neat village, with the advantage of a good market, and of, what an European at least would consider, a fine climate. In the shops refreshments, consisting of tea, rice, and other articles, were ready laid out for travellers, of which we saw a good number in the course of this day's and yesterday's journey. These persons, among whom were women and children, travelled unarmed, and without guards, and apparently without apprehension. This, at least, was a favourable sign of the vigilance and energy of the Government.

As soon as we had reached the summit of the hill, we enjoyed a grand and extensive prospect, which exhibited at one view the bay and peninsula of Touran, the bay of Faifo, and the marble rocks which lie between them. The rest of our route was a rapid and not very easy descent to the western shore of the bay of Touran. This occupied an hour and a half. At ten o'clock we reached the little cove which I had visited on the 23d of September. Here we breakfasted, and embarking at twelve o'clock, after a beating passage against a strong sea-breeze, reached the ship at four o'clock in the afternoon, and had the happiness to join our friends and to find them all well.

The geological formation of the country which we passed in this journey is entirely primitive. The extremity of a small ridge of hills, which terminates at the side of the river opposite the palace, we found upon examination to be quartz rock. Throughout the rest of our journey granite, with occasional beds of horn-blende rock, were the only formations which occurred. In the vicinity of the capital there seems to be more variety, for we found besides quartz and granite, specimens of mountain lime-stone, which we were told had been brought from a distance of no more than ten or twelve miles.

Oct. 20.—Early this morning the military Mandarin of Touran came on board to congratulate us upon our return, and to inform us that the presents from the King for the officers of the Mission were ready to be delivered, and that it would be necessary for us to go on shore to receive them. We agreed to do so, and landed at ten o'clock. We were formally received by the two Mandarins of the place, and by one of the assistants of the first Minister, who had come down from the capital for the express purpose of delivering the presents. The presents for the Envoy consisted of a pair of elephant's teeth, the horn of a rhinoceros, five catties of cinnamon of the second quality, and five of the third quality. We were perfectly satisfied at being told that all was right; but the Mandarins insisted upon our opening every box separately, and examining the articles one by one. The presents of provisions consisted of ten bullocks, ten goats, ten hogs, one hundred ducks, one hundred fowls, and one hundred and twenty measures of rice, amounting to about eight thousand pounds. The Mandarins, by way of demonstrating to us that there was no foul play, would have us to examine these articles also in detail; but this we positively declined. There is a paltryness and want of delicacy, or even decorum, in the conduct of these people, in matters of this nature, which is quite surprising. We presented the assistant of the Minister with a piece of broad cloth and some British cottons. He had been little accustomed to a gift of this magnitude, and received it thankfully, but was very anxious that the circumstance should be kept strictly secret.

Oct. 21.—A party from the ship ascended this morning the hill opposite to the anchoring-place. The whole peninsula of Touran is one long mountainous range of granite, the most elevated parts of which are about two thousand feet in height. On the brow of the hill, about a quarter of a mile up, we found a little temple of Buddha, the exterior of which was little better in appearance than a common hut. It contained a sitting image of the god, and an erect one of one of his disciples. These were of porcelain, and were of a manufacture much superior to what might have been expected from the situation they were in. We were afterwards told that the late King had caused them to be brought from China, and placed here, in gratitude for his final triumph over the Taysons. The kings of

Cochin China, however, are not of the Buddhist religion; but, I presume, that, like the ancient polytheists, they are inclined to honour every mode of worship followed by their subjects; hoping, no doubt, that this indiscriminate piety may sometimes prove profitable to them in a temporal point of view.

Oct. 22.—While at Hué, we had obtained leave to visit the town of Faifo. This place is one of the principal seats of Chinese commerce, and for this reason we were anxious to be acquainted with it. Mr. Rutherford, Captain Brown, the commander of the ship, and myself, accordingly left Touran at five o'clock this morning, in two boats, on our voyage to it. Touran and Faifo are connected with each other by a salt-water creek, or a natural canal, running all the way parallel to the shore, and separated from it by a range of sand-hills from a mile to a mile and a half broad. At nine o'clock we reached a singular group of rocks, situated on this narrow strip of land,—rising in a bold and picturesque manner from among the sand-hills, and altogether unconnected with the nearest range of mountains, which I think cannot be less than fifteen or twenty miles distant. These rocks are six in number, of an oblong form, and all running in a direction nearly east and west. They rise from the sands almost perpendicularly. Wherever there is shelter or room for a little soil to rest, they are covered with a luxuriant vegetation of arborescent plants. Most generally, however, they are quite naked. They consist of crystallized limestone, or marble, which has no regular appearance of stratification, but rises in perpendicular columns, presenting at the summits a serrated appearance. We made a geometrical measurement of two of them with much care. The lowest of these was 212 feet from its base, and the highest 300. On the almost perpendicular face of the loftiest was seen a herd of small monkeys clambering up and down with as much *sang-froid* as if they were upon the level ground. Another rock, and the most singular of the group, appeared to us to be about fifty feet higher than this last; but as it did not afford the same conveniences for measurement, we did not ascertain its exact height. We had been told that there were some caves in these rocks, containing images which were worshipped by the natives, but this circumstance was not noticed in such a manner as to excite in us much curiosity. We resolved, however, to see them, and were well rewarded for our trouble. They are contained in the highest and largest portion of the range which lies nearest the sea. We walked up a steep ascent of sand-hills, which covered the base of the rocks to a considerable height, and entered them by a rent or chasm, which forms a bold and striking approach. Inside we were surprised to find some dwellings, surrounded by very neat gardens. A guide, whom we found here, led us to the principal cave. The approach to this was by a natural gallery in the rock, partly open and partly closed at top, 180 feet long. As we came near the termination of this, we had a view of the grotto itself, to which we descended by a flight of thirty seven artificial steps. The cave measures eighty-four feet in length, and seventy-two in breadth. The height appeared to be not less than eighty or ninety feet. The top is a natural dome, with three or four wide rents in it, which let in a sufficiency of light. The parasitical plants growing without, struck down their shoots in various directions through these, and some even took root at the very bottom of the cave. The interior presented the appearance of rude natural columns, or rather pilasters, and in general had the venerable look of a Gothic ruin. The north-east side was occupied by a temple dedicated to the religion of Buddha, a form of worship that, in theory at least, delights in the recesses of rocks, mountains, and forests. On the principal altar, there were two gilded figures of Buddha in the common sitting attitude; and near him, in stone, were two figures of his ministers or disciples. On another altar, to the right hand, was a gilt female figure, also in a sitting attitude. This, I suppose, may have been the tutelary deity of the rocks. Two monstrous figures stood as warders at the entrance of the grotto, and two more in front of the temple of Buddha. Such figures as these seem never to be wanting in Buddhist temples of any magnitude.

From this grotto we were led to other parts of the same group of rocks. In one place we were conducted through a natural arched gateway into a square enclosure, which seemed about one hundred and fifty feet in every direction, having perpendicular walls, not less than seventy or eighty feet high. Opposite the gateway by which we entered this enclosure was a second gateway, from which we had a noble view of the sea, not above three hundred yards distant from us,—of the Chamcal-lao islands directly before us, and of the beach, lashed, at the time, by a loud surge.

From this portion of the rocks we descended, and turning to the north-east, passed through some more gardens and habitations, and entered another fine cave, although inferior in size to the first. This was nearly open at top, but shaded by the foliage and branches of a number of fine trees growing over the rocks. One side of this cave was occupied by a temple, in which was a single female figure, similar to that in the first temple.

This, we were informed by our conductors, was the divinity of the place, the protectress of the grotto. This temple, in opposition to the one before mentioned, appeared to be Cochin Chinese, and to have no marks of Buddhism about it.

The neighbourhood of these rocks, although there is scarcely any thing to be seen but naked sand, is inhabited, and several villages lie immediately under the rocks themselves. The inhabitants of these are principally fishermen, and a few of them seem to gain a livelihood by making small culinary utensils out of the marble. This material is in some places white, in others streaked with a bluish vein, but more commonly it is of a grey or bluish colour. I am told that it is inferior to the marble of Tonquin, principally because, from the frequent fissures in it, it does not admit of being cut into blocks of sufficient magnitude. After breakfasting under shelter of one of the rocks, we set off for Faifo at one o'clock, and reached it at half-past ten at night.

Oct. 23.—We spent this day, notwithstanding that it rained incessantly, in visiting every part of Faifo. This is almost entirely a Chinese establishment, being principally inhabited by that people or their descendants. It lies upon the west bank of the creek, or that farthest from the coast, and consists of a single street, about three quarters of a mile in length. The whole permanent population was stated to us to amount to about five thousand. It contains six hundred Chinese families, and is the principal mart of the foreign commerce of this part of the kingdom. Our visit was made in a very dull and uninteresting period; but in the season of the junks it is a busy place, a kind of fair being held at it, at which, including the crews of the junks and the inhabitants themselves, not less than ten thousand Chinese are alleged to be collected. Sugar and cinnamon are the great articles of exportation.

The Chinese houses of Faifo are all built of stone and lime, and very neatly and substantially roofed with tile. That which we occupied might, with little arrangement, have been made a very comfortable residence. Faifo contains two handsome Chinese temples, dedicated, we were told, to the Protectress of Commerce and Navigation. The principal of them was built, about a century ago, at the cost of a Chinese merchant, who brought from China the principal materials, and even the artisans who constructed it. In this temple we saw an immense iron vase, eight feet high, and in the broadest part about four feet in diameter. This also was the workmanship of China. It stood in front of the altar; behind it was a fountain, in which fifteen or twenty small land tortoises were sporting. At Faifo also we saw the largest temple of Buddha which we had met with in Cochin China. There was a single gilded image of Buddha in it, behind which was a painting probably representing one of his disciples. This last was remarkable for being exhibited in a crimson drapery, with a gold embroidery upon it.

I may here remark, that all the figures of Buddha, which we saw in Cochin China, differed materially in appearance from the common representations in Siam and Western India. The Cochin Chinese Buddha had Tartar or Chinese features, instead of Hindu, and a drapery thrown over both shoulders instead of one. It resembled the common Buddha in attitude, in the pendant ears, and in the mode in which the head is dressed. Some of these images were fabricated in China. May not the Buddhist worship of the Chinese and Cochin Chinese be that of the first Buddha, received direct from Tartary? and may not the Buddhism of Siam and other western countries be the modification of it, introduced by the second or Indian Buddha, the Prince of Magadha or Behar? This is a plausible supposition, but not corroborated by any historical facts. On inquiry, we found, for the first time, that to the temple just alluded to there were priests attached. They were unluckily all absent, however, upon a pilgrimage to a place in the mountains, six or seven days' journey from Faifo. The following account of them was given to us, viz., that they lived in a state of celibacy—that they did not destroy animal life, or even eat animal food—that they wore a peculiar cap as a

DEVOTEE. COCHIN CHINESE PRIEST OF FO. NOVICIATES.

head-dress—that either yellow or red was the colour of their garments, and that the Buddhists of Cochin China burnt the dead bodies of their priests, but not of the laity.

Faifo is not the capital of the province in which it is situated. The Governor resides at a fortified place, about six miles distant from it, called Fu-chi-am, and which is in consequence considered as the principal place. The whole province is called Cham, and extends to the range of mountains which borders the south-west side of the Bay of Touran. It is said to contain 50,000 inhabitants.

Oct. 24.—We left Faifo this morning at six o'clock, and arrived at Touran at five in the evening. The north-east monsoon having regularly set in, and with considerable violence, we had some difficulty in making the ship, well sheltered as that part of the Bay of Touran is, where she lay. Judging from the rate at which we travelled on our return, and the time our journey occupied, I imagine the whole distance from Faifo to Touran is about thirty-five miles. Faifo is however six or eight miles from the sea; so that the whole length of the creek which connects the two places, cannot be less than forty miles. Towards both extremities, with the exception of the sand-bars at the entrances, there are at least three fathoms water, and it is between two and three hundred yards broad. For a short way however, towards the middle of its course, it contracts to a breadth of between twenty and thirty yards, and at high-water there are not here above two or three feet of depth. In going up, although we had very flat boats, we were detained for two hours at this part, and had to drag our boats over the shallowest portions. A considerable number of boats were to be seen passing and repassing the creek, both sides of which, but particularly the land side, were well inhabited; and although the soil was uncommonly thin and scanty, every practicable spot was cultivated. There was evidently no want of industry among the people. The poverty of the soil was attempted to be remedied by manuring it with a species of alga, or sea-weed, fished up from the bottom of the creek. In ploughing, we noticed that the same person held the plough and drove the cattle, an improvement which I have nowhere else seen in India. The corn too was neatly stacked, as in Europe; and the villages altogether presented the same neat and clean appearance which had, in other parts of this country, attracted our notice. It was the fisheries however, and not the land, which had encouraged the people to settle on the banks of the creek. From Touran to Faifo, and, I suppose, through the rest of its course, the creek is filled, and indeed in some places almost choked up, with various contrivances for catching fish. The most considerable of these are a sort of stake-nets, consisting of a series of compartments, diminishing in size until they end in a small trap, where the fish is finally taken. A series of these snares is placed on each side of the river, opening in opposite directions, and leaving but a narrow channel in the middle of the stream for boats to pass. In other situations, faggots of bamboo canes, with the branches on, were fixed in the middle of the creek, forming thick circular bushes, which allured the fish by the cool retreat they afforded. When the fish are to be taken, these bushes are surrounded by nets, and the prey scared out and taken. Another mode of fishing was practised here, and is frequent in all parts of the coast of Cochin China. It consisted of a net affixed to a long crane and lever, from the bow of a boat, which, by being well-balanced, was sunk and raised without difficulty. With this machine prawns and other small fish only were caught, its use being confined to shallow water. In other situations there were ponds on the banks of the creek for feeding and preserving fish, such as are common in some parts of Java, and in that country extremely productive. The banks of the creek abounded with mews, coots, and other common water-fowl, and with two large species of crane, of which we shot specimens.

Oct. 31.—On the twenty-seventh we were ready to sail, but about twelve o'clock of the night of the twenty-sixth, a heavy gale came on from the north-east, accompanied with torrents of rain. This was a true Typhoon. The gale did not abate until early yesterday morning, nor was there the least cessation of rain until twelve o'clock of the same day. In short, it rained heavily and incessantly for a period of eighty-two hours. We observed upon this occasion a phenomenon which I had never noticed any where before, nor indeed heard of. The quantity of rain was so great, that it covered the whole bay with a stratum of fresh water; so that we filled our cask alongside the ship, with water good enough for the cattle and poultry. During the height of the gale, the harbour of Touran where we lay was quite undisturbed, and we experienced no inconvenience whatever from the fury of the gale.

At half-past twelve to-day we weighed anchor, and stood on our course to Singapore, on our return to Bengal; our long detention at Siam having brought the season unluckily to so advanced a period, as to render it impossible for us to follow the route of the Phillippines and Dampier's Straits, according to our first intentions. Complimentary messages passed between us and the Mandarins of Touran before parting.

The bay of Touran, or more correctly the bay of Han, may be described in a few words. It is of great extent, but this, instead of being an advantage, is its principal defect. Its entrance is to the north, between a high island to the right, and the high land of the extremity of the peninsula of Han to the left. This channel cannot be less than five miles broad: from the entrance to the bottom of the bay at the village of Touran, the distance is not less than twelve miles. Across the bay, from east to west, the breadth is at least eight miles. To the east, the bay is formed by the high land of the peninsula of Han; and to the west, by a range of mountains still higher. The south and south-east sides alone are formed by low sandy land. The anchorage notwithstanding the great size of the bay is but of moderate extent. It lies to the north-east angle, within a few hundred yards of the high land of the peninsula; and behind a small promontory, off which there is a stony islet. In sailing in, the best anchorage is determined as soon as the entrance of the bay is closed in. To the southern side, the extent of the harbour is limited by a low flat sand coming out from the entrance of the creek. Upon the whole, it is not above a mile and a half in extent in any direction, notwithstanding the spaciousness of the bay itself. Every other part of the bay except the small cove where the village is situated, which forms the last stage from Hué, is just as exposed as the open sea, and upon the western coast especially, a formidable surf always prevails, which renders landing both difficult and dangerous, even in the finest weather. We left the ship one morning when it was perfectly calm, and after a long continuance of fine weather, with an intention of exploring this part of the bay; but found the swell and the surf running so high, that we dared not attempt to land, although we approached within a few yards of the shore.

Nov. 2.—The wind with which we were beating out of the bay of Touran on the 31st, having failed us on the same evening, we were compelled to come to an anchor, but at twelve o'clock at night a strong breeze having sprung up from the north-west, which soon increased to a fresh gale, we made sail. At noon, on the 1st of November, we were in the latitude of 15° 18′ North, and to-day, assisted by the same favourable wind, and by a strong current setting with the monsoon, we ran the extraordinary distance of two hundred and forty-nine miles of latitude, and found ourselves, by our meridian observation, in 11° 9′. At sunset we were in sight of Pulo Sapata, one of the three islands, or rather rocks, called The Catwicks, and which are considered by navigators the southern limit of hurricanes or Typhoons. Pulo Sapata, the second of the same name mentioned in this journal, is a bare inaccessible rock, visible thirty miles off from a ship's deck, and is the undisturbed habitation of thousands of sea-fowl. We were to-day, for the first time for near nine months, in the ordinary track of European navigation.

Nov. 6.—We lost the regular monsoon on the 2d, and ever since had nothing but light airs and calms, the season being too early for the setting in of the regular periodical wind so far to the south. At noon to-day, our latitude was 5° 13′, and our longitude 106° 3′. At daylight two European sail were in sight, the first we had seen for near nine months. In the course of the day we spoke the American brig Comet, of Salem, direct from Canton, but obtained no news from her. The other vessel had the appearance of a British ship bound for India. Within the last few days, although distant at least two hundred miles from any land, we were accompanied by an extraordinary number of land-birds, such as swallows, yellow-hammers, and hawks. Of all these we caught specimens, as they lay asleep on the rigging, exhausted by fatigue. Of hawks, we caught in this manner no less than six of two species. These animals, notwithstanding the precarious situation they were in, hunted the smaller birds, and caught them in our presence as coolly as if they were in their native woods and hills. It is remarkable, that at the same time we did not see any water-fowl, with the exception of a single pelican.

Nov. 7.—The group of islands called the Anambas, being little out of our course, and imperfectly known, we considered that a visit to them would prove of some interest, and accordingly stood down for them in the course of yesterday. Early this morning they were in sight, appearing more numerous and more extensive than they are represented in the common charts. By noon we were close to one of the most northern group, when our latitude was 3° 26′ North, and our longitude by chronometer, 105° 56′ East. At five in the evening we were within 300 yards of a small island; and the wind being then unfavourable, we would have anchored for the night, but there was no ground in less than thirty-seven fathoms. As we passed the eastern side of this island, a little sandy cove was opposite to us, immediately above the beach of which, but in no other part of the island, was a grove of old cocoa-nut trees. There was no sign of dwellings, but it is probable, from the appearance of the cocoa-nut trees, that the place was once inhabited; yet the island is extremely small and steep, and the bay could have afforded no shelter for fishermen or their boats in the north-east monsoon. Upon this beach the surf ran so high, although it had the appearance of being sheltered, that we were unable to effect a landing. The rock formation appeared to be sand-stone.

Nov. 9.—During the night of the 7th we lay off and on, not being able to come to an anchor from the great depth of water. In the morning we found ourselves in an extensive basin, closed in on all sides, except the north and north-west, by groups and chains of islands. During the day we endeavoured to reach a long chain which lay to the west of us, and which from appearance promised to contain what we were most anxious to find—a secure harbour. Contrary and baffling winds, and a heavy swell, made it however impossible for us to reach it, and we came to an anchor at night in thirty-two fathoms. This morning the same unfavourable weather still continued, and our time admitting of no longer delay, we were reluctantly compelled to quit the islands, without making those inquiries which we were so anxious about, and we made sail, continuing our route towards the Straits of Singapore.

The islands, called by European navigators the Anambas, a name not known to the Malays of the country, are properly called by the various names of Siantan, Jamajah, and Sarasan, which make the northern, middle, and southern Anambas of our charts. They are, in all, about fifty in number, and form, along with the other islands between the Malay peninsula and Borneo, from the longitude of 104° to 110° East, dependencies of the principality of Jehor. They are generally hilly and sterile, and inhabited by true Malays, always poor, and commonly inoffensive. These people cultivate a little mountain rice and maize, cocoa-nuts, and sago; and their shores afford the tripang, or holothurion. The population of the Anambas Islands is said to amount to fifteen hundred. They carry on a traffic with the Straits of Malacca, which has considerably increased since the establishment of the new settlement of Singapore.

Nov. 13.—Ever since we left the Anambas, we encountered nothing but calms, or light and baffling airs. To-day, at noon, we were in latitude 2° 17′ Bintang Hill, in the Straits of Malacca, visible from the mast-head before us, and the islands Timun (Tioman), Pisang, Aor (Awar), and Pulo Tingi, in sight to the north. The islands now named, except Pisang, are scantily inhabited by Malay fishermen, who cultivate a few roots and ordinary fruits, but none of them contain a harbour. Pulo Aor is of importance to navigation, as being the universal point of departure for ships bound to China, as well as the mark by which, on their return, they steer for the Straits of Malacca and the Java seas.

Nov. 16.—On the 14th, we passed the white rock, which lies in the very entrance of the Straits of Malacca, and which is so well known to European navigators under the Portuguese name of Pedro Branco; and this morning we had the pleasure of seeing the British flag flying at the new settlement of Singapore. We anchored in the course of the day, and landed in the evening. We had now, after an absence of nine months, and after being without any accounts from England for a whole year, the pleasure to receive the numerous communications of our Indian and English correspondents, with files of Indian and English journals and periodical publications.

Nov. 23.—After a stay of six days at Singapore,* and after witnessing the rapid improvements which had been effected in this flourishing settlement even during the short period of our own absence, we embarked last night, in pursuance of our voyage, and made sail at daylight this morning. Dr. Wallich, the Superintendent of the Botanical Garden at Calcutta, whom we found at Singapore, where he had come for the restoration of his health, became the companion of our voyage to Bengal. In the evening, it falling calm after we had passed the channel of the Rabbit and Coney, we followed our usual practice, and landed. Dr. Wallich accompanied Mr. Finlayson and myself. The island which we visited is called in the charts Alligator Island, and lies close to another which is known by the name of Barren Island. The first consists of a mass of sandstone of various colours and textures, in which are frequent veins of clay

* An ample account of Singapore will be found in a subsequent chapter.

iron-ore, the formation in fact differing in no way, as far as we could discover, from that of Singapore. Dr. Wallich described the vegetable productions of all these islands as equally rich and novel, and was, in fact, carrying back with him a curious and extensive botanical collection.

Nov. 25.—Last night we passed Malacca, and at noon to-day were off Cape Rachado. Here the Straits are not above thirty miles broad, and while we pass within a few miles of the coast of the continent, the Sumatran shore is distinctly visible. Dr. Wallich and I landed in the evening, and made a short examination of Cape Rachado. This is a promontory, rising boldly from the sea to the height of one hundred and fifty feet. Its geological formation is quartz rock, interspersed with frequent veins of clay iron-ore. It appears to be the extremity of a ramification of the great chain of primitive mountains, which runs thus far throughout the whole Malayan peninsula. Beyond it, and all the way down to Point Romania, there are detached hills, but no continuous range of high mountains. A rapid current passes Cape Rachado, occasioning a swell of the sea even during a calm, as was the case when we now visited it. On each side of the Cape there is a sandy cove. We landed on that to the N.W., which we found wild, romantic, and very pretty.

Here, as every where else, we added many novelties to our botanical collection.

Nov. 29.—The island of Dinding or Pangkur having proved in our outward voyage so rich a field for botany, we were induced to touch at it last night for a few hours. A party landed near the ruins of the Dutch fort, and was very successful in obtaining specimens of living plants for the Botanical Garden at Calcutta. Among others, we procured several fine ones of the splendid epidendron, which Mr. Finlayson had discovered in our former visit.

Dec. 2.—This morning we anchored in the harbour of Penang, having come in by the southern channel. After breakfast we landed, and at the delightful mansion of the Governor, Mr. Phillips, were received with the same hospitality and kindness as on our first visit, just one year before.

Dec. 5.—I paid a visit this morning, at the suggestion of the Governor, to the Raja of Queda, accompanied by the Secretary, Mr. Cracroft. This chief was an old acquaintance: I had paid him a visit at Queda in the year 1810. At that time he was a young man of little more than thirty, of goodly appearance, and extremely fair for a Malay. He was now very much changed, indeed, and although only forty-two or forty-three, had the appearance of sixty. His manners, like those of all Malays of rank, and generally, indeed, like those of the whole race, were soft, pleasing, and unassuming. I had the mortification of being the channel of communicating to him the result of my unsuccessful efforts at Siam in his behalf. He received my statement with composure, and said that, with the assistance of his friends, the Princes of Perak, Salangor, and Siak, he would make an effort to recover his country; which, after laying it waste, and driving the population into exile, the Siamese themselves had now in a great measure abandoned.

Dec. 8.—Having communicated with the Government of Prince of Wales's Island respecting the result of my Mission to Siam, and afforded every necessary explanation, we embarked this morning for Bengal, and at eleven o'clock quitted the harbour. Besides a great quantity of dried specimens of plants, we brought with us from Penang for the Botanical Garden at Calcutta, fourteen large boxes of living plants.

Dec. 10.—The coast of Queda, between Penang and Junk-Ceylon, is fronted by numerous islands of various sizes. The principal of these are the Ladas which mean the Pepper Islands, Lang-kawi, Trutao, and Butong. Yesterday morning we were within two miles of the most southern, or Lada Islands. Between these is a fine harbour, very conveniently situated for the common track of navigation. This is called, by the English, Bass Harbour. The country, notwithstanding the deceitful appearance of its luxuriant forests, so apt to mislead an European stranger, appears so steep, so rugged, and so inhospitable, that it is difficult to imagine it capable of being converted to any useful purpose in the present state of society in these regions. Lang-kawi is the largest island of the group, and is said to contain from four to five thousand inhabitants, all Malays. This population is situated upon the eastern or sheltered side of the island, opposite to the main-land. During our absence, the Siamese invaded the island, and took possession of it. In consequence of this, a great number of the inhabitants fled to Prince of Wales's Island. From these, and other refugees from the Queda territory, the Government of Penang has established a colony on the narrow strip of land which we hold upon the Peninsula, and which, at the period of our visit, already amounted to nine thousand persons. It may here be worth mentioning, that Lang-kawi, an island now so little frequented, was visited in 1672 by Commodore Beaulieu, the sensible and intelligent Frenchman who conducted the first adventure of his nation to the Indies. It was then celebrated for its production of pepper, a commodity which it now affords in too inconsiderable a quantity even to deserve mention. Trutao, commonly called by us Trotto, is scantily inhabited by a peculiar race, who have the physical appearance of the Malays, speak a dialect of the same language, but have not yet adopted the Mahometan religion. They are strictly fishermen, living as much as possible on a fish diet, and almost entirely neglecting the cultivation of a soil, which indeed appears to offer them little temptation. They are called, by the Malays, Orang Laut, or Men of the Sea; the same denomination by which the fishermen of the opposite extremity of the Straits of Malacca are also known, and which indeed is frequently applied to races of similar habits in other parts of the Archipelago.

Dec. 12.—To-day we passed along the coast of the Island of Junk-Ceylon, called by the Siamese Talang. The Malays, who, from the narrowness of the strait, which divides it from the continent, can hardly be induced to consider it an island, have corrupted it into Ujung Salang, which means the point or cape of Salang, which our mariners, and after them our geographical writers, have converted, with no small violence to orthography, into its present name. We were again, therefore, in the vicinity of our friends the Siamese, for this island belongs to Siam, and its native inhabitants are the Siamese race. Geographically, it runs in a direction nearly north and south, between the latitudes of 7° 46′ and 8° 9′, and in the longitude of 98° 20′. It is twenty-four miles long, and about nine miles broad. On the western side it presents a mountainous, bold, woody, and uncultivated aspect. The eastern side, lying opposite to the large island of Pulo Panjang, is the cultivated and inhabited portion, and contains several bays or harbours, the most considerable one of which is about four leagues from the south-east extremity. This last is a good harbour, and the principal town or village of the island, called Teroa, is situated about a mile and a half up a small river which falls into it. Junk-Ceylon is divided from the main land by the Straits of Papra, about fifteen miles in length. The eastern extremity of these straits forms a good harbour.

The mountains of Junk-Ceylon are granitic, and it is highly probable, therefore, that the soil is scanty and far from being fertile. It abounds, however, in tin, and is probably, next to Banca, the most productive country in the East, in this metal. In the year 1787, according to the description of Mr. Francis Light, the first Governor of Prince of Wales's Island, the whole produce of the island amounted to four thousand piculs of tin, or to two hundred and thirty-eight tons. I have no means of ascertaining its present produce. Mr. Light also gives a description of the process of mining, from which it appears that the ore is found in a situation exactly similar to that of Banca, viz. in alluvial soil, at from ten to thirty feet below the surface, and often close to the sea-side. The stratum of ore is, as in that island, mixed with fragments of granite and quartz, and as there too, always lies upon a bed of white friable clay. From this statement, there can be little doubt of the fertility of the mines. The account which Mr. Light gives of the economy of the mines, and of the process of working them, shows that they are wretchedly managed, compared even with those of Banca; a matter easily accounted for, since the first are under the direction of the Siamese, and the latter managed by the intelligent and industrious Chinese.

During the last fifty years, Junk-Ceylon has been a frequent bone of contention between the Siamese and Burmans. In 1810, the Burmans invaded and captured it with a very large force; but in the course of a few months, they were compelled to surrender to the Siamese at discretion, to the number of 4,000. The chiefs, on this occasion, were all beheaded, and the lower classes carried into captivity. We saw a few of the survivors working in chains in Siam when we were there.

Dec. 16.—In the latitude of Junk-Ceylon, and up to the Seyer Islands, we had variable winds and a good deal of rain. On the evening of the 13th, we passed between the latter islands and the main-land. We then got the regular north-east monsoon, which is a fair wind between the Straits of Malacca and Bengal, both going and coming; and towards the east side of the Bay always brings with it, during the months of December, January, and February, serene and delightful weather, such as we now experienced. Last night, we passed the Island of Narcondam at no great distance; this morning, the Cocos, and in the evening the Preparis. The Cocos are two small woody islands which form a portion of the Andaman chain, being connected with them by soundings of no great depth. They take their name from a few cocoa-nut trees seen upon the beach, but they are uninhabited.

Dec. 29.—From the 16th to the 27th we had fine weather, but light and baffling winds. On the latter day we received a pilot. On the 28th, having reached the Island of Saugor, I embarked for expedition in a native boat, and, rowing all night, reached Calcutta on the afternoon of the 29th, after an absence from that place of above thirteen months. On the same day, I made my report to the Marquess of Hastings, whom I found on the point of sailing for England. His Lordship was pleased to approve of the discretion with which, under many difficult and embarrassing circumstances, the affairs of the Mission had been conducted; and I had afterwards the honour of receiving the official approbation of his immediate successor, my amiable and lamented friend the late Mr. Acland.

Before bringing this narrative to a close, it will be necessary briefly to advert to the subsequent circumstances of our connexion with Siam and Cochin China, chiefly in so far as they relate to the Mission. We left on our departure from Siam the British trading-vessel already mentioned at that place. Her commander and supercargo, very discreet and respectable men, had presented to the King upon their arrival an Indian horse of no great value, and chiefly selected on their part on account of his colour, which was white. The King had accepted the offering, and kept the horse for several months; but pretending to discover that he had unlucky marks, and in reality finding that he was much inferior in value to the horse presented by the Governor-general, he was unceremoniously returned just as the ship was on the point of sailing. The vessel was small, deeply laden, and had, on her return, to beat against the monsoon. It was, therefore, impossible to accommodate the animal, and it was resolved to destroy him. Very imprudently, and in ignorance of the religious prejudices of the Siamese, this was done publicly, and without any precaution. The officers of the Siamese Government took high offence, and resolved to punish the authors of the alleged sacrilege. They had not, however, the courage to venture upon this step publicly, and therefore, under a false pretext, seduced the commander and supercargo to the house of the Prince

Krom-Chiat. Here they were beset by hundreds of persons, jostled, thrown down, brutally beaten, put in irons, imprisoned four days, and, finally, compelled to sign an unqualified apology, written in the Siamese language, not one word of which they either understood, or was explained to them. The Siamese Government, however, had some misgivings of the prudence of this proceeding, and thought it necessary to address an apologetic letter to the Governor-general, in which the conduct of the commander and supercargo was, with a good deal of address, represented in aggravated and false colours. The Prah-klang, the writer of this letter, insisted that the crime of killing a horse was worthy of death, and that had it been committed by a native of the country, it would inevitably have been followed by that punishment.

The letter of the Prah-klang also contained accusations against the officers of the Mission and other persons connected with it. The matter of these, notwithstanding the precautions taken to disarm the jealousy of the Government, chiefly referred to the inquiries which we had made respecting the geography and statistics of the country, few and guarded as these were. Our interpreters in the Malay and Siamese languages not being wanted for the remainder of our voyage, had, at their own request, when we proceeded to Cochin China, been left at Siam, with the view of enabling them, by an overland journey, to return the sooner home. These persons, it was pretended by the Siamese Government, had given the most unfavourable representation of the objects of the Mission. Extracts of the letter of the Prah-klang will be found in the Appendix, as well as the reply made to it by the Governor-general.

During the period that I was Resident at Singapore, as Agent to the Governor-general for Siam, Cochin China, &c. I carried on a frequent and friendly correspondence with this same Prah-klang, whom I found, as during my residence in Siam, a shrewd, wary, and very mercenary personage. He, as well as the other officers of the Court, traded extensively with Singapore, and it would have been impossible to gather from his conduct or correspondence that he had ever expressed a sinister opinion, either of our policy or commerce.

After the breaking out of the Burmese war, a second mission was sent by the Governor-general, the object of which was to gain the assistance of the Siamese, and to improve our commercial relations. The first object might have been gained by giving up to the Siamese our conquests on the coast of Tenaserim; but this was a measure which could not be taken without compromising our honour; for it was discovered, on the occupation of the country in question, that the inhabitants, either themselves

Burmese, or long reconciled to the Government of Ava, bore a rancorous hatred to the Siamese, which would have made their surrender to this power, on any terms, a measure of cruelty and discredit. The Siamese sent armies into the field, and showed a disposition to cooperate with us, but when they found there was nothing substantial to be gained, they withdrew, and stood neuter, making warm professions of friendship to both the belligerent parties, but obviously more apprehensive of us, in the long run, than of their hereditary and inveterate enemy, the Burmese.

In a commercial point of view, the result of the last mission was a consolidation, without any reduction of the duties and charges. This, has been accompanied by no beneficial results, nor is it likely to be. In consequence of the expectation of extending British commerce with Siam by a direct intercourse, some intelligent, enterprising, and extensive efforts were made with this view by the merchants of Singapore, backed by the capital of London and Liverpool. They may be said, however, to have totally failed, and one establishment, after an experience of two or three years' actual residence, has recently, and since the date of the last treaty, abandoned the undertaking as hopeless. In fact, the residence of English merchants, owing to the political fears of the Siamese, is extremely repugnant to the wishes of the Government of the country, while the free and independent conduct of our countrymen is so incompatible with the servility and obsequiousness which is looked for, not only from natives but from strangers, that it must, of necessity, prove repulsive and offensive to the pride and prejudices of the Siamese chiefs. To these obstacles to the establishment of a free trade on our part, must be added the strong motive to counteract it which exists in the personal interests of the chief officers, who now enjoy a monopoly of lucrative privileges, which any approach to free trade would impair or destroy.

One object of the last Mission was the restoration of the Prince of Queda to his throne, and the emancipation of the Malayan tributaries of Siam from its thraldom. These objects were not only not attained, but we bound ourselves by the stipulations of a treaty from all future interference. As a specimen of the political sagacity and shrewdness of the Siamese Court, I give in the Appendix its reply to the memorial of the Envoy, adding my conviction that the conduct of this officer throughout was not only able but highly prudent and discreet.

With respect to Cochin China, I have but few observations to make. The repeated professions of the foreign minister, as well as of the Governor of Kamboja, tendering offers of protection and assistance to such British merchants as might frequent the country, induced me, not long after I took charge of Singapore, to furnish the supercargo of a British merchant-ship proceeding to Hue and Saigun, with letters of introduction. The Governor of Kamboja received the letter, addressed to him, with great civility and replied to it, and a friendly correspondence ensued. The reception of my letter to the foreign minister was very different. The bearer of it was declared to have violated the laws of the Empire in bringing a letter from a stranger, and, in fact, to have committed such an offence as, with a native of the country, would have entitled him to capital punishment. This however, it must be added, amounted only to a threat or insinuation, for no violence was offered to himself, or real impediment thrown in the way of his business.

I shall conclude with a few remarks upon the most expedient and suitable manner of maintaining our future political and commercial relations with the Courts of Siam and Cochin China. With the strong excitement which our conquests in Hindostan has produced, probably the most prudent, if not the most profitable, mode of conducting our trade will be through the channel of the Chinese junks. This is an intercourse which, as it offers no offence to their manners or political prejudices, they are not less anxious to promote than ourselves. In reality, it not only increases in amount from year to year, but considerable improvements have taken place even in the mode of conducting it, which promise to render it in no long time equally extensive and advantageous.

Our political relations with the Siamese must, from their nature, be left to the management of the Governor-general of India, whether our territorial acquisitions be under the direct administration of the crown, or the delegated one of the East India Company. The necessity for this arises from the recent extension of the British as well as Siamese dominions, an extension through which we have become immediate neighbours, and which consequently brings the Siamese within the pale of our Indian diplomacy. The details of our diplomatic intercourse in this quarter may, with propriety and convenience, be entrusted to the local officers on the British frontier; and it appears to me that either an envoy, or a resident agent at the court of Siam, will not only, in general, be unnecessary, but even a source of jealousy and irritation. The sea on one quarter, and impracticable mountains and forests on another, are barriers which, together with the fears and discretion of the Siamese Government, will in all likelihood preserve us long at peace with this people. Another motive will tend to the same effect · there is no territorial acquisition which we could make from them, with the exception, perhaps, of a good port among the islands at the upper end of the gulf of Siam, which would not prove both useless and burthensome.

The circumstances of the Cochin Chinese are very different; they are not our immediate neighbours, but far removed from the sphere of our Indian politics. The cautious and prudent foreign policy of this people is sufficiently shown by the history of their relations with China and with France, as well as by that of our own and of the recent Burmese Missions. They have nothing to apprehend from us, nor do I conceive that our Indian power can ever have any thing to apprehend from them. The fears entertained by our Government, at one period, always exaggerated, arose from the existence of a French party in Cochin China. This party is now extinct; and I have no doubt, in the present state of the Government of that country, that its prudence is such that it would maintain a strict neutrality in the event of future hostilities between us and France. Another revolution in Cochin China, and the formation of another French party, which would very probably follow it, would be the only event likely to prove inconvenient to us. The numerous and fine harbours of Cochin China might in such a case prove safe and convenient retreats, from which a French navy might harass or destroy our commerce with China. But this evil might be readily averted, and the Cochin Chinese Government reduced to almost any terms, by the easy and practicable blockade of two or three of the principal ports from which the capital and other portions of the kingdom derive their food and other resources. As to any formidable danger to our Indian Empire from so poor a country as Cochin China, with its scanty and unwarlike population, even if the whole kingdom were a province of France, I conceive it to be quite visionary; for what could be the resources of such a country, in comparison with our extensive, productive, and populous territorial acquisitions in Hindostan, long, permanently and regularly organized?

The reluctance of the Cochin Chinese Government to maintain any diplomatic intercourse with the delegated Government of India, was sufficiently displayed in the history of our own Mission, as well as in that which preceded it; nor do I see any advantage, but the contrary, in attempting to persevere in it. It is another serious objection, that all the acts of the Indian Government are at once associated in the minds of the Cochin Chinese with our territorial aggrandisement. A direct intercourse with the Crown has not this disadvantage; and, as it would conciliate and flatter the Court of Cochin China, and thus tend to extend and improve our commercial relations, it ought, I think, occasionally to be cultivated. In the present state of that country we have nothing to ask, and the intercourse therefore would be purely complimentary. The delivery of a letter, and a trifling present from the King, will require no extraordinary selection of diplomatic talents. An intelligent and prudent commander of one of His Majesty's ships on the Indian station, would be both the fittest and the cheapest ambassador to employ on such an occasion. Two or three of his officers, and a few marines, would form an appropriate suite, sufficient to ensure respect and attention; and the only extra assistance necessary, would be a Chinese interpreter understanding the English language, always readily obtained at Singapore, or Prince of Wales's Island, both of which lie in the route to Cochin China.

END OF THE FIRST VOLUME.